MW00846175

COMPUTER PROGRAMMING

FUNDAMENTAL CONCEPTS USING JAVA®

Rachel M. Jones

Y. Daniel Liang

Armstrong Atlantic State University

Boston • Columbus • Indianapolis • New York • San Francisco • Amsterdam
Cape Town • Dubai • London • Madrid • Milan • Munich • Paris • Montréal • Toronto
Delhi • Mexico City • São Paulo • Sydney • Hong Kong • Seoul • Singapore • Taipei • Tokyo

330 Hudson Street, New York, NY 10013
Hardcover ISBN 10: 0-13-444434-5
Hardcover ISBN 13: 978-0-13-444434-5
1 16

BRIEF CONTENTS

TABLE OF CONTENTS

CHAPTER 6

CHAPTER 7

CHAPTER 8

CHAPTER 9

PREFACE

This book is an introduction to computer programming fundamentals. The intended audience of this book is students who desire a basic understanding of computer programming. It lays a foundation for more advanced courses at both the high school and college level, or for those seeking an entry-level position in the computer software industry.

The content begins by identifying expectations in the workplace, and the skills required of computer programmers. Students will learn about the differences between various programming languages and their common uses. An introduction to the software life-cycle approach to designing an application is also covered. The first step in learning computer programming is to understand how to analyze and solve problems in a logical way. Students will learn how to create algorithms to analyze and solve problems.

Basic programming concepts such as selection statements, looping, and array data structures are introduced using the Java programming language. Students gain hands on experience through examples and programming exercises throughout the book. The earlier chapters provide a solid foundation for the introduction of more advanced topics covered in chapters 8 and 9. These latter two chapters introduce modular, object-oriented programming. The final chapter provides a foundation for developing and implementing a risk assessment strategy, tactics for reducing security risks, and understanding state and federal laws surrounding the industry. Several supplemental chapters are included. The intent of this supplemental material is to provide deeper understanding and advanced study at the discretion of both teachers and students. The supplements include topics such as algorithmic thinking, multi-dimensional arrays, variable scoping, and nested loops.

Much of the content is an adaptation from Y. Daniel Liang's *Introduction to Java Programming, Brief Version, Tenth Edition*. Additionally, adaptations of Lawrence Snyder's *Fluency 6 With Information Technology* is included in the algorithmic thinking and security sections of the book. It is with great admiration and appreciation for Professor Liang and Professor Snyder's groundwork that this book is created for you.

I would like to thank Felicia Carmouche of Katy, Texas Independent School District (KISD), Karen Misler, and Suzanne Weixel for their contributions to this book, and *Emergent Learning, LLC* for the opportunity to be involved in this project. I owe my deepest gratitude to Chuck, Robbi, and Chris for enduring the long hours in the "code cave" over the years.

It is our passion to encourage bright, young minds to enter into this fascinating and rewarding industry of software development. We hope this book lights a spark!

Sincerely,

Rachel M. Jones
twitter: @rachelmcjones

Pedagogical Features

The pedagogical approach is an introduction of topics through text narrative, coding examples, and case studies followed by hands-on coding exercises. Section assessments and end-of-chapter reviews provide additional learning reinforcement.

Objectives at the beginning of each chapter list what students should learn from the chapter. This will help them determine whether they have met the objectives after completing the chapter.

Key Points are included at the beginning of each section. Each key point highlights an important takeaway for the section.

Margin Terms provide a quick glance at key concepts. Readers can use the margin words as a reference locator of key concepts.

Section Assessments provide review questions to help students individually track their understanding of the material, or they can be used as assignments to measure student progress.

Case Studies and Examples highlight real-world application of the material and provide hands-on learning.

Notes, Tips, and Cautions are included throughout the book to offer valuable advice about computer programming, the work environment, and tools used in designing an application.

Chapter Review and Assessment sections at the end of each chapter include the following:

- **Key Terms** is a listing of important terms. The ability to describe the terms and apply them to exercises provides a minimal baseline metric for successful completion of the chapter.
- **Chapter Summary** reviews the important subjects that students should understand and remember. It helps them reinforce the key concepts they have learned in the chapter.
- **Programming Exercises** provide hands-on experience to apply the new skills learned. Answers to exercises are provided at the end of the Teacher's Edition, but are not included in the book.
- **Group exercises** are included in some chapters to emulate real-world experience of working on a team project.

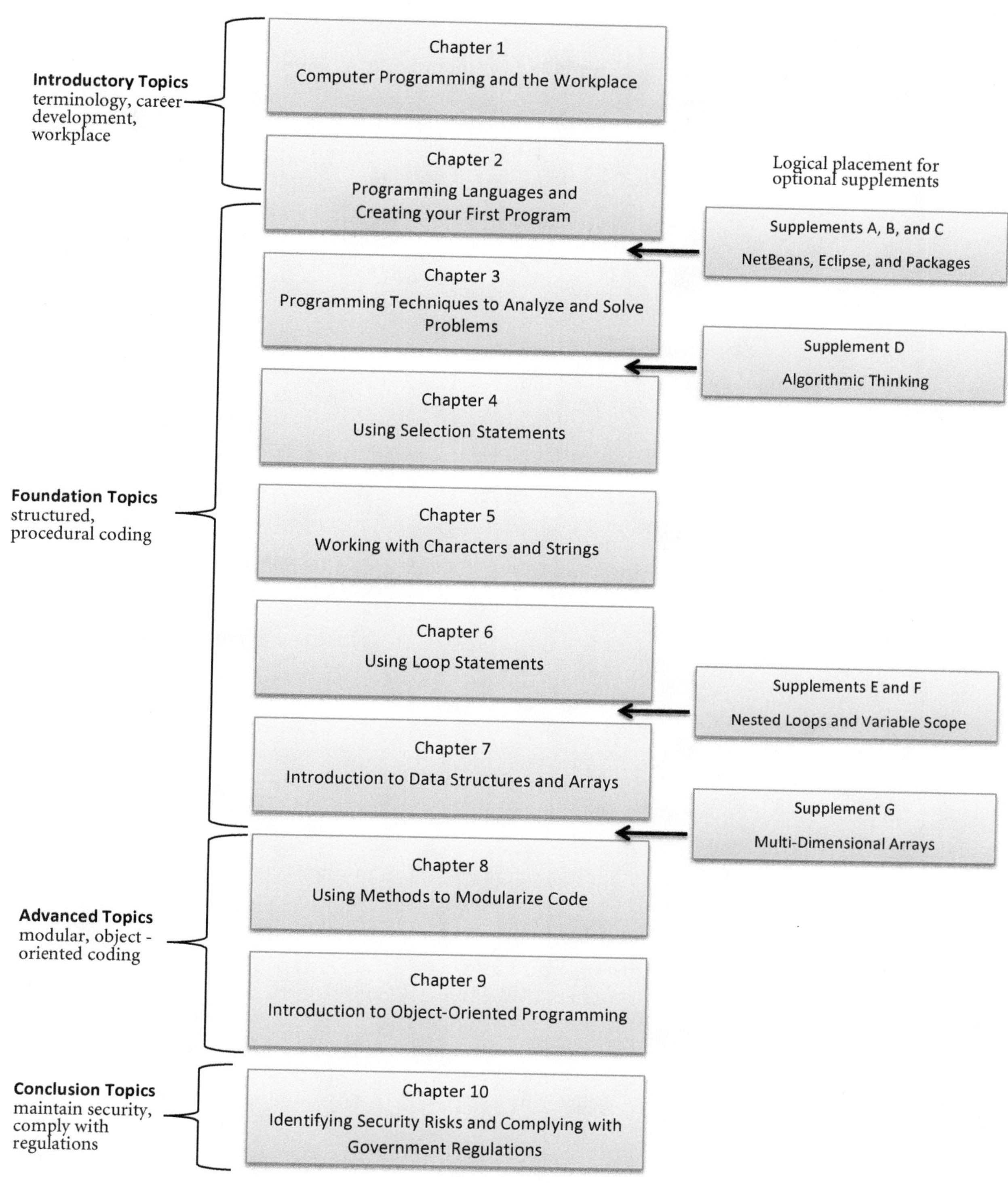
Introductory Topics
terminology, career development, workplace
Chapter 1
Computer Programming and the Workplace
Chapter 2
Programming Languages and Creating your First Program
Logical placement for optional supplements
Supplements A, B, and C
NetBeans, Eclipse, and Packages
Chapter 3
Programming Techniques to Analyze and Solve Problems
Supplement D
Algorithmic Thinking
Chapter 4
Using Selection Statements
Foundation Topics
structured, procedural coding
Chapter 5
Working with Characters and Strings
Chapter 6
Using Loop Statements
Supplements E and F
Nested Loops and Variable Scope
Chapter 7
Introduction to Data Structures and Arrays
Supplement G
Multi-Dimensional Arrays
Chapter 8
Using Methods to Modularize Code
Advanced Topics
modular, object - oriented coding
Chapter 9
Introduction to Object-Oriented Programming
Conclusion Topics
maintain security, comply with regulations
Chapter 10
Identifying Security Risks and Complying with Government Regulations

CHAPTER 1

COMPUTER PROGRAMMING AND THE WORKPLACE

Objectives

- Understand basic computer terminology.
- Understand the basic *hardware and software components* of a computer.
- Identify *job opportunities* that require computer programming skills.
- Identify the necessary *skills* for a job in computer programming.
- Understand the *steps to problem solving.*
- Understand the definition of business *ethics.*
- Distinguish between *ethical and unethical business practices* in the information technology industry.
- Examine software *copyright* and *licensing* issues.

1.1 Concepts and Terminology of a Computer

The central theme of this book is to learn how to solve problems by writing a program.

programming

program

This book is about programming. So, what is programming? The term *programming* means to create (or develop) software, which is also called a *program*. In basic terms, software contains the instructions that tell a computer—or a computerized device—what to do.

Software is all around you, even in devices that you might not think would need it. Of course, you expect to find and use software on a personal computer, but software also plays a role in running airplanes, cars, cell phones, and even toasters. On a personal computer, you use word processors to write documents, Web browsers to explore the Internet, and e-mail programs to send and receive messages. These programs are all examples of software. Software developers create software with the help of powerful tools called *programming languages*.

programming languages

This book teaches you how to create programs by using the Java programming language. There are many programming languages, some of which are decades old. Each language was invented for a specific purpose—to build on the strengths of a previous language, for example, or to give the programmer a new and unique set of tools. Knowing that there are so many programming languages available, it would be natural for you to wonder which one is best. But, in truth, there is no "best" language. Each one has its own strengths and weaknesses. Experienced programmers know that one language might work well in some situations, whereas a different language may be more appropriate in other situations. For this reason, seasoned programmers try to master as many different programming languages as they can, giving them access to a vast arsenal of software-development tools.

If you learn to program using one language, you should find it easy to pick up other languages. The key is to learn how to solve problems using a programming approach. That is the main theme of this book.

You are about to begin an exciting journey: learning how to program. At the outset, it is helpful to review computer basics, programs, and operating systems.

What Is a Computer?

A computer is an electronic device that stores and processes data.

hardware

software

A computer includes both *hardware* and *software*. In general, hardware comprises the visible, physical elements of the computer, and software provides the invisible instructions that control the hardware and make it perform specific tasks. Knowing computer hardware isn't essential to learning a programming language, but it can help you better understand the effects that a program's instructions have on the computer and its components. This section introduces computer hardware components and their functions.

A computer consists of the following major hardware components (Figure 1.1):

- A central processing unit (CPU)
- Memory (main memory)
- Storage devices (such as disks and CDs)

- Input devices (such as the mouse and keyboard)
- Output devices (such as monitors and printers)
- Communication devices (such as modems and network interface cards)

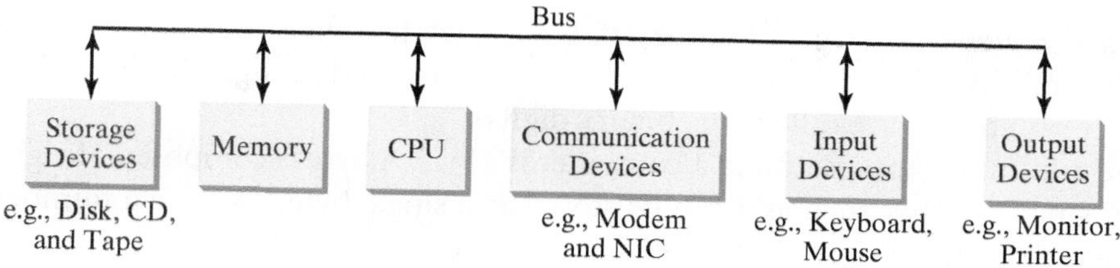

FIGURE 1.1 A computer consists of a CPU, memory, storage devices, input devices, output devices, and communication devices.

A computer's components are interconnected by a subsystem called a *bus*. You can think of a bus as a sort of system of roads running among the computer's components. Data and power travel along the bus from one part of the computer to another. In personal computers, the bus is built into the computer's *motherboard*, which is a circuit case that connects all of the parts of a computer together.

bus

motherboard

Central Processing Unit

The *central processing unit (CPU)* is the computer's brain. It retrieves instructions from memory and executes them. The CPU usually has two components: a *control unit* and an *arithmetic/logic unit*. The control unit controls and coordinates the actions of the other components. The arithmetic/logic unit performs numeric operations (addition, subtraction, multiplication, division) and logical operations (comparisons).

CPU

control unit

arithmetic/logic unit

Today's CPUs are built on small silicon semiconductor chips that contain millions of tiny electric switches, called *transistors*, for processing information.

transistors

Every computer has an internal clock, which emits electronic pulses at a constant rate. These pulses are used to control and synchronize the pace of operations. A higher clock *speed* enables more instructions to be executed in a given period of time. The unit of measurement of clock speed is the *hertz (Hz)*, with 1 hertz equaling 1 pulse per second. In the 1990s, computers measured clocked speed in *megahertz (MHz)*, but CPU speed has been improving continuously; the clock speed of a computer is now usually stated in *gigahertz (GHz)*. Intel's newest processors run at about 3 GHz.

speed

hertz

megahertz

gigahertz

CPUs were originally developed with only one core. The *core* is the part of the processor that performs the reading and executing of instructions. In order to increase CPU processing power, chip manufacturers are now producing CPUs that contain multiple cores. A multicore CPU is a single component with two or more independent cores. Today's consumer computers typically have two, three, and even four separate cores. Soon, CPUs with dozens or even hundreds of cores will be affordable.

core

Bits and Bytes

Before we discuss memory, let's look at how information (data and programs) are stored in a computer.

A computer is really nothing more than a series of switches. Each switch exists in two states: on or off. Storing information in a computer is simply a matter of setting a sequence of switches on or off. If the switch is on, its value is 1. If the switch is off, its value is 0. These 0s and 1s are interpreted as digits in the binary number system and are called *bits* (binary digits).

bits

byte

The minimum storage unit in a computer is a *byte*. A byte is composed of eight bits. A small number such as `3` can be stored as a single byte. To store a number that cannot fit into a single byte, the computer uses several bytes.

Data of various kinds, such as numbers and characters, are encoded as a series of bytes. As a programmer, you don't need to worry about the encoding and decoding of data, which the computer system performs automatically, based on the encoding scheme. An *encoding scheme* is a set of rules that govern how a computer translates characters, numbers, and symbols into data the computer can actually work with. Most schemes translate each character into a predetermined string of bits. In the popular ASCII encoding scheme, for example, the character `C` is represented as `01000011` in one byte.

encoding scheme

A computer's storage capacity is measured in bytes and multiples of the byte, as follows:

kilobyte (KB)

megabyte (MB)

gigabyte (GB)

terabyte (TB)

- A *kilobyte (KB)* is about 1,000 bytes.
- A *megabyte (MB)* is about 1 million bytes.
- A *gigabyte (GB)* is about 1 billion bytes.
- A *terabyte (TB)* is about 1 trillion bytes.

A typical one-page word document might take 20 KB. Therefore, 1 MB can store 50 pages of documents and 1 GB can store 50,000 pages of documents. A typical two-hour high-resolution movie might take 8 GB, so it would require 160 GB to store 20 movies.

Memory

memory

A computer's *memory* consists of an ordered sequence of bytes for storing programs as well as data that the program is working with. You can think of memory as the computer's work area for executing a program. A program and its data must be moved into the computer's memory before they can be executed by the CPU.

unique address

Every byte in the memory has a *unique address*, as shown in Figure 1.2. The address is used to locate the byte for storing and retrieving the data. Since the bytes in the memory can be accessed in any order, the memory is also referred to as *random-access memory (RAM)*.

RAM

Generally speaking, the more RAM a computer has, the faster it can operate, but there are limits to this simple rule of thumb.

A memory byte is never empty, but its initial content may be meaningless to your program. The current content of a memory byte is lost whenever new information is placed in it.

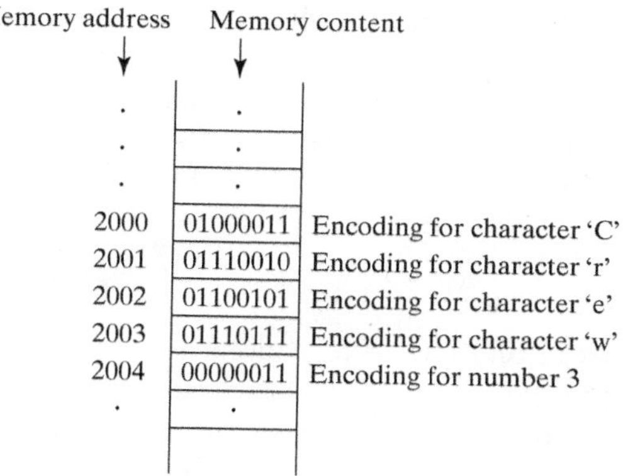

FIGURE 1.2 Memory stores data and program instructions in uniquely addressed memory locations.

Like the CPU, memory is built on silicon semiconductor chips that have millions of transistors embedded on their surface. Compared to CPU chips, memory chips are less complicated, slower, and less expensive.

Storage Devices

A computer's memory (RAM) is a volatile form of data storage: any information that has been stored in memory (i.e., saved) is lost when the system's power is turned off. Programs and data are permanently stored on *storage devices* and are moved, when the computer actually uses them, to memory, which operates at much faster speeds than permanent storage devices can. storage devices

There are three main types of storage devices:

- Magnetic disk drives
- Optical disc drives (CD and DVD)
- USB flash drives

Drives are devices for operating a medium, such as disks and CDs. A storage medium physically stores data and program instructions. The drive reads data from the medium and writes data onto the medium. drive

Disks

A computer usually has at least one hard disk drive. *Hard disks* are used for permanently storing data and programs. Newer computers have hard disks that can store from 500 gigabytes to several terabytes of data. Hard disk drives are usually encased inside the computer, but removable hard disks are also available. hard disk

CDs and DVDs

CD stands for compact disc. There are two types of CD drives: CD-R and CD-RW. A *CD-R* is for read-only permanent storage; the user cannot modify its contents once they are recorded. A *CD-RW* can be used like a hard disk; that is, you can write data onto the disc, and then overwrite that data with new data. CD-R CD-RW

A single CD can hold up to 700 MB. Most new PCs are equipped with a CD-RW drive that can work with both CD-R and CD-RW discs.

DVD

DVD stands for digital versatile disc or digital video disc. DVDs and CDs look alike, and you can use either to store data. A DVD can hold more information than a CD. Like CDs, there are two types of DVDs: DVD-R (read-only) and DVD-RW (rewritable).

USB Flash Drives

Universal serial bus (USB) connectors allow the user to attach many kinds of peripheral devices to the computer. You can use a USB to connect a printer, digital camera, mouse, external hard disk drive, and other devices to the computer.

A USB *flash drive* is a device for storing and transporting data. A flash drive is small—about the size of a pack of gum. It acts like a portable hard drive that can be plugged into your computer's USB port.

Communication Devices

Computers can be networked through communication devices, such as a wired network interface card, or a wireless adapter.

network interface card (NIC)
local area network (LAN)
million bits per second (mbps)

- A *network interface card (NIC)* is a device that connects a computer to a *local area network (LAN)*. It requires the use of physical Ethernet wiring to connect and network two or more computers. A high-speed NIC called *1000BaseT* can transfer data at 1,000 *million bits per second (mbps)*.
- Wireless networking is now extremely popular in homes, businesses, and schools. Every laptop computer sold today is equipped with a wireless adapter that enables the computer to connect to a local area network and the Internet.

✓ Section 1.1 Assessment

1. What are hardware and software?
2. List five major hardware components of a computer.
3. What does the acronym "CPU" stand for?
4. What unit is used to measure CPU speed?
5. What is a bit? What is a byte?
6. What is memory for? What does RAM stand for? Why is memory called RAM?
7. What unit is used to measure memory size?
8. What unit is used to measure disk size?
9. What is the primary difference between memory and a storage device?

1.2 Exploring Careers and the Workplace

Careers in computer programming require problem-solving, time-management, teamwork, and leadership.

A *career* is a chosen field of work in which you try to advance over time by gaining responsibility and earning more money. The career you choose has a major impact on the kind of life you will lead. It determines the type of training and education you will need. It might impact where you live and the type of lifestyle you achieve.

career

The U.S. Department of Education organizes careers into 16 clusters. A *cluster* is a group of similar items. Career clusters help you sort the career possibilities into 16 manageable groups. Within each of the 16 career clusters are related job, industry, and occupation types called pathways. Each pathway offers a variety of careers you might choose. Programming and software development is a pathway within the Information Technology career cluster. Careers in this pathway involve the design, development, implementation, and maintenance of computer systems and software.

cluster

Identifying Job Opportunities

Computer programmers create, test, and run the programs that make computer applications work. Some typical tasks include working alone or with others to write computer code, develop diagrams and flowcharts, document design and development procedures, and test systems to make sure they work as expected. Programmers must be detail-oriented, able to meet strict deadlines, and have strong teamwork, communications, and problem-solving skills.

Every industry that uses computer technology needs computer programmers. Examples include video game development, health care, financial institutions, and government agencies. There are also companies that exist to develop software. Some develop applications, while others develop system software. All of these companies need computer programmers.

Entry-level positions generally require a bachelor's degree. A master's degree may be required for advancement. According to the U.S. Bureau of Labor Statistics (BLS), in 2014 the median annual salary for computer programmers was about $77,500. Programmers usually work in an office but may be home-based.

A knowledge of computer programming can help you succeed in many careers. Even if you do not work as a programmer, the logic and problem-solving skills you learn by programming are highly valued by employers in many industries and will make you a strong candidate for other positions.

Teamwork and Leadership

A *team* is a group of two or more people who work together to achieve a common goal. When you are part of a team, you have access to all the knowledge, experience, and abilities of your teammates. Together you can have more ideas, achieve more goals, and solve more problems.

team

Most programming projects require teamwork. Depending on the project, programmers may work with a partner, or with a group of other programmers, usually under the direction of a team leader or project manager. But, no matter who is on the team and what the team is doing, the interactions between team members will be most productive if the members of the team:

- Listen to each other
- Respect each other's opinions
- Recognize each other's skills and abilities
- Share the work load
- Share responsibility

leader

Even when all members of a team have an equal role in decision making and problem solving, it is important to have a leader. A *leader* is a type of manager who knows how to use available resources to help others achieve their goals.

Leaders exhibit positive qualities that other people respect, such as self-confidence, honesty, effective listening and speaking skills, decisiveness, respect for others, and open-mindedness. They are organized and supportive of the other team members.

Although you might have heard that someone is a "born leader," that's not usually the case. Becoming a leader takes time and patience. Leaders have to prove that they can make decisions, set goals, and solve problems. You can develop leadership characteristics by recognizing and modeling positive leadership qualities. One way to do this is by participating in student leadership and professional development opportunities. For example, you can join clubs and activities such as your school robotics team, and volunteer for leadership roles. You might also join a career technical student organization (CTSO) such as Technology Student Association (TSA) or SkillsUSA. CTSOs offer members a range of individual and group programs, activities, and competitions designed to build professional skills as well as leadership qualities.

While a strong leader is important to the success of a team, team members must also be committed to the group's success. An effective team member helps teammates if they need help, does not blame teammates for problems or mistakes, and offers ideas and suggestions instead of criticism. Effective team members use critical-thinking skills and interpersonal skills to identify and solve problems and achieve their goals.

You are a good team member if you are:

- Open minded
- Willing to compromise
- Cooperative
- Friendly
- Trustworthy

Project Management

Employers value employees who know how to use planning and project management skills to make sure work is completed on time. *Project management* is a process used to take a project from conception to completion. There are four basic parts to the process:

project management

- **Identifying measurable objectives.** An *objective* is a short-term goal used to keep a project on track for completion. A measurable objective can be evaluated by specific standards.

objective

- **Identifying deliverables.** A *deliverable* is a product, or segment of a product, that can be provided to an employer, customer, or the public.

deliverable

- **Setting a schedule.** The schedule should include a timeline with a final deadline, as well as milestones for achieving each objective. It involves setting *priorities*—which means deciding which tasks must be completed first.

priorities

- **Developing supporting plans.** Supporting plans usually specify items like how to allocate resources such as funds and technology, how to identify and manage risk, and methods for communication.

Many companies have project management software for scheduling, organizing, coordinating, and tracking project tasks. You can find basic project management templates in programs such as Microsoft Excel. There are also specific tools for project management, such as a *Gantt chart* (Figure 1.3a) and a PERT chart (Figure 1.3b). A Gantt chart, developed by Henry L. Gantt in 1917, is a horizontal bar chart that shows a graphical illustration of a schedule. A *PERT chart* (Program Evaluation Review Technique), developed by the U.S. Navy in the 1950s, shows project tasks, the order in which they must be completed, and the time requirements.

Gantt chart

PERT chart

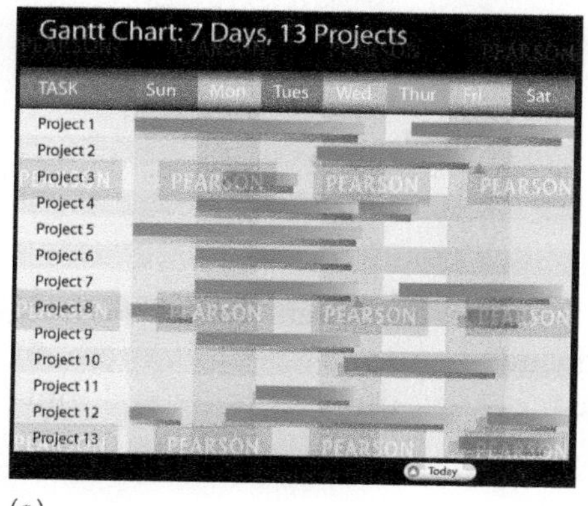

(a)

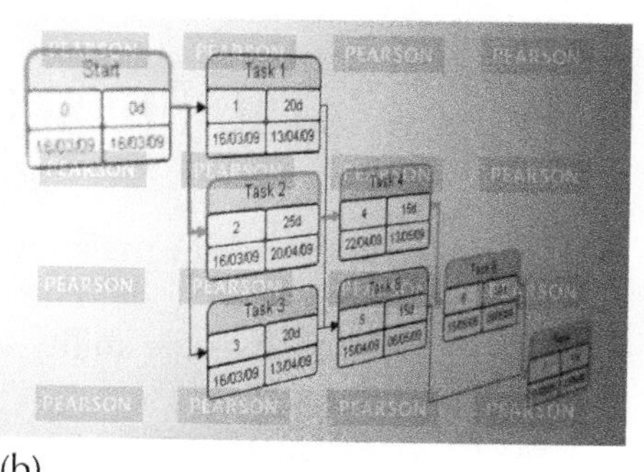

(b)

FIGURE 1.3 (a) Gantt chart and (b) PERT chart

Time Management

Time management is a critical skill for both finding a career and succeeding at work. During a career search, you can use schedules and to-do lists to keep yourself organized and on-track. Combining goal-setting with time management is a very effective way to make sure you get things done. Each time you set a goal, such as contacting a prospective employer or revising your resume, you can include a realistic time frame.

At work, you can use schedules and goal-setting to keep you focused on the tasks at hand. Computer programs can help you organize and meet your responsibilities.

- Set realistic and attainable goals using daily, weekly, and monthly schedules. Different schedules can help you identify tasks that must be accomplished within a specific timeframe.
- Make use of the calendar program on your computer or handheld device. You can enter schedules, phone calls, and appointments. Use the tasks list feature to record and prioritize the tasks you need to accomplish. Set the program to display a message or make a sound to remind you of deadlines.

It is also important to respect time in the workplace. It shows that you respect your co-workers. It also demonstrates to your employer that you take your responsibilities seriously and proves that you are ready for new challenges such as those that might come from a promotion.

To show that you respect time at work:

- Arrive on time.
- Notify your supervisor if you will be late.
- Take your lunch hour and other breaks at the designated time and return promptly.
- Do not leave until the end of the work day.
- Meet your deadlines.
- Do not conduct personal business during work hours.

1.3 Employability Skills

Employability means having and using skills and abilities to be hired and stay hired.

transferable skills

Employability skills include the knowledge for a specific career—such as writing and debugging computer code. They also include *transferable skills* that you can use in any career, such as the ability to solve problems, think critically, and communicate effectively.

Effective Communication

Communication is a process that involves an exchange of information between a sender and a recipient. The sender transmits the message with a specific intent. The recipient interprets the message and responds.

Effective communication occurs when the receiver interprets the message the way the sender intended. Ineffective communication occurs when the receiver misinterprets the message. Sometimes the sender thinks the message is clear, but in fact it might confuse or mislead the receiver.

In order to ensure effective communication:

- The message must be clear.
- The sender must be able to deliver the message in a concise and accurate manner.
- The receiver must be able to hear and receive the message.
- The receiver must be able to interpret the message correctly.

You can communicate effectively by using a six-step process:

1. **Be clear.** The receiver is more likely to get your message if you deliver it in a way he or she can understand. Speak slowly. Consider who he or she is. You probably use different language when you talk to a teacher than when you talk to a friend. You might even use a completely different type of communication —face-to-face instead of a social networking site.
2. **Be personal.** Use the other person's name—then he or she will know you are communicating with him or her. Use an "I" statement—a statement that starts with the word "I"—to frame the statement in terms of you and your goals. An "I" statement indicates that you are taking responsibility for your thoughts and feelings. It helps the receiver understand your point of view and respond to you, instead of focusing on himself or herself and how your statement affects him or her.
3. **Be positive.** Phrase your message in positive terms. Say what you want, not what you don't want.
4. **Get to the point.** Follow the "I" statement with an explanation of the message you are sending. Explain how or why you feel a certain way, or how or why you think a certain thing.
5. **Actively listen to the response.** Pay attention and make sure you hear the response.
6. **Think before you respond.** Make sure you understand the message. Repeat it, if necessary, and ask questions for clarification. Use critical thinking to make sure you are not letting emotions and preconceived ideas get in the way.

Verbal and Nonverbal Communications

Verbal communication is the exchange of messages by speaking, reading, or writing. For most of us, verbal communication is the most common way we stay in touch with other people in our lives. We talk face to face or on the phone. We send text messages, e-mails, and instant messages. We write blogs, tweet, pass notes, and send cards.

Talking is usually a very effective form of verbal communication. When you speak clearly and use language the receiver understands, he or she almost always gets the message the way you intend it.

Nonverbal communication helps put words into context. This form of communication includes visual messages that the receiver can see, such as a smile when you are talking. It also includes physical messages, such as a pat on the back.

During a conversation, the tone of your voice and the language you use combine to provide context for the words.

Writing is also verbal communication. Effective writing is simple, clear, and to the point. It is free from spelling and grammatical errors. Effective writing usually uses the *active voice* rather than the *passive voice*. In the active voice, the subject takes action. In the passive voice, the subject is acted upon. For example, *She threw the ball*, is in the active voice; *The ball was thrown by her*, is in the passive voice.

When you write, you lose some of the context, which can make the communication less effective. Exchanging written messages doesn't take place face to face. It might be across great distances. When the receiver can't hear your voice, he or she might misinterpret the message.

There are different ways to read, depending on what you are reading. Passive reading is the kind of reading you do for entertainment, such as when you read a magazine or a comic book. In this kind of reading, you are just taking in information or following the plot. When you read critically, you take time to really think about what is written and why. Critical reading happens when you are actively engaging the subject as you read.

Critical reading is essential for success. Following are three steps you can use to be sure you are reading critically:

- Determine the best reading strategy for the text. This means that you need to figure out whether to skim the text, read closely for detail, or read for meaning or critical analysis.
- As you read, stop and think about what is being said and try to put it in your own words, or rephrase it from your own point of view.
- Take notes while you are reading to make sure you are understanding and remembering the main points.

Active Listening

Active listening is an important part of effective communication. When you are an active listener, you pay attention to the speaker, and make sure you hear and understand the message.

Use these skills to be an active listener:

- Show interest using eye contact and positive nonverbal messages.
- Let the other person finish speaking before you respond.
- Ignore distractions such as cell phones and other people.
- Set your predetermined opinions and emotions aside.
- Repeat the message that you hear out loud, to make sure you received it correctly.

Active listening is a sign of respect. It shows you are willing to communicate and that you care about the speaker and the message. When you listen actively, the other person is more likely to listen when you speak, too.

Solving Problems

A *problem*—or challenge—is a difficulty that you must resolve before you can make progress. In other words, any barrier or obstacle between you and a goal is a problem. To overcome a problem, you can use a process to figure out the best solution:

problem

1. **Identify the problem.** This is your chance to be honest, acknowledge the problem, and determine what goal it is blocking.
2. **Consider all possible solutions.** There may be one obvious solution, or there may be many possible solutions. Write down as many as you can think of. You will need to consider your values, standards, and resources, too. Some solutions might be harder to make happen, or take longer than others. Some might cost money and some might be free. Some might solve only part of the problem.
3. **Identify the consequences of each solution.** Like decisions, each solution will have consequences, and it is important to recognize how the consequences will affect you and others. Again, write them down.
4. **Select the best solution.** The best solution offers the best possible opportunity for you to continue your progress toward your goal.
5. **Make and implement a plan of action.** Recognizing and selecting a solution are only part of the process. You must take the necessary steps to make the solution real.
6. **Evaluate the solution, process, and outcome.** Did your solution work? Did you achieve your goal? Would you do anything differently if you had the same problem again?

Basically, computer programming is problem-solving. The programmer identifies the challenge—how to get the computer to perform a specific task—and then sets about identifying the best solution and writing the code to make it happen.

Thinking Critically

Critical thinking can help you evaluate your options in many situations. You can use it when you are making decisions, setting goals, and solving problems. When you think critically, you are honest, rational, and open-minded about your options. You try not to let emotions get in the way of choosing the best course of action.

- Being honest means acknowledging selfish feelings and preexisting opinions.
- Being rational means relying on reason and thought instead of on emotion or impulse.
- Being open-minded means being willing to evaluate all possible options—even those that are unpopular.

When you think critically, you consider all possible options and other points of view. You look objectively at information. *Objective* means fairly, without emotion or prejudice. Then, you use your values, standards, and ethics to interpret the information subjectively. *Subjective* means affected by existing opinions, feelings, and beliefs. Looking at things both objectively and subjectively can help you make choices that are right for you.

objective

subjective

Thinking critically doesn't mean you should ignore emotions, or any other influence factors. It just means you should consider all possibilities before rushing to judgment.

You can think critically about a lot of things, not just decisions and problems. You don't have to believe everything you hear or read. You can question a news report or information you find on a Web site, look deeper into the meaning of a magazine article, or investigate the truth behind a rumor.

1.4 Ethical Responsibilities

Information technology professionals, including computer programmers, have many legal and ethical responsibilities.

ethics

work ethics

Ethics are a set of beliefs about what is right and what is wrong. *Work ethics* are moral principles, or beliefs and behaviors about what is right and wrong in a work environment. When you behave ethically at work, others will trust and respect you. Most work ethics are the same ethics from other areas of life that you apply to your workplace. Some typical business ethics are:

- Respect the rules and policies of your employer.
- Respect the authority of your supervisor.
- Respect your co-workers.
- Respect company property.
- Be honest.
- Obey the law.

Business Ethics

business ethics

Business ethics are moral principles applied to business issues and actions. When a company acts ethically, it treats employees, clients, and other businesses honestly and with respect. It obeys all laws and regulations governing its business. But, not all businesses behave ethically. They may use dishonest business practices to cheat clients, steal work from other companies or individuals, and advance their own interests. For example, a company might use someone else's copyrighted software code to develop its own product.

Unethical and dishonest business practices might seem to help a company in the short term, but in the long run the consequences can be severe. Businesses that do not obey laws and regulations might be forced to pay large fines and other penalties. They may be trapped in lengthy and expensive legal battles. In addition, the executives responsible for making the decisions that lead to illegal and unethical behavior may end up facing criminal charges.

Employees at companies that engage in unethical business practices often end up acting unethically in their own positions. They may believe that since the company is unethical, they can be, too. They may not respect their managers or the company executives. As a result, they may be less productive, causing the company to lose money. Clients and business partners may also lose respect for the unethical company, and make the decision to take their business elsewhere.

Copyright and Licensing

Federal laws that involve copyright protect individuals and companies from the theft or misuse of their intellectual property, such as creative, literary, or artistic work. This includes software code. Copyright exists as soon as a work is created, but the creator can register it with the U.S. Copyright Office. It is a crime to copy this kind of work without the permission of the person who owns the copyright to it. Penalties include paying a large fine and possibly jail time.

Copyright laws protect software developers from the misuse of their intellectual property by others. Someone who pretends that another person's work is his or her own has broken the law by committing copyright infringement. He or she has stolen another person's work. If you copy someone else's code and try to pass it off as your own, or use it in your own product, you are breaking the law. If you want to use content created by someone else, such as software code, you must obtain permission from the copyright holder.

Software must be legally licensed before it can be installed and used. A *software license* is a legally binding agreement between the software producer and the user. It specifies the terms of use and defines the rights of both the software producer and the user. The license permits the buyer to use and install the program, and sometimes entitles the buyer to receive free or reduced cost support and updates.

software license

Individuals might buy a single-user license for one copy of the program, or a single-seat license to install the program on a single computer. Organizations such as schools or businesses usually buy a volume or site license which lets them install on multiple systems or a network for multiple users. Network licensing generally costs less per user and allows users to share resources.

Creative Commons is a license that lets software copyright holders open some of their work for public use while letting them hold onto other parts of their work.

TABLE 1.1 Types of Software

Commercial software	Copyrighted software, also called proprietary software. The company, or individual, that developed the software owns the copyright. This means it is illegal for others to sell it, give it away, or even share it. When you buy commercial software, you are paying for the right to use the software, not necessarily for the right to the software's code. Software where the user doesn't gain access to the program's code is also called closed-source software.
Shareware	Copyrighted software that you can use on a try-before-you-buy basis. If you decide to keep it, you must pay a fee.
Freeware	Copyrighted software that the copyright owner gives away for free on the condition that users do not resell it.
Open-source software	A program, like proprietary software, and you may have to pay for it. Unlike proprietary software, it makes the source code available to the public. The idea is that the software will improve and benefit from the innovations of users, who troubleshoot weak points and expand features.
Public domain software	Software that the developers or authors allow others to use, copy, share, and even alter for free.

Legal and Ethical Responsibilities in Information Technology

Information technology professionals, including computer programmers, have many legal and ethical responsibilities. Some are the same as in any industry, such as treating co-workers and clients with respect, obeying all laws and regulations, and calling attention to negligent, illegal, unethical, abusive, or dangerous business practices. Some, however, are unique to IT.

One of the most significant legal and ethical responsibilities for an IT worker is to stop software piracy, which is the act of enabling access to software illegally. This is an area in which IT workers may be tempted to violate laws and policies for personal gain, but should also recognize the harm it does their own profession.

Another legal and ethical responsibility is to protect proprietary information. IT workers may have access to a company's trade secrets and other confidential information. In addition to legally protected information such as copyrighted code, it includes business information that is generally not available to the public, that has some degree of uniqueness, and that requires cost or effort to develop. Many companies require employees to sign a non-disclosure agreement that prohibits them from sharing proprietary information. However, there may be temptations for an employee to break that agreement. He or she may leave and start working at a competitor, or even be offered money to share the information.

Many IT workers also have access to employee and client personal information. It is imperative that they follow all security protocols to maintain an individual's right to privacy. Identity theft and fraud are serious crimes. IT workers may be responsible for protecting systems from security breaches which could compromise personal data.

To help IT professionals recognize and adhere to their legal and ethical responsibilities, some professional associations, including the Association of Information Technology Professionals (AITP) and the Association for Computing Machinery (ACM), have developed their own codes of ethics and professional conduct. These codes include standards such as the following:

- Not misrepresenting or withholding information concerning the capabilities of equipment, software, or systems
- Not using or taking credit for the work of others without specific acknowledgement and authorization
- Protecting the privacy and confidentiality of all information
- Not exploiting the weakness of a computer system for personal gain or personal satisfaction

Chapter 1 — Review and Assessment

Key Terms

bits 4
bus 3
business ethics 14
byte 4
career 7
central processing unit (CPU) 3
cluster 7
core 3
drive 5
encoding scheme 4
ethics 14
Gantt chart 9
gigabyte (GB) 4
gigahertz 3
hard disk 5
hardware 2
hertz 3
kilobyte (KB) 4
leader 8
local area network (LAN) 6
megabyte (MB) 4
megahertz 3
memory 4
million bits per second (mbps) 6
motherboard 3
network interface card (NIC) 6
objective 13
PERT chart 9
priorities 9
problem 13
program 2
programming 2
programming languages 2
project management 9
RAM 4
software 2
software license 15
speed 3
storage devices 5
subjective 13
team 7
terabyte (TB) 4
transistors 3
unique address 4
work ethics 14

Chapter Summary

1. A computer is an electronic device that stores and processes data.
2. A computer includes both *hardware* and *software.*
3. Hardware is the physical aspect of the computer that can be touched.
4. Computer *programs*, known as *software*, are the invisible instructions that control the hardware and make it perform tasks.
5. Computer *programming* is the writing of instructions (i.e., code) for computers to perform.
6. The *central processing unit (CPU)* is a computer's brain. It retrieves instructions from *memory* and executes them.

7. Computers use zeros and ones because digital devices have two stable states, referred to by convention as zero and one.

8. A *bit* is a binary digit 0 or 1.

9. A *byte* is a sequence of 8 bits.

10. A *kilobyte* is about 1,000 bytes, a *megabyte* about 1 million bytes, a *gigabyte* about 1 billion bytes, and a *terabyte* about 1,000 gigabytes.

11. *Memory* stores data and program instructions for the CPU to execute.

12. A *memory unit* is an ordered sequence of bytes.

13. Memory is volatile, because information is lost when the power is turned off.

14. Programs and data are permanently stored on *storage devices* and are moved to memory when the computer actually uses them.

15. *Computer programmers* create, test, and run the programs that make computer applications work.

16. Every industry that uses computer technology needs computer programmers, and other industries seek employees with skills developed by learning computer programming.

17. Most programming projects require *teamwork*.

18. *Leaders* exhibit positive qualities that other people respect, such as self-confidence, honesty, effective listening and speaking skills, decisiveness, respect for others, and open-mindedness.

19. Planning and time management skills such as *project management* are critical for both finding a career and succeeding at work

20. *Employability skills* include effective reading and writing skills, as well as verbal and nonverbal communication skills.

21. Employers value employees who can *solve problems* and *think critically*.

22. *Business ethics* are moral principles applied to business issues and actions.

23. *Copyright laws* protect software developers from the misuse of their intellectual property by others.

24. Software must be *legally licensed* before it can be installed and used.

25. Information technology professionals, including computer programmers, have many legal and *ethical responsibilities*, including stopping software piracy, protecting confidential information, and protecting the privacy of others.

CHAPTER ASSESSMENT

1. List five major hardware components of a computer and explain their purpose.
2. Make a three column chart. In one column, list at least three jobs available in the programming and software development pathway. In the second column, list the type of business or industry in which that person might work. In the third column, list the job duties and tasks.
3. Define business ethics.
4. Explain the effects of unethical practices on a business.
5. Explain how copyright laws affect the software industry.
6. What is a software license? List at least three types of software licensing.
7. Explain the difference between honest and dishonest business practices. Give at least two examples of each.
8. Write a paragraph explaining legal and ethical responsibilities in relation to the field of information technology.

GROUP EXERCISE

Working in small teams, plan a presentation about legal and ethical responsibilities in relation to the field of information technology. Use problem-solving, planning, and time-management skills such as project management to organize the project. You may want to use a project management template in a program such as Excel. Take turns so each team member has the opportunity to demonstrate team leadership skills. Research the topic using effective reading skills. Use critical thinking to evaluate the information that you find, and only use content that is valid and accurate. Record and cite all source information. When your research is complete, compile the information into a presentation. Use effective writing skills to develop a script to accompany the slides. Take turns using verbal and nonverbal communications skills to read the script out loud and deliver the presentation.

CHAPTER

2

Comparing Programming Languages and Creating your First Java Program

Objectives

- Understand computer basics, programs, and operating systems.
- Understand differences of language styles, such as structured, procedural, event-driven, and object-oriented.
- Identify current programming languages and their uses.
- Practice writing an algorithm to explain the steps of a problem.
- Understand the meaning of Java language specification, API, JDK, and IDE.
- Write a simple Java program.
- Display output on the console.
- Explain the basic syntax of a Java program.
- Create, compile, and run Java programs.
- Learn to structure and document code with standard styling techniques.
- Explain the differences between syntax errors, runtime errors, and logic errors.
- Develop Java programs using NetBeans.
- Develop Java programs using Eclipse.

2.1 Types of Programming Languages and Their Uses

Computer programs, known as software, are instructions that tell a computer what to do.

Computers do not understand human languages, so programs must be written in a language a computer can use. There are hundreds of programming languages, and they were developed to make the programming process easier for people. However, all programs must be converted into instructions the computer can execute.

Machine Language

machine language

A computer's native language, which differs among different types of computers, is its *machine language*—a set of built-in primitive instructions. These instructions are in the form of binary code, so if you want to give a computer an instruction in its native language, you have to enter the instruction as binary code. For example, to add two numbers, you might have to write an instruction in binary code, like this:

```
1101101010011010
```

Assembly Language

assembly language

Programming in machine language is a tedious process. Moreover, programs written in machine language are very difficult to read and modify. For this reason, *assembly language* was created in the early days of computing as an alternative to machine languages. Assembly language uses a short descriptive word, known as a *mnemonic*, to represent each of the machine-language instructions. For example, the mnemonic `add` typically means to add numbers and `sub` means to subtract numbers. To add the numbers `2` and `3` and get the result, you might write an instruction in assembly code like this:

```
add 2, 3, result
```

assembler

Assembly languages were developed to make programming easier. However, because the computer cannot execute assembly language, another program—called an *assembler*—is used to translate assembly-language programs into machine code, as shown in Figure 2.1.

low-level language

Writing code in assembly language is easier than in machine language. However, it is still tedious to write code in assembly language. An instruction in assembly language essentially corresponds to an instruction in machine code. Writing in assembly requires that you know how the CPU works. Assembly language is referred to as a *low-level language*, because assembly language is close in nature to machine language and is machine dependent.

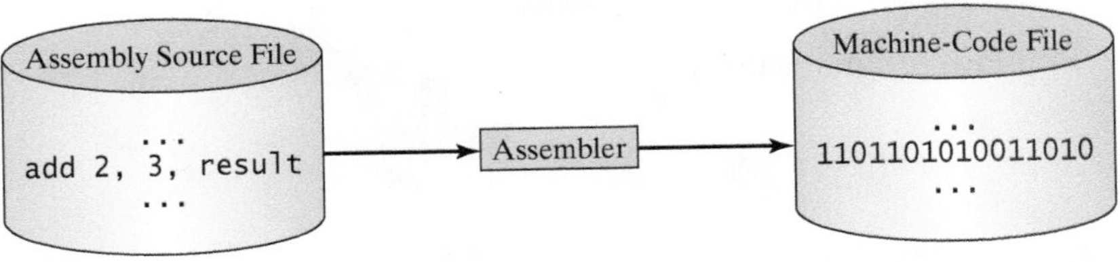

FIGURE 2.1 An assembler translates assembly-language instructions into machine code.

High-Level Language

In the 1950s, a new generation of programming languages known as *high-level languages* emerged. They are platform independent, which means that you can write a program in a high-level language and run it in different types of machines. High-level languages are English-like and easy to learn and use. The instructions in a high-level programming language are called *statements.* Here, for example, is a high-level language statement that computes the area of a circle with a radius of 5:

high-level language

statement

```
area = 5 * 5 * 3.14159;
```

There are many high-level programming languages, and each was designed for a specific purpose. Table 2.1 on the next page lists some popular ones and describes common environments for which they are used.

To execute any of the high-level programming languages listed in Table 2.1, an operating system must exist. The operating system (OS) is the most important program that runs on a computer. The OS manages and controls a computer's activities.

The popular *operating systems* for general-purpose computers are Microsoft Windows, Mac OS, and Linux. Application programs, such as a Web browser or a word processor, cannot run unless an operating system is installed and running on the computer.

operating system

A program written in a high-level language is called a *source program* or *source code.* Because a computer cannot execute a source program, a source program must be translated into machine code for execution. The translation can be done using another programming tool called an *interpreter* or a *compiler.*

source code
interpreter
compiler

- An interpreter reads one statement from the source code, translates it to the machine code or virtual machine code, and then executes it right away, as shown in Figure 2.2a. Note that a statement from the source code may be translated into several machine instructions.
- A compiler translates the entire source code into a machine-code file, and the machine-code file is then executed, as shown in Figure 2.2b.

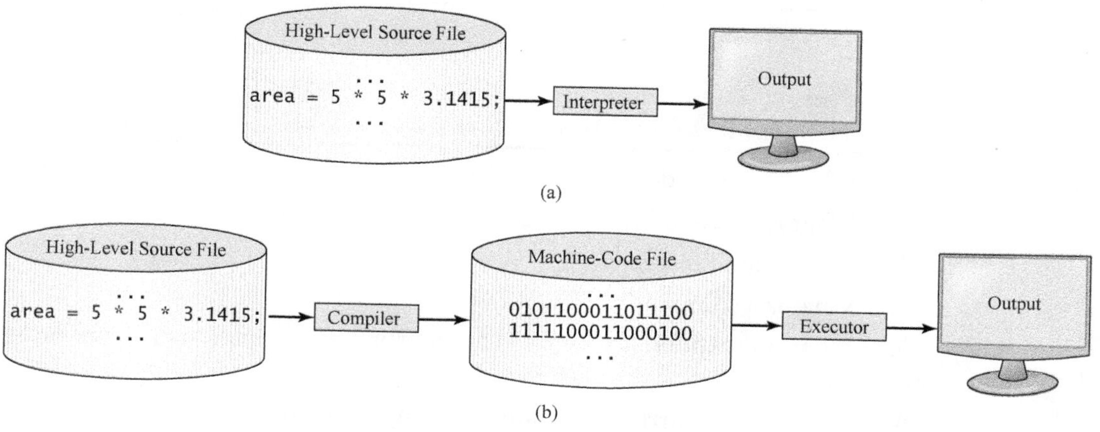

Figure 2.2 (a) An interpreter translates and executes a program one statement at a time. (b) A compiler translates the entire source program into a machine-language file for execution.

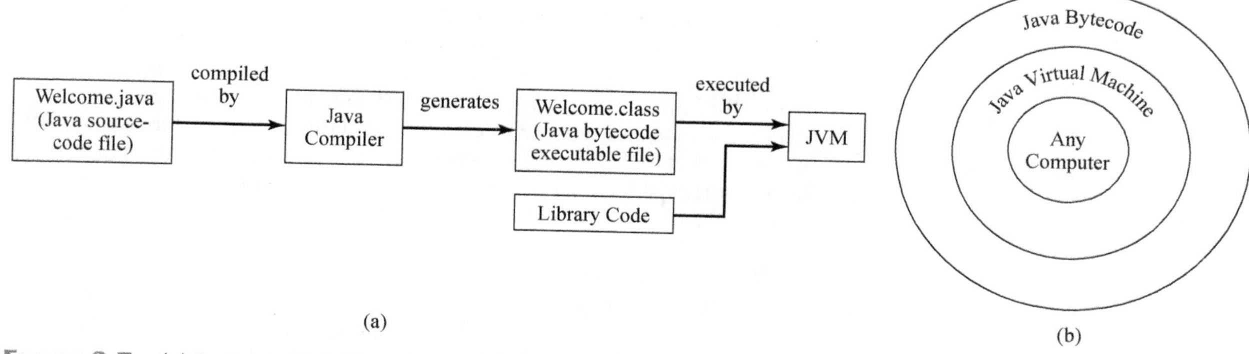

FIGURE 2.7 (a) Java source code is translated into bytecode. (b) Java bytecode can be executed on any computer with a Java Virtual Machine.

Note

For simplicity and consistency, all source-code and class files used in this book are placed under **c:\book** unless specified otherwise.

c:\book

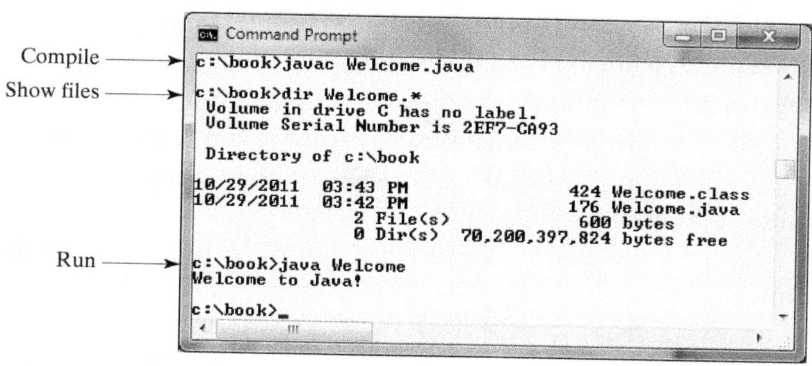

FIGURE 2.8 The output of Listing 2.1 displays the message "Welcome to Java!"

Caution

Do not use the extension `.class` in the command line when executing the program. Use `java ClassName` to run the program. If you use `java ClassName.class` in the command line, the system will attempt to fetch `ClassName.class.class`.

`java ClassName`

Tip

If you execute a class file that does not exist, a `NoClassDefFoundError` will occur. If you execute a class file that does not have a `main` method or you mistype the `main` method (e.g., by typing `Main` instead of `main`), a `NoSuchMethodError` will occur.

`NoClassDefFoundError`

`NoSuchMethodError`

Note

class loader

bytecode verifier

When executing a Java program, the JVM first loads the bytecode of the class to memory using a program called the *class loader*. If your program uses other classes, the class loader dynamically loads them just before they are needed. After a class is loaded, the JVM uses a program called the *bytecode verifier* to check the validity of the bytecode and to ensure that the bytecode does not violate Java's security restrictions. Java enforces strict security to make sure that Java class files are not tampered with and do not harm your computer.

Pedagogical Note

Your instructor may require you to use packages for organizing programs. For example, you may place all programs in this chapter in a package named *chapter1*. For instructions on how to use packages, see Supplement C, Using Packages to Organize Classes.

✓ Section 2.5 Assessment

1. What is the Java source filename extension, and what is the Java bytecode filename extension?
2. What are the input and output of a Java compiler?
3. What is the command to compile a Java program?
4. What is the command to run a Java program?
5. What is the JVM?
6. Can Java run on any machine? What is needed to run Java on a computer?
7. If a `NoClassDefFoundError` occurs when you run a program, what is the cause of the error?
8. If a `NoSuchMethodError` occurs when you run a program, what is the cause of the error?

2.6 Documenting your Program using a Defined Standard and Style

A standard programming style and documentation should be implemented beginning with the initial design and throughout the development of your application.

programming style

documentation

Programming style deals with what programs look like. A program can compile and run properly even if written on only one line, but writing it all on one line would be bad programming style because it would be hard to read. *Documentation* is the body of explanatory remarks and comments pertaining to a program. Programming style and documentation are as important as coding. Good programming style and appropriate documentation reduce the chance of errors and make programs easy to read. This section gives several guidelines.

Appropriate Comments and Comment Styles

Include a summary at the beginning of the program that explains what the program does, its key features, and any unique techniques it uses. In a long program, you should also include comments that introduce each major step and explain anything that is difficult to read. It is important to make comments concise so that they do not crowd the program or make it difficult to read.

In addition to line comments (beginning with //) and block comments (beginning with /*), Java supports comments of a special type, referred to as *javadoc comments*. javadoc comments begin with /** and end with */. They can be extracted into an HTML file using the JDK's `javadoc` command.

javadoc comment

Use javadoc comments (/** ... */) for commenting on an entire class or an entire method. These comments must precede the class or the method header in order to be extracted into a javadoc HTML file. For commenting on steps inside a method, use line comments (//).

Proper Indentation and Spacing

A consistent indentation style makes programs clear and easy to read, debug, and maintain. *Indentation* is used to illustrate the structural relationships between a program's components or statements. Java can read the program even if all of the statements are on the same long line, but humans find it easier to read and maintain code that is aligned properly. Indent each subcomponent or statement at least *two* spaces more than the construct within which it is nested.

indent code

A single space should be added on both sides of a binary operator, as shown in the following statement:

```
System.out.println(3+4*4);          Bad style

System.out.println(3 + 4 * 4);      Good style
```

Block Styles

A *block* is a group of statements surrounded by braces. There are two popular styles, *next-line* style and *end-of-line* style, as shown below.

```
public class Test
{
  public static void main(String[] args)
  {
    System.out.println("Block Styles");
  }
}
```

Next-line style

```
public class Test {
  public static void main(String[] args) {
    System.out.println("Block Styles");
  }
}
```

End-of-line style

The next-line style aligns braces vertically and makes programs easy to read, whereas the end-of-line style saves space and may help avoid some subtle programming errors. Both are acceptable block styles. The choice depends on personal or organizational preference. You should use a block style consistently—mixing styles is not recommended. This book uses the *end-of-line* style to be consistent with the Java API source code.

✓ Section 2.6 Assessment

1. Reformat the following program according to the programming style and documentation guidelines. Use the end-of-line brace style.

```
public class Test
{
  // Main method
  public static void main(String[] args) {
  /** Display output */
  System.out.println("Welcome to Java");
  }
}
```

2.7 Testing your Program and Understanding Programming Errors

Key Point

Programming errors can be categorized into three types: syntax errors, runtime errors, and logic errors.

Syntax Errors

syntax errors
compile errors

Errors that are detected by the compiler are called *syntax errors* or *compile errors.* Syntax errors result from errors in code construction, such as mistyping a keyword, omitting some necessary punctuation, or using an opening brace without a corresponding closing brace. These errors are usually easy to detect because the compiler tells you where they are and what caused them. For example, the program in Listing 2.4 has a syntax error, as shown in Figure 2.9.

Listing 2.4 ShowSyntaxErrors.java

```
public class ShowSyntaxErrors {
  public static main(String[] args) {
    System.out.println("Welcome to Java);
  }
}
```

Compile

```
Administrator: Command Prompt
c:\book>javac ShowSyntaxErrors.java
ShowSyntaxErrors.java:2: error: invalid method declaration; return type required

  public static main(String[] args) {
                ^
ShowSyntaxErrors.java:3: error: unclosed string literal
    System.out.println("Welcome to Java);
                       ^
ShowSyntaxErrors.java:3: error: ';' expected
    System.out.println("Welcome to Java);
                                         ^
ShowSyntaxErrors.java:5: error: reached end of file while parsing
}
 ^
4 errors

c:\book>_
```

Figure 2.9 The compiler reports syntax errors.

Four errors are reported, but the program actually has two errors:

- The keyword `void` is missing before `main` in line 2.
- The string `Welcome to Java` should be closed with a closing quotation mark in line 3.

Since a single error will often display many lines of compile errors, it is a good practice to fix errors from the top line and work downward. Fixing errors that occur earlier in the program may also fix additional errors that occur later.

Tip

If you don't know how to correct it, compare your program closely, character by character, with similar examples in the text. In the first few weeks of this course, you will probably spend a lot of time fixing syntax errors. Soon you will be familiar with Java syntax and can quickly fix syntax errors.

Runtime Errors

runtime errors

Runtime errors are errors that cause a program to terminate abnormally. They occur while a program is running if the environment detects an operation that is impossible to carry out. Input mistakes typically cause runtime errors. An *input error* occurs when the program is waiting for the user to enter a value, but the user enters a value that the program cannot handle. For instance, if the program expects to read in a number, but instead the user enters a string, this causes a data-type mismatch and a runtime error occurs.

Another example of runtime errors is division by zero. This happens when the divisor is zero for integer divisions. For instance, the program in Listing 2.5 would cause a runtime error, as shown in Figure 2.10.

LISTING 2.5 ShowRuntimeErrors.java

```
public class ShowRuntimeErrors {
  public static void main(String[] args) {
    System.out.println(1 / 0);
  }
}
```

runtime error

Run →

```
Administrator: Command Prompt
c:\book>java ShowRuntimeErrors
Exception in thread "main" java.lang.ArithmeticException: / by zero
        at ShowRuntimeErrors.main(ShowRuntimeErrors.java:4)

c:\book>_
```

FIGURE 2.10 The runtime error causes the program to terminate abnormally.

Logic Errors

logic errors

Logic errors occur when a program does not perform the way it was intended to. Errors of this kind occur for many different reasons. For example, suppose you wrote the program in Listing 2.6 to convert Celsius 35 degrees to a Fahrenheit degree:

Listing 2.6 ShowLogicErrors.java

```
public class ShowLogicErrors {
  public static void main(String[] args) {
    System.out.println("Celsius 35 is Fahrenheit degree ");
    System.out.println((9 / 5) * 35 + 32);
  }
}
```

```
Celsius 35 is Fahrenheit degree
67
```

You will get Fahrenheit 67 degrees, which is wrong. It should be 95.0. In Java, the division for integers is the quotient—the fractional part is truncated—so in Java 9 / 5 is 1. To get the correct result, you need to use 9.0 / 5, which results in 1.8.

In general, syntax errors are easy to find and easy to correct because the compiler gives indications as to where the errors came from and why they are wrong. Runtime errors are not difficult to find, either, since the reasons and locations for the errors are displayed on the console when the program aborts. Finding logic errors, on the other hand, can be very challenging. In the upcoming chapters, you will learn the techniques of tracing programs and finding logic errors.

Common Errors

Missing a closing brace, missing a semicolon, missing quotation marks for strings, and misspelling names are common errors for new programmers.

Common Error 1: Missing Braces

The braces are used to denote a block in the program. Each opening brace must be matched by a closing brace. A common error is missing the closing brace. To avoid this error, type a closing brace whenever an opening brace is typed, as shown in the following example.

```
public class Welcome {

}  ←—Type this closing brace right away to match the opening brace
```

If you use an IDE such as NetBeans and Eclipse, the IDE automatically inserts a closing brace for each opening brace typed.

Common Error 2: Missing Semicolons

Each statement ends with a statement terminator (;). Often, a new programmer forgets to place a statement terminator for the last statement in a block, as shown in the following example.

```
public static void main(String[] args) {
  System.out.println("Programming is fun!");
  System.out.println("Fundamentals First");
  System.out.println("Problem Driven")
}
```

Missing a semicolon

Common Error 3: Missing Quotation Marks

A string must be placed inside the quotation marks. Often, a new programmer forgets to place a quotation mark at the end of a string, as shown in the following example.

```
System.out.println("Problem Driven );
```

Missing a quotation mark

If you use an IDE such as NetBeans and Eclipse, the IDE automatically inserts a closing quotation mark for each opening quotation mark typed.

Common Error 4: Misspelling Names

Java is case sensitive. Misspelling names is a common error for new programmers. For example, the word `main` is misspelled as `Main` and `String` is misspelled as `string` in the following code.

```
public class Test {
  public static void Main(string[] args) {
    System.out.println((10.5 + 2 * 3) / (45 - 3.5));
  }
}
```

✓ Section 2.7 Assessment

1. What are syntax errors (compile errors), runtime errors, and logic errors?
2. Give examples of syntax errors, runtime errors, and logic errors.
3. If you forget to put a closing quotation mark on a string, what kind of error will be raised?
4. If your program needs to read integers, but the user entered strings, an error would occur when running this program. What kind of error is this?
5. Suppose you write a program for computing the perimeter of a rectangle and you mistakenly write your program so that it computes the area of a rectangle. What kind of error is this?
6. Identify and fix the errors in the following code:

```
public class Welcome {
  public void Main(String[] args) {
    System.out.println('Welcome to Java!);
  }
}
```

2.8 Developing Java Programs Using NetBeans

You can edit, compile, run, and debug Java Programs using NetBeans.

NetBeans and Eclipse are two free popular integrated development environments for developing Java programs. They are easy to learn if you follow simple instructions. We recommend that you use either one for developing Java programs. This section gives the essential instructions to guide new users to create a project, create a class, compile, and run a class in NetBeans. The use of Eclipse will be introduced in the next section. For instructions on downloading and installing the latest version of NetBeans, see Supplement A.

Creating a Java Project

Before you can create Java programs, you need to first create a project. A project is like a folder to hold Java programs and all supporting files. You need to create a project only once. Here are the steps to create a Java project:

1. Choose *File*, *New Project* to display the New Project dialog box, as shown in Figure 2.11.

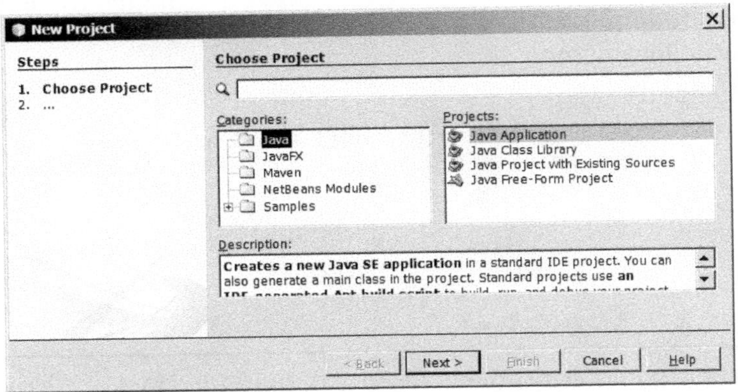

FIGURE 2.11 The New Project dialog is used to create a new project and specify a project type.

2. Select Java in the Categories section and Java Application in the Projects section and click *Next* to display the New Java Application dialog box, as shown in Figure 2.12.
3. Type `demo` in the Project Name field and `c:\michael` in Project Location field. Uncheck *Use Dedicated Folder for Storing Libraries* and uncheck *Create Main Class*.
4. Click *Finish* to create the project, as shown in Figure 2.13.

Creating a Java Class

After a project is created, you can create Java programs in the project using the following steps:

1. Right-click the demo node in the project pane to display a context menu. Choose *New*, *Java Class* to display the New Java Class dialog box, as shown in Figure 2.14.

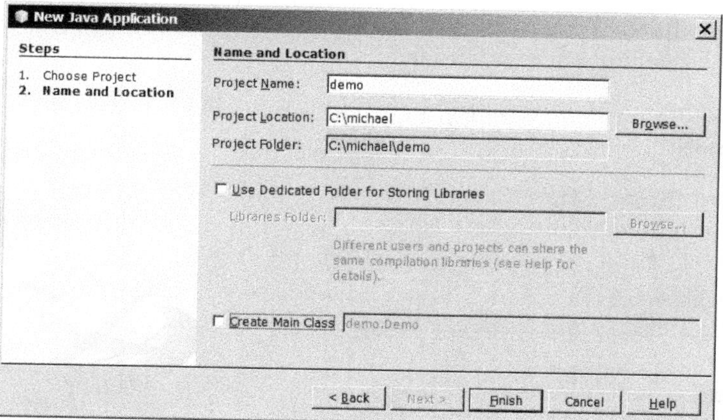

FIGURE 2.12 The New Java Application dialog is for specifying a project name and location.

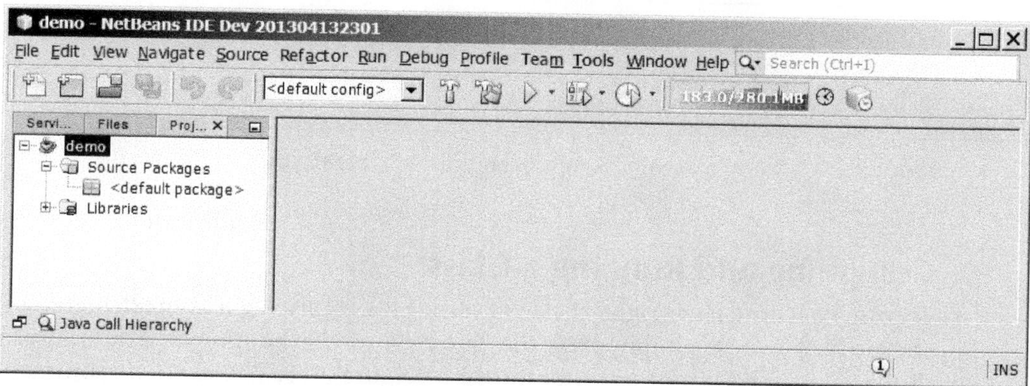

FIGURE 2.13 A New Java project named demo is created.

New Java Class

Steps

1. Choose File Type
2. Name and Location

Name and Location

Class Name: Welcome

Project: demo

Location: Source Packages

Package:

Created File: C:\michael\demo\src\Welcome.java

Warning: It is highly recommended that you do NOT

< Back | Next > | Finish | Cancel | Help

FIGURE 2.14 The New Java Class dialog box is used to create a new Java class.

2. Type `Welcome` in the Class Name field and select the Source Packages in the Location field. Leave the Package field blank. This will create a class in the default package.

3. Click *Finish* to create the Welcome class. The source code file Welcome.java is placed under the <default package> node.
4. Modify the code in the Welcome class to match Listing 2.1 in the text, as shown in Figure 2.15.

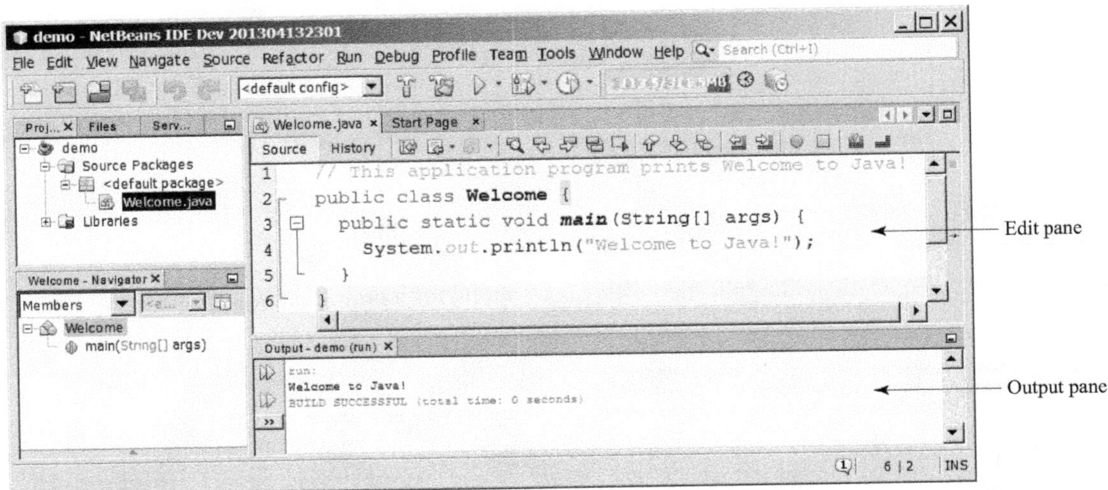

FIGURE 2.15 You can edit a program and run it in NetBeans.

Compiling and Running a Class

To run **Welcome.java**, right-click Welcome.java to display a context menu and choose *Run File*, or simply press the green arrow on the toolbar. The output is displayed in the Output pane, as shown in Figure 2.15. The *Run File* command automatically compiles the program if the program has been changed.

2.9 Developing Java Programs Using Eclipse

You can edit, compile, run, and debug Java Programs using Eclipse.

The preceding section introduced developing Java programs using NetBeans. You can also use Eclipse to develop Java programs. This section gives the essential instructions to guide new users to create a project, create a class, compile and run a class in Eclipse. All exercises in the book can be done in either NetBeans or Eclipse. Your teacher may make Section 2.9 optional, or provide you with further instructions on the IDE choice that aligns with the lab setup. Further instructions on installing and using Eclipse can be found in Supplement B at the back of the book.

Creating a Java Project

Before creating Java programs in Eclipse, you need to first create a project to hold all files. Here are the steps to create a Java project in Eclipse:

1. Choose *File*, *New*, *Java Project* to display the New Project wizard, as shown in Figure 2.16.
2. Type demo in the Project name field. As you type, the Location field is automatically set by default. You may customize the location for your project.

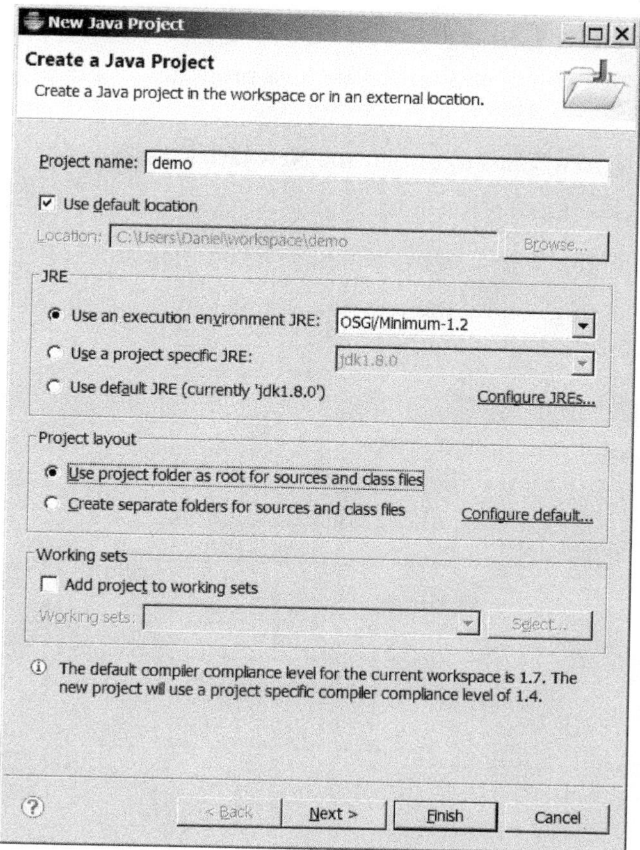

FIGURE 2.16 The New Java Project dialog is for specifying a project name and properties.

3. Make sure that you selected the options *Use project folder as root for sources and class files* so that the .java and .class files are in the same folder for easy access.
4. Click *Finish* to create the project, as shown in Figure 2.17.

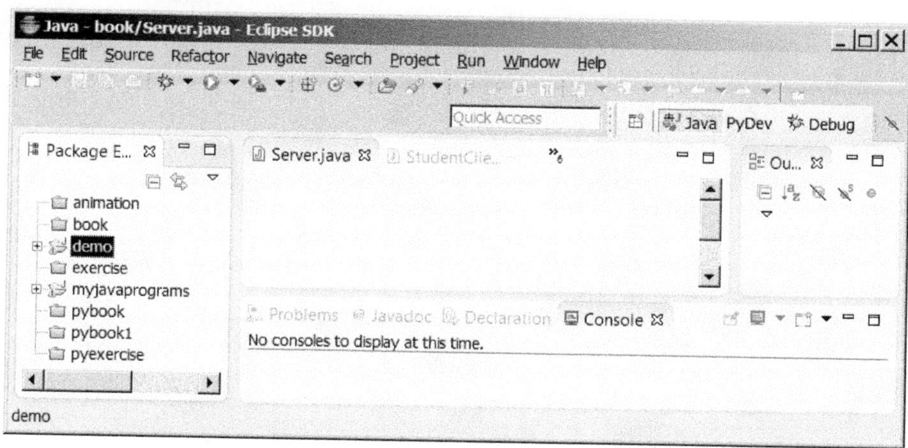

FIGURE 2.17 A New Java project named demo is created.

Creating a Java Class

After a project is created, you can create Java programs in the project using the following steps:

1. Choose *File*, *New*, *Class* to display the New Java Class wizard.
2. Type `Welcome` in the Name field.
3. Check the option *public static void main(String[] args)*.
4. Click *Finish* to generate the template for the source code Welcome.java, as shown in Figure 2.18.

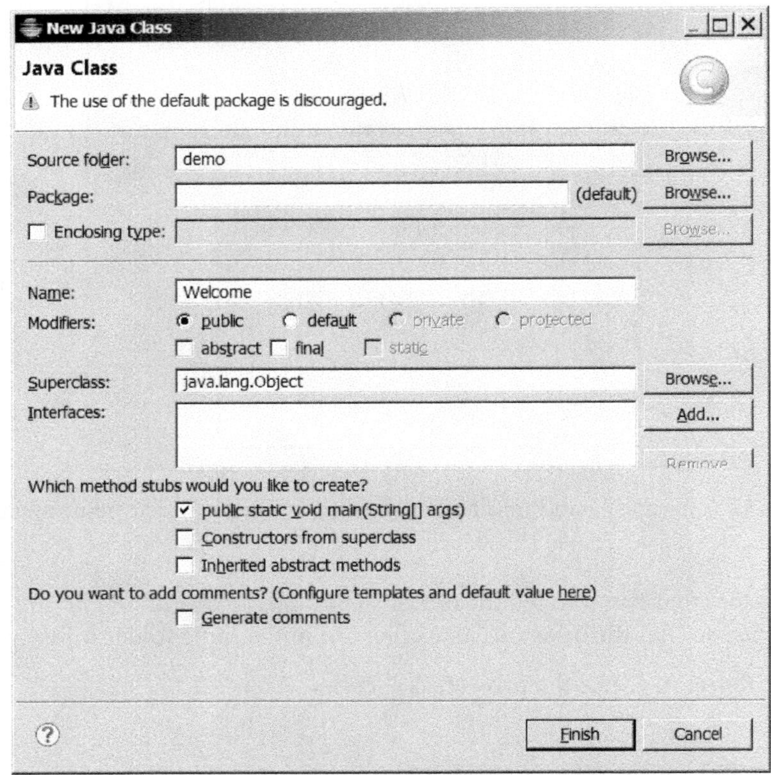

FIGURE 2.18 The New Java Class dialog box is used to create a new Java class.

Compiling and Running a Class

To run the program, right-click the class in the project to display a context menu. Choose *Run, Java Application* in the context menu to run the class. The output is displayed in the Console pane, as shown in Figure 2.19.

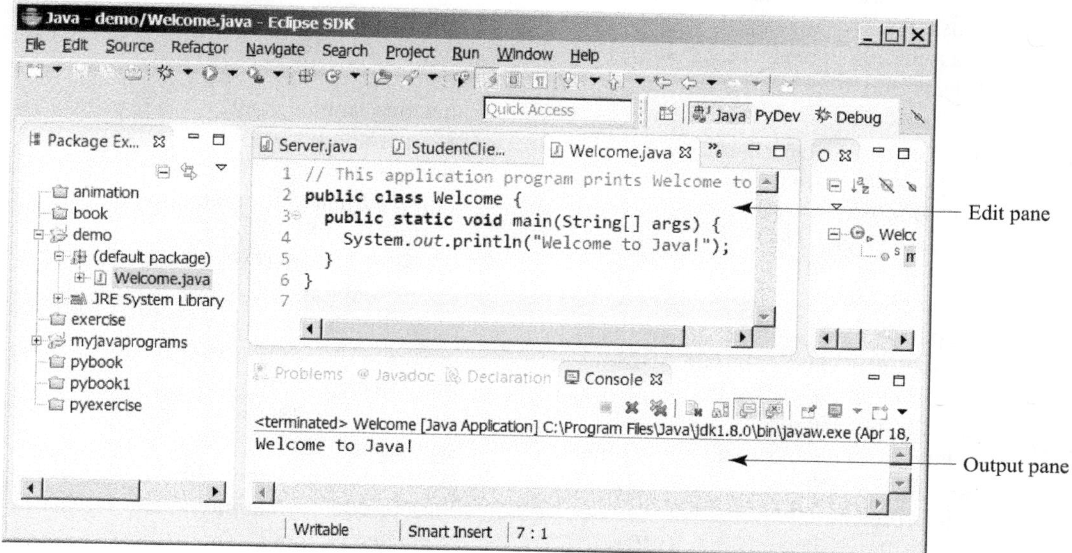

FIGURE 2.19 You can edit a program and run it in Eclipse.

Chapter 2 — Review and Assessment

Key Terms

Application Program Interface (API) 29
assembler 22
assembly language 22
back-end 25
block 31
bytecode 34
bytecode verifier 36
case sensitive 31
class loader 36
comment 30
compiler 23
console 30
event-driven programming 28
front-end 25
high-level language 23
integrated development environment (IDE) 29
interpreter 23
Java Development Toolkit (JDK) 29
Java Virtual Machine (JVM) 34
`javac` command 34
keyword (or reserved word) 30
library 29
logic error 40
low-level language 22
machine language 22
`main` method 30
modular design 25
Object-Oriented Programming (OOP) 28
operating system (OS) 23
Procedural Language 27
programming paradigm 26
programming style 36
runtime error 39
source code 23
statement 23
statement terminator 30
Structured Programming 26
syntax error 38
Unstructured Programming 26

Chapter Summary

1. The *machine language* is a set of primitive instructions built into every computer.
2. *Assembly language* is a *low-level programming language* in which a mnemonic is used to represent each machine-language instruction.
3. *High-level languages* are English-like and easy to learn and program.
4. A program written in a high-level language is called a *source program.*
5. A *compiler* is a software program that translates the source program into a *machine-language program.*
6. The *operating system (OS)* is a program that manages and controls a computer's activities.
7. Java is platform independent, meaning that you can write a program once and run it on any computer.

8. Java programs can be embedded in HTML pages and downloaded by Web browsers to bring live animation and interaction to Web clients.

9. The Java source file name must match the public class name in the program. Java source code files must end with the `.java` extension.

10. Every class is compiled into a separate bytecode file that has the same name as the class and ends with the `.class` extension.

11. To compile a Java source-code file from the command line, use the **javac** command.

12. To run a Java class from the command line, use the **java** command.

13. Every Java program is a set of class definitions. The keyword `class` introduces a class definition. The contents of the class are included in a *block.*

14. A block begins with an opening brace (`{`) and ends with a closing brace (`}`).

15. Methods are contained in a class. To run a Java program, the program must have a `main` method. The `main` method is the entry point where the program starts when it is executed.

16. Every *statement* in Java ends with a semicolon (`;`), known as the *statement terminator.*

17. *Reserved words,* or *keywords,* have a specific meaning to the compiler and cannot be used for other purposes in the program.

18. In Java, comments are preceded by two slashes (`//`) on a line, called a *line comment,* or enclosed between `/*` and `*/` on one or several lines, called a *block comment* or *paragraph comment.* Comments are ignored by the compiler.

19. Java source programs are case sensitive.

20. Programming errors can be categorized into three types: *syntax errors, runtime errors,* and *logic errors.* Errors reported by a compiler are called syntax errors or *compile errors.* Runtime errors are errors that cause a program to terminate abnormally. Logic errors occur when a program does not perform the way it was intended to.

21. *Modular design* is the practice of dividing your application into smaller, reusable units that work together as a whole.

22. Programming languages have evolved over time. Types of language styles include *unstructured, structured, event-driven,* and *object-oriented.*

Programming Exercises

1. (*Display three messages*) Write a program that displays `Welcome to Java`, `Welcome to Computer Science`, and `Programming is fun`.

2. (*Display five messages*) Write a program that displays `Welcome to Java` five times.

3. (*Print a table*) Write a program that displays the following table:

```
a      a^2    a^3
1      1      1
2      4      8
3      9      27
4      16     64
```

4. (*Compute expressions*) Write a program that displays the result of
$$\frac{9.5 \times 4.5 - 2.5 \times 3}{45.5 - 3.5}.$$

5. (*Summation of a series*) Write a program that displays the result of
$$1 + 2 + 3 + 4 + 5 + 6 + 7 + 8 + 9.$$

6. (*Approximate* π) π computed using the following formula:
$$\pi = 4 \times \left(1 - \frac{1}{3} + \frac{1}{5} - \frac{1}{7} + \frac{1}{9} - \frac{1}{11} + \ldots\right)$$
Write a program that displays the result of $4 \times \left(1 - \frac{1}{3} + \frac{1}{5} - \frac{1}{7} + \frac{1}{9} - \frac{1}{11}\right)$ and $4 \times \left(1 - \frac{1}{3} + \frac{1}{5} - \frac{1}{7} + \frac{1}{9} - \frac{1}{11} + \frac{1}{13}\right)$. Use `1.0` instead of `1` in your program.

7. (*Area and perimeter of a circle*) Write a program that displays the area and perimeter of a circle that has a radius of `5.5` using the following formula:
$$perimeter = 2 \times radius \times \pi$$
$$area = radius \times radius \times \pi$$

8. (*Area and perimeter of a rectangle*) Write a program that displays the area and perimeter of a rectangle with the width of `4.5` and height of `7.9` using the following formula:
$$area = radius \times radius \times \pi$$

9. (*Average speed in miles*) Assume a runner runs `14` kilometers in `45` minutes and `30` seconds. Write a program that displays the average speed in miles per hour. (Note that `1` mile is `1.6` kilometers.)

10. (*Average speed in kilometers*) Assume a runner runs `24` miles in `1` hour, `40` minutes, and `35` seconds. Write a program that displays the average speed in kilometers per hour. (Note that `1` mile is `1.6` kilometers.)

Programming Techniques to Analyze and Solve Problems

CHAPTER

3

Objectives

- Identify input that is required, and retrieve input using the `Scanner` class.
- Identify output that is required, and write it to the console.
- Write programming code using assignment statements and assignment expressions.
- Use constants to store permanent data.
- Use variable to store data.
- Use appropriate style and clarity when naming variables, constants, methods, and classes.
- Follow defined, standard procedures to document your project.
- Explore Java numeric primitive data types: `byte`, `short`, `int`, `long`, `float`, and `double`.
- Perform operations using operators `+`, `-`, `*`, `/`
- Describe the Software Development Life Cycle process.
- Design an application using a Software Development Life Cycle approach.
- Explain the quality assurance process.
- Test your application for quality assurance.

3.1 Introduction

The focus of this chapter is on learning beginning programming techniques to solve problems.

In Chapter 1 you learned how to create, compile, and run very basic Java programs. Now you will learn how to solve problems by writing programs. Through these problems, you will learn elementary programming using primitive data types, variables, constants, operators, expressions, and input and output.

Suppose, for example, that you need to take out a student loan. Given the loan amount, loan term, and annual interest rate, can you write a program to compute the monthly payment and total payment? This chapter shows you how to write programs like this. Along the way, you learn the basic steps that go into analyzing a problem, designing a solution, and implementing the solution by creating a program.

3.2 Writing a Simple Program

Writing a program involves designing a strategy for solving the problem and then using a programming language to implement that strategy.

Let's first consider the simple problem of computing the area of a circle. How do we write a program for solving this problem?

algorithm

Writing a program involves designing algorithms and translating algorithms into programming instructions, or code. An *algorithm* describes how a problem is solved by listing the actions that need to be taken and the order of their execution. Algorithms can help the programmer plan a program before writing it in a programming language. Algorithms can be described in natural languages or in *pseudocode*. You may recall from Chapter 2 that pseudocode is a tool used to explain the logical steps of a program by using natural language mixed with some programming code. The algorithm for calculating the area of a circle can be described as follows:

pseudocode

1. Read in the circle's radius.
2. Compute the area using the following formula:

$$area = radius * radius * \pi$$

3. Display the result.

Tip
It's always good practice to outline your program (or its underlying problem) in the form of an algorithm before you begin coding.

When you *code*—that is, when you write a program—you translate an algorithm into a program. You already know that every Java program begins with a class definition in which the keyword `class` is followed by the class name. Assume that you have chosen `ComputeArea` as the class name. The outline of the program would look like this:

```
public class ComputeArea {
  // Details to be given later
}
```

As you know, every Java program must have a `main` method where program execution begins. The program is then expanded as follows:

```
public class ComputeArea {
  public static void main(String[] args) {
    // Step 1: Read in radius

    // Step 2: Compute area
    // Step 3: Display the area
  }
}
```

Step 1 in the preceding code identifies the input requirements. The program needs to read the radius entered by the user from the keyboard. This raises two important issues:

- Reading the radius.
- Storing the radius in the program.

Let's address the second issue first. In order to store the radius, the program needs to declare a symbol called a *variable*. A variable represents a value stored in the computer's memory.

variable

Rather than using `x` and `y` as variable names, choose descriptive names: in this case, `radius` for radius, and `area` for area. To let the compiler know what `radius` and `area` are, specify their data types. That is the kind of data stored in a variable, whether integer, real number, or something else. This is known as *declaring variables.* Java provides simple data types for representing integers, real numbers, characters, and Boolean types. These types are known as *primitive data types* or *fundamental types.*

descriptive names

data type

declare variables

primitive data types

Real numbers (i.e., numbers with a decimal point) are represented using a method known as *floating-point* in computers. So, the real numbers are also called *floating-point numbers.* In Java, you can use the keyword `double` to declare a floating-point variable. Declare `radius` and `area` as `double`. The program can be expanded as follows:

floating-point number

```
public class ComputeArea {
  public static void main(String[] args) {
    double radius;
    double area;

    // Step 1: Read in radius

    // Step 2: Compute area

    // Step 3: Display the area
  }
}
```

The program declares `radius` and `area` as variables. The reserved word `double` indicates that `radius` and `area` are floating-point values stored in the computer.

The first step is to prompt the user to designate the circle's `radius`. You will soon learn how to prompt the user for information. For now, to learn how variables work, you can assign a fixed value to `radius` in the program as you write the code; later, you'll modify the program to prompt the user for this value.

The second step is to compute area by assigning the result of the expression radius * radius * 3.14159 to area.

The final step displays the output requirements. The program will display the value of area on the console by using the System.out.println method.

Listing 3.1 shows the complete program, and a sample run of the program is shown in Figure 3.1.

LISTING 3.1 ComputeArea.java

```
1  public class ComputeArea {
2    public static void main(String[] args) {
3      double radius; // Declare radius
4      double area; // Declare area
5
6      // Assign a radius
7      radius = 20; // radius is now 20
8
9      // Compute area
10     area = radius * radius * 3.14159;
11
12     // Display results
13     System.out.println("The area for the circle of radius " +
14       radius + " is " + area);
15   }
16 }
```

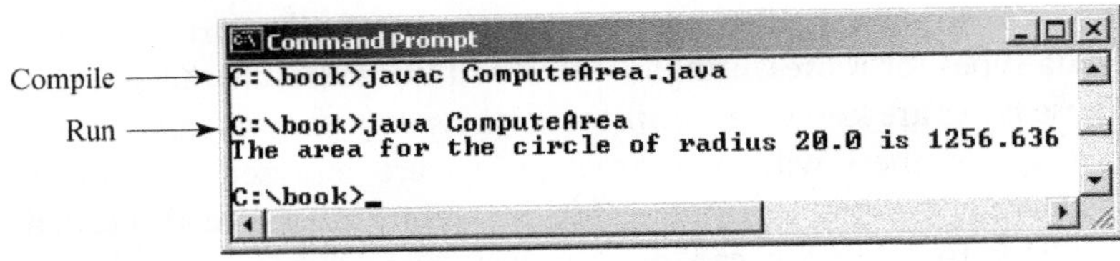
Compile
Run
Command Prompt
C:\book>javac ComputeArea.java
C:\book>java ComputeArea
The area for the circle of radius 20.0 is 1256.636
C:\book>_

FIGURE 3.1 The program displays the area of a circle.

declare variable

assign value

Variables such as radius and area correspond to memory locations. Every variable has a name, a type, a size, and a value. Line 3 declares that radius can store a double value. The value is not defined until you assign a value. Line 7 assigns 20 into variable radius. Similarly, line 4 declares variable area, and line 10 assigns a value into area. The following table shows the value in the memory for area and radius as the program is executed. Each row in the table shows the values of variables after the statement in the corresponding line in the program is executed. This method of reviewing how a program works is called *tracing a program.* Tracing programs are helpful for understanding how programs work, and they are useful tools for comparing actual results to anticipated results.

tracing program

compare results

line#	radius	area
3	no value	
4		no value
7	20	
10		1256.636

3.7 Named Constants

A named constant is an identifier that represents a permanent value.

constant

The value of a variable may change during the execution of a program, but a *named constant,* or simply *constant,* represents permanent data that never changes. In our `ComputeArea` program, π is constant. If you use it frequently, you don't want to keep typing `3.14159`; instead, you can declare a constant for π. Here is the syntax for declaring a constant:

```
final datatype CONSTANTNAME = value;
```

`final` keyword

A constant must be declared and initialized in the same statement. The word `final` is a Java keyword for declaring a constant. For example, you can declare π as a constant and rewrite Listing 3.1 as in Listing 3.4.

LISTING 3.4 ComputeAreaWithConstant.java

```
import java.util.Scanner; // Scanner is in the java.util package

public class ComputeAreaWithConstant {
  public static void main(String[] args) {
    final double PI = 3.14159; // Declare a constant

    // Create a Scanner object
    Scanner input = new Scanner(System.in);

    // Prompt the user to enter a radius
    System.out.print("Enter a number for radius: ");
    double radius = input.nextDouble();

    // Compute area
    double area = radius * radius * PI;

    // Display result
    System.out.println("The area for the circle of radius " +
      radius + " is " + area);
  }
}
```

benefits of constants

There are three benefits of using constants:

1. You don't have to repeatedly type the same value if it is used multiple times.
2. If you have to change the constant value (e.g., from `3.14` to `3.14159` for `PI`), you need to change it only in a single location in the source code.
3. A descriptive name for a constant makes the program easy to read.

3.8 Follow Defined Standards to Document Your Design

Following common industry standards helps document your program design. Following the standard Java naming convention is a meaningful way to document your program. It makes your programs easy to read and avoids errors.

Make sure that you choose descriptive names with straightforward meanings for the variables, constants, classes, and methods in your program. As mentioned earlier, names are case sensitive. Listed below are the standard conventions for naming variables, methods, and classes.

name variables and methods

- Use lowercase for variables and methods. If a name consists of several words, concatenate them into one, making the first word lowercase and capitalizing the first letter of each subsequent word—for example, the variables `radius` and `area` and the method `print`.

name classes

- Capitalize the first letter of each word in a class name—for example, the class names `ComputeArea` and `System`.

name constants

- Capitalize every letter in a constant, and use underscores between words —for example, the constants `PI` and `MAX_VALUE`.

It is important to follow the naming conventions to make your programs easy to read.

name classes

Caution

Do not choose class names that are already used in the Java library. For example, since the `System` class is defined in Java, you should not name your class `System`.

✓ Section 3.8 Assessment

1. What are the benefits of using constants? Declare an `int` constant `SIZE` with value `20`.
2. What are the naming conventions for class names, method names, constants, and variables? Which of the following items can be a constant, a method, a variable, or a class according to the Java naming conventions?

   `MAX_VALUE`, `Test`, `read`, `readDouble`
3. Translate the following algorithm into Java code:

   Step 1: Declare a `double` variable named `miles` with initial value `100`.

   Step 2: Declare a `double` constant named `KILOMETERS_PER_MILE` with value `1.609`.

   Step 3: Declare a `double` variable named `kilometers`, multiply `miles` and `KILOMETERS_PER_MILE`, and assign the result to `kilometers`.

   Step 4: Display `kilometers` to the console.

   What is `kilometers` after Step 4?

3.9 Numeric Data Types and Operations

*Java has six numeric types for integers and floating-point numbers with operators +, -, *, /, and %.*

Numeric Types

Every data type has a range of values. The compiler allocates memory space for each variable or constant according to its data type. Java provides eight primitive data types for numeric values, characters, and Boolean values. This section introduces numeric data types and operators.

Table 3.1 lists the six numeric data types, their ranges, and their storage sizes.

TABLE 3.1 Numeric Data Types

Name	*Range*	*Storage Size*	
`byte`	-2^7 to $2^7 - 1$ (–128 to 127)	8-bit signed	`byte` type
`short`	-2^{15} to $2^{15} - 1$ (–32768 to 32767)	16-bit signed	`short` type
`int`	-2^{31} to $2^{31} - 1$ (–2147483648 to 2147483647)	32-bit signed	`int` type
`long`	-2^{63} to $2^{63} - 1$	64-bit signed	`long` type
	(i.e., –9223372036854775808 to 9223372036854775807)		
`float`	Negative range: –3.4028235E + 38 to –1.4E – 45	32-bit IEEE 754	`float` type
	Positive range: 1.4E – 45 to 3.4028235E + 38		
`double`	Negative range: –1.7976931348623157E + 308 to –4.9E – 324	64-bit IEEE 754	`double` type
	Positive range: 49E – 324 to 1.7976931348623157E + 308		

integer types

Java uses four types for integers: `byte`, `short`, `int`, and `long`. Choose the type that is most appropriate for your variable. For example, if you know an integer stored in a variable is within a range of a byte, declare the variable as a `byte`. For simplicity and consistency, we will use `int` for integers most of the time in this book.

floating-point types

Java uses two types for floating-point numbers: `float` and `double`. The `double` type is twice as big as `float`, so the `double` is known as *double precision* and `float` as *single precision*. Normally, you should use the `double` type, because it is more accurate than the `float` type.

Reading Numbers from the Keyboard

You know how to use the `nextDouble()` method in the `Scanner` class to read a double value from the keyboard. You can also use the methods listed in Table 3.2 to read a number of the `byte`, `short`, `int`, `long`, and `float` type.

TABLE 3.2 Methods for Scanner Objects

Method	*Description*
`nextByte()`	reads an integer of the `byte` type.
`nextShort()`	reads an integer of the `short` type.
`nextInt()`	reads an integer of the `int` type.
`nextLong()`	reads an integer of the `long` type.
`nextFloat()`	reads a number of the `float` type.
`nextDouble()`	reads a number of the `double` type.

Here are examples for reading values of various types from the keyboard:

```
 1  Scanner input = new Scanner(System.in);
 2  System.out.print("Enter a byte value: ");
 3  byte byteValue = input.nextByte();
 4
 5  System.out.print("Enter a short value: ");
 6  short shortValue = input.nextShort();
 7
 8  System.out.print("Enter an int value: ");
 9  int intValue = input.nextInt();
10
11  System.out.print("Enter a long value: ");
12  long longValue = input.nextLong();
13
14  System.out.print("Enter a float value: ");
15  float floatValue = input.nextFloat();
```

If you enter a value with an incorrect range or format, a runtime error would occur. For example, if you enter a value `128` for line 3, an error would occur because `128` is out of range for a `byte` type integer.

Numeric Operators

operators +, -, *, /, %

operand

The operators for numeric data types include the standard arithmetic operators: addition (+), subtraction (-), multiplication (*), division (/), and remainder (%), as shown in Table 3.3. The *operands* are the values operated by an operator.

TABLE 3.3 Numeric Operators

Name	*Meaning*	*Example*	*Result*
+	Addition	34 + 1	35
-	Subtraction	34.0 – 0.1	33.9
*	Multiplication	300 * 30	9000
/	Division	1.0 / 2.0	0.5
%	Remainder	20 % 3	2

When both operands of a division are integers, the result of the division is the quotient and the fractional part is truncated. For example, `5 / 2` yields `2`, not `2.5`, and `-5 / 2` yields `-2`, not `-2.5`. To perform a float-point division, one of the operands must be a floating-point number. For example, `5.0 / 2` yields `2.5`.

The `%` operator, known as *remainder* or *modulo* operator, yields the remainder after division. The operand on the left is the dividend and the operand on the right is the divisor. Therefore, `7 % 3` yields `1`, `3 % 7` yields `3`, `12 % 4` yields `0`, `26 % 8` yields `2`, and `20 % 13` yields `7`.

```
   2        0        3        3                      1  <-- Quotient
3 / 7    7 / 3    4 / 12   8 / 26   Divisor --> 13 / 20 <-- Dividend
    6        0       12       24                    13
   --       --       --       --                    --
    1        3        0        2                     7  <-- Remainder
```

The `%` operator is often used for positive integers, but it can also be used with negative integers and floating-point values. The remainder is negative only if the dividend is negative. For example, `-7 % 3` yields `-1`, `-12 % 4` yields `0`, `-26 % -8` yields `-2`, and `20 % -13` yields `7`.

✓ Section 3.9 Assessment

1. You are designing input requirements for an application. You need to store decimal numbers and ensure the highest accuracy. Which data type should you use?
2. You are designing input requirements for an application. What data type should you use to store a student's current age?
3. You are designing the output requirements for an application. What data type should you use to print a student ID ranging from 1000 - 100,000?
4. What is the output value of: `5 * 10 / 2`?

3.10 Evaluating Expressions and Operator Precedence

Java expressions are evaluated in the same way as arithmetic expressions.

In Java programming, operators contained within pairs of parentheses are evaluated first. Parentheses can be nested, in which case the expression in the inner parentheses is evaluated first. When more than one operator is used in an expression, the following operator precedence rule is used to determine the order of evaluation.

evaluating an expression

operator precedence rule

- Multiplication, division, and remainder operators are applied first. If an expression contains several multiplication, division, and remainder operators, they are applied from left to right.
- Addition and subtraction operators are applied last. If an expression contains several addition and subtraction operators, they are applied from left to right.

Here is an example of how an expression is evaluated:

```
3 + 4 * 4 + 5 * (4 + 3) - 1
                   ↑ (1) inside parentheses first
3 + 4 * 4 + 5 * 7 - 1
      ↑ (2) multiplication
3 + 16 + 5 * 7 - 1
           ↑ (3) multiplication
3 + 16 + 35 - 1
  ↑ (4) addition
19 + 35 - 1
   ↑ (5) addition
    54 - 1
       ↑ (6) subtraction
    53
```

Listing 3.5 gives a program that converts a Fahrenheit degree to Celsius using the formula celsius = $(\frac{5}{9})$(fahrenheit = 32).

LISTING 3.5 FahrenheitToCelsius.java

divide

```
1  import java.util.Scanner;
2
3  public class FahrenheitToCelsius {
4    public static void main(String[] args) {
5      Scanner input = new Scanner(System.in);
6
7      System.out.print("Enter a degree in Fahrenheit: ");
8      double fahrenheit = input.nextDouble();
9
10     // Convert Fahrenheit to Celsius
11     double celsius = (5.0 / 9) * (fahrenheit - 32);
12     System.out.println("Fahrenheit " + fahrenheit + " is " +
13       celsius + " in Celsius");
14   }
15 }
```

```
Enter a degree in Fahrenheit: 100 ↵Enter
Fahrenheit 100.0 is 37.77777777777778 in Celsius
```

line#	fahrenheit	celsius
8	100	
11		37.77777777777778

integer vs. floating-point division

Be careful when applying division. Division of two integers yields an integer in Java. $\frac{5}{9}$ is translated to `5.0 / 9` instead of `5 / 9` in line 11, because `5 / 9` yields `0` in Java.

So, the input needed for the program is the monthly interest rate, the length of the loan in years, and the loan amount.

Note

The requirements specification says that the user must enter the annual interest rate, the loan amount, and the number of years for which payments will be made. During analysis, however, it is possible that you may discover that input is not sufficient or that some values are unnecessary for the output. If this happens, you can go back and modify the requirements specification.

Note

In the real world, you will work with customers from all walks of life. You may develop software for chemists, physicists, engineers, economists, and psychologists, and of course you will not have (or need) complete knowledge of all these fields. Therefore, you don't have to know how formulas are derived, but given the monthly interest rate, the number of years, and the loan amount, you can compute the monthly payment in this program. You will, however, need to communicate with customers and understand how a mathematical model works for the system.

Stage 3: System Design—Identify the Software Process, Required Input/Output, and Possible Issues

During system design, you identify the steps in the program.

Step 1. Prompt the user to enter the annual interest rate, the number of years, and the loan amount.

(The interest rate is commonly expressed as a percentage of the principal for a period of one year. This is known as the *annual interest rate.*)

Step 2. The input for the annual interest rate is a number in percent format, such as 4.5%. The program needs to convert it into a decimal by dividing it by `100`. To obtain the monthly interest rate from the annual interest rate, divide it by `12`, since a year has 12 months. So, to obtain the monthly interest rate in decimal format, you need to divide the annual interest rate in percentage by `1200`. For example, if the annual interest rate is 4.5%, then the monthly interest rate is 4.5/1200 = 0.00375.

Step 3. To avoid issues while performing calculations on numerical values, be sure to choose the most appropriate data type. Use *Casting* to help solve this issue. A limitation, or constraint of this application, is that the user must enter the values in the correct format.

Step 4. Compute the monthly payment using the preceding formula.

Step 5. Compute the total payment, which is the monthly payment multiplied by `12` and multiplied by the number of years.

Step 6. Display the monthly payment and total payment.

Stage 4: Implementation

Implementation is also known as *coding* (writing the code). In the formula, you have to compute $(1 + monthlyInterestRate)^{numberOfYears \times 12}$, which can be obtained using `Math.pow(1 + monthlyInterestRate, numberOfYears * 12)`.

`Math.pow(a, b)` method

Listing 3.8 gives the complete program.

LISTING 3.8 ComputeLoan.java

import class · create a `Scanner` · enter interest rate · enter years · enter loan amount · `monthlyPayment` · `totalPayment` · casting · casting

```
1  import java.util.Scanner;
2
3  public class ComputeLoan {
4    public static void main(String[] args) {
5      // Create a Scanner
6      Scanner input = new Scanner(System.in);
7
8      // Enter annual interest rate in percentage, e.g., 7.25%
9      System.out.print("Enter annual interest rate, e.g., 7.25%: ");
10     double annualInterestRate = input.nextDouble();
11
12     // Obtain monthly interest rate
13     double monthlyInterestRate = annualInterestRate / 1200;
14
15     // Enter number of years
16     System.out.print(
17       "Enter number of years as an integer, e.g., 5: ");
18     int numberOfYears = input.nextInt();
19
20     // Enter loan amount
21     System.out.print("Enter loan amount, e.g., 120000.95: ");
22     double loanAmount = input.nextDouble();
23
24     // Calculate payment
25     double monthlyPayment = loanAmount * monthlyInterestRate / (1
26       - 1 / Math.pow(1 + monthlyInterestRate, numberOfYears * 12));
27     double totalPayment = monthlyPayment * numberOfYears * 12;
28
29     // Display results
30     System.out.println("The monthly payment is $" +
31       (int)(monthlyPayment * 100) / 100.0);
32     System.out.println("The total payment is $" +
33       (int)(totalPayment * 100) / 100.0);
34   }
35 }
```

```
Enter annual interest rate, e.g., 5.75%: 5.75 ↵Enter
Enter number of years as an integer, e.g., 5: 15 ↵Enter
Enter loan amount, e.g., 120000.95: 250000 ↵Enter
The monthly payment is $2076.02
The total payment is $373684.53
```

Line 10 reads the annual interest rate, which is converted into the monthly interest rate in line 13.

Choose the most appropriate data type for the variable. For example, `numberOfYears` is best declared as an `int` (line 18), although it could be declared as a `long`, `float`, or `double`. Note that `byte` might be the most appropriate for `numberOfYears`. For simplicity, however, the examples in this book will use `int` for integer and `double` for floating-point values.

The formula for computing the monthly payment is translated into Java code in lines 25–27.

Casting is used in lines 31 and 33 to obtain a new `monthlyPayment` and `totalPayment` with two digits after the decimal points.

The program uses the `Scanner` class, imported in line 1. The program also uses the `Math` class, and you might be wondering why that class isn't imported into the program. The `Math` class is in the `java.lang` package, and all classes in the `java.lang` package are implicitly imported. Therefore, you don't need to explicitly import the `Math` class.

`java.lang` package

Stage 5: Testing—Assure Project Quality by Identifying Problems and Resolutions
Quality assurance is the process of monitoring a project to ensure the software design plan is followed and the expected results are achieved. Quality assurance reviews should occur throughout the project life cycle. Some of the techniques discussed in this chapter such as following a project plan, using standard coding practices, choosing standard and meaningful naming conventions, documenting your coding steps, and testing your code are all ways to maintain the quality of your project. Testing your application with some sample data and verifying the output is an important step in quality assurance.

quality assurance

✓ Section 3.16 Assessment

1. Explain the Software Development Life Cycle and identify the stages.
2. Explain the Quality Assurance process.
3. Create a quality assurance tracking table like the one that follows. Test and document the results of the **computeloan.java** example by filling in the results into the proper cell in the table.
   - **a.** What is the value of *annualInterestRate* after line 10 is executed?
   - **b.** What is the value of *monthlyInterestRate* after line 13 is executed?
   - **c.** What is the value of *numberOfYears* after line 18 is executed?
   - **d.** What is the value of *loanAmount* after line 22 is executed?
   - **e.** What is the value of *monthlyPayment* after line 25 is executed?
   - **f.** What is the value of totalPayment after line 27 is executed?

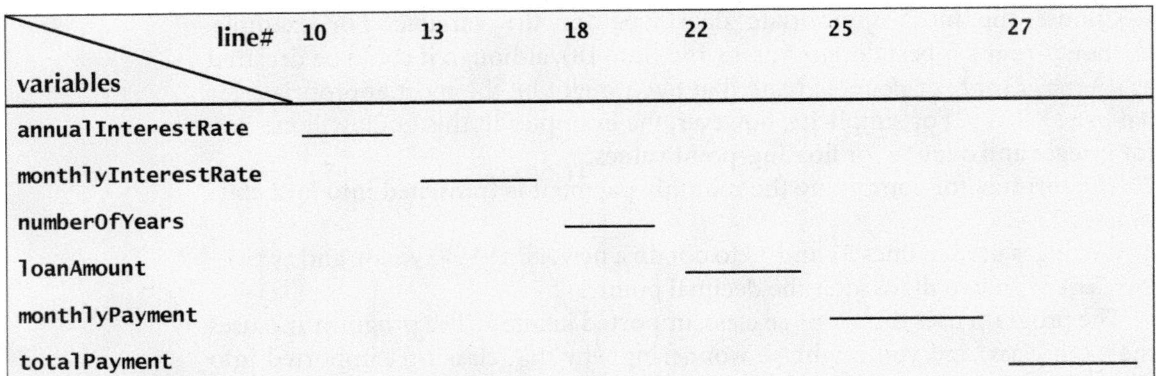

variables \ line#	10	13	18	22	25	27
annualInterestRate	______					
monthlyInterestRate		______				
numberOfYears			______			
loanAmount				______		
monthlyPayment					______	
totalPayment						______

3.17 Case Study: Counting Monetary Units

This section presents a program that breaks a large amount of money into smaller units.

Suppose you want to develop a program that changes a given amount of money into smaller monetary units. The program lets the user enter an amount as a `double` value representing a total in dollars and cents, and outputs a report listing the monetary equivalent in the maximum number of dollars, quarters, dimes, nickels, and pennies, in this order, to result in the minimum number of coins.

Here are the steps in developing the program:

1. Prompt the user to enter the amount as a decimal number, such as `11.56`.
2. Convert the amount (e.g., `11.56`) into cents (`1156`).
3. Divide the cents by `100` to find the number of dollars. Obtain the remaining cents using the cents remainder `100`.
4. Divide the remaining cents by `25` to find the number of quarters. Obtain the remaining cents using the remaining cents remainder `25`.
5. Divide the remaining cents by `10` to find the number of dimes. Obtain the remaining cents using the remaining cents remainder `10`.
6. Divide the remaining cents by `5` to find the number of nickels. Obtain the remaining cents using the remaining cents remainder `5`.
7. The remaining cents are the pennies.
8. Display the result.

The complete program is given in Listing 3.9.

LISTING 3.9 ComputeChange.java

```
import java.util.Scanner;

public class ComputeChange {
  public static void main(String[] args) {
    // Create a Scanner
    Scanner input = new Scanner(System.in);

    // Receive the amount
    System.out.print(
      "Enter an amount in double, for example 11.56: ");
    double amount = input.nextDouble();

    int remainingAmount = (int)(amount * 100);

    // Find the number of one dollars
    int numberOfOneDollars = remainingAmount / 100;
    remainingAmount = remainingAmount % 100;

    // Find the number of quarters in the remaining amount
    int numberOfQuarters = remainingAmount / 25;
    remainingAmount = remainingAmount % 25;

    // Find the number of dimes in the remaining amount
    int numberOfDimes = remainingAmount / 10;
    remainingAmount = remainingAmount % 10;

    // Find the number of nickels in the remaining amount
    int numberOfNickels = remainingAmount / 5;
    remainingAmount = remainingAmount % 5;

    // Find the number of pennies in the remaining amount
    int numberOfPennies = remainingAmount;

    // Display results
    System.out.println("Your amount " + amount + " consists of");
    System.out.println("    " + numberOfOneDollars + " dollars");
    System.out.println("    " + numberOfQuarters + " quarters ");
    System.out.println("    " + numberOfDimes + " dimes");
    System.out.println("    " + numberOfNickels + " nickels");
    System.out.println("    " + numberOfPennies + " pennies");
  }
}
```

import class

enter input

dollars

quarters

dimes

nickels

pennies

output

```
Enter an amount, for example, 11.56: 11.56 ↵Enter
Your amount 11.56 consists of
    11 dollars
    2 quarters
    0 dimes
    1 nickels
    1 pennies
```

variables \ line#	11	13	16	17	20	21	24	25	28	29	32
`amount`	11.56										
`remainingAmount`		1156		56		6		6		1	
`numberOfOneDollars`			11								
`numberOfQuarters`					2						
`numberOfDimes`							0				
`numberOfNickels`									1		
`numberOfPennies`											1

The variable `amount` stores the amount entered from the console (line 11). This variable is not changed, because the amount has to be used at the end of the program to display the results. The program introduces the variable `remainingAmount` (line 13) to store the changing remaining amount.

The variable `amount` is a `double` decimal representing dollars and cents. It is converted to an `int` variable `remainingAmount`, which represents all the cents. For instance, if `amount` is `11.56`, then the initial `remainingAmount` is `1156`. The division operator yields the integer part of the division, so `1156 / 100` is `11`. The remainder operator obtains the remainder of the division, so `1156 % 100` is `56`.

The program extracts the maximum number of singles from the remaining amount and obtains a new remaining amount in the variable `remainingAmount` (lines 16–17). It then extracts the maximum number of quarters from `remainingAmount` and obtains a new `remainingAmount` (lines 20–21). Continuing the same process, the program finds the maximum number of dimes, nickels, and pennies in the remaining amount.

loss of precision

One serious problem with this example is the possible loss of precision when casting a `double` amount to an `int remainingAmount`. This could lead to an inaccurate result. If you try to enter the amount `10.03`, `10.03 * 100` becomes `1002.9999999999999`. You will find that the program displays `10` dollars and `2` pennies. To fix the problem, enter the amount as an integer value representing cents. As an example, `10.03` is represented as `1003` cents.

✓ Section 3.17 Assessment

1. Show the output with the input value `1.99`.

3.18 Testing Your Program for Common Errors and Pitfalls

When you are testing your application, you should start by looking for common errors. Common errors are often caused by undeclared variables, uninitialized variables, integer overflow, unintended integer division, and round-off errors.

Common Error 1: Undeclared/Uninitialized Variables and Unused Variables

A variable must be declared with a type and assigned a value before using it. A common error is not declaring a variable or initializing a variable. Consider the following code:

```
double interestRate = 0.05;
double interest = interestrate * 45;
```

This code is wrong, because `interestRate` is assigned a value `0.05`; but `interestrate` has not been declared and initialized. Java is case sensitive, so it considers `interestRate` and `interestrate` to be two different variables.

If a variable is declared, but not used in the program, it might be a potential programming error. So, you should remove the unused variable from your program. For example, in the following code, `taxRate` is never used. It should be removed from the code.

```
double interestRate = 0.05;
double taxRate = 0.05;
double interest = interestRate * 45;
System.out.println("Interest is " + interest);
```

If you use an IDE such as Eclipse and NetBeans, you will receive a warning on unused variables.

Common Error 2: Integer Overflow

Numbers are stored with a limited numbers of digits. When a variable is assigned a value that is too large (*in size*) to be stored, it causes *overflow*. For example, executing the following statement causes overflow, because the largest value that can be stored in a variable of the `int` type is `2147483647`. `2147483648` will be too large for an `int` value.

what is overflow?

```
int value = 2147483647 + 1;
// value will actually be -2147483648
```

Likewise, executing the following statement causes overflow, because the smallest value that can be stored in a variable of the `int` type is `-2147483648`. `-2147483649` is too large in size to be stored in an `int` variable.

```
int value = -2147483648 - 1;
// value will actually be 2147483647
```

Java does not report warnings or errors on overflow, so be careful when working with numbers close to the maximum or minimum range of a given type.

what is underflow?

When a floating-point number is too small (i.e., too close to zero) to be stored, it causes *underflow*. Java approximates it to zero, so normally you don't need to be concerned about underflow.

Common Error 3: Round-off Errors

round-off error

A *round-off error*, also called a *rounding error*, is the difference between the calculated approximation of a number and its exact mathematical value. For example, 1/3 is approximately 0.333 if you keep three decimal places, and is 0.3333333 if you keep seven decimal places. Since the number of digits that can be stored in a variable is limited, round-off errors are inevitable. Calculations involving floating-point numbers are approximated because these numbers are not stored with complete accuracy. For example,

```
System.out.println(1.0 - 0.1 - 0.1 - 0.1 - 0.1 - 0.1);
```

displays `0.5000000000000001`, not `0.5`, and

```
System.out.println(1.0 - 0.9);
```

displays `0.09999999999999998`, not `0.1`. Integers are stored precisely. Therefore, calculations with integers yield a precise integer result.

Common Error 4: Unintended Integer Division

Java uses the same divide operator, namely `/`, to perform both integer and floating-point division. When two operands are integers, the `/` operator performs an integer division. The result of the operation is an integer. The fractional part is truncated. To force two integers to perform a floating-point division, make one of the integers into a floating-point number. For example, the code in (a) displays that average is `1` and the code in (b) displays that average is `1.5`.

```
int number1 = 1;
int number2 = 2;
double average = (number1 + number2) / 2;
System.out.println(average);
```

(a)

```
int number1 = 1;
int number2 = 2;
double average = (number1 + number2) / 2.0;
System.out.println(average);
```

(b)

Common Pitfall 1: Redundant Input Objects

New programmers often write the code to create multiple input objects for each input. For example, the following code reads an integer and a double value.

```
Scanner input = new Scanner(System.in);
System.out.print("Enter an integer: ");
int v1 = input.nextInt();

Scanner input1 = new Scanner(System.in);
System.out.print("Enter a double value: ");
double v2 = input1.nextDouble();
```

BAD CODE

The code is not wrong, but inefficient. It creates two input objects unnecessarily and may lead to some subtle errors. You should rewrite the code as follows:

```
Scanner input = new Scanner(System.in);
System.out.print("Enter an integer: ");
int v1 = input.nextInt();
System.out.print("Enter a double value: ");
double v2 = input.nextDouble();
```

GOOD CODE

✓ Section 3.18 Assessment

1. Can you declare a variable as `int` and later redeclare it as `double`?
2. What is an integer overflow? Can floating-point operations cause overflow?
3. Will overflow cause a runtime error?
4. What is a round-off error? Can integer operations cause round-off errors? Can floating-point operations cause round-off errors?

Chapter 3 — Review and Assessment

Key Terms

algorithm 52
assignment operator (=) 61
assignment statement 61
`byte` type 65
casting 74
constant 63
data type 53
declare variables 53
decrement operator (--) 72
`double` type 65
expression 61
`final` keyword 63
`float` type 65
floating-point number 53
identifier 59
increment operator (++) 72
initialize variables 60
`int` type 65
integer overflow 85
IPO 58
`long` type 65
operators 66
postdecrement 72
postincrement 72
predecrement 72
preincrement 72
primitive data type 53
pseudocode 52
quality assurance 81
requirements specification 77
round-off error 86
`short` type 65
software development lifecycle 77
specific import 57
system analysis 77
system design 77
tracing program 54
UNIX epoch 69
variable 53
wildcard import 57

Chapter Summary

1. *Identifiers* are names for naming elements such as variables, constants, methods, classes, packages in a program.
2. An identifier is a sequence of characters that consists of letters, digits, underscores (_), and dollar signs ($). An identifier must start with a letter or an underscore. It cannot start with a digit. An identifier cannot be a reserved word. An identifier can be of any length.
3. *Variables* are used to store data in a program. To declare a variable is to tell the compiler what type of data a variable can hold.
4. There are two types of `import` statements: *specific import* and *wildcard import.* The specific import specifies a single class in the import statement; the wildcard import imports all the classes in a package.
5. In Java, the equal sign (=) is used as the *assignment operator.*
6. A variable declared in a method must be assigned a value before it can be used.

7. A *named constant* (or simply a *constant*) represents permanent data that never changes.

8. A named constant is declared by using the keyword `final`.

9. Java provides four integer types (`byte`, `short`, `int`, and `long`) that represent integers of four different sizes.

10. Java provides two *floating-point types* (`float` and `double`) that represent floating-point numbers of two different precisions.

11. Java provides *operators* that perform numeric operations: + (addition), - (subtraction), * (multiplication), / (division), and % (remainder).

12. Integer arithmetic (/) yields an integer result.

13. The numeric operators in a Java expression are applied the same way as in an arithmetic expression.

14. Java provides the augmented assignment operators += (addition assignment), -= (subtraction assignment), *= (multiplication assignment), /= (division assignment), and %= (remainder assignment).

15. The *increment operator* (++) and the *decrement operator* (--) increment or decrement a variable by 1.

16. When evaluating an expression with values of mixed types, Java automatically converts the operands to appropriate types.

17. You can explicitly convert a value from one type to another using the `(type)value` notation.

18. *Casting* a variable of a type with a small range to a variable of a type with a larger range is known as *widening a type.*

19. Casting a variable of a type with a large range to a variable of a type with a smaller range is known as *narrowing a type.*

20. Widening a type can be performed automatically without explicit casting. Narrowing a type must be performed explicitly.

21. In computer science, midnight of January 1, 1970, is known as the *UNIX epoch.*

22. *Quality assurance* is the process of monitoring a project throughout the software life-cycle process. Following standard coding practices and thoroughly testing the output of your project helps maintain quality. *Tracing* can be used to compare actual output with expected output.

Programming Exercises

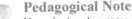

Debugging TIP

learn from examples

The compiler usually gives a reason for a syntax error. If you don't know how to correct it, compare your program closely, character by character, with similar examples in the text.

Pedagogical Note

document analysis and design

Your instructor may ask you to document your analysis and design for selected exercises. Use your own words to analyze the problem, including the input, output, and what needs to be computed, and describe how to solve the problem in pseudocode.

1. (*Convert Celsius to Fahrenheit*) Write a program that reads a Celsius degree in a `double` value from the console, then converts it to Fahrenheit and displays the result. The formula for the conversion is as follows:

   ```
   fahrenheit = (9 / 5) * celsius + 32
   ```

   Hint: In Java, `9 / 5` is `1`, but `9.0 / 5` is `1.8`.

   Here is a sample run:

```
Enter a degree in Celsius: 43 ↵Enter
43 Celsius is 109.4 Fahrenheit
```

2. (*Compute the volume of a cylinder*) Write a program that reads in the radius and length of a cylinder and computes the area and volume using the following formulas:

   ```
   area = radius * radius * π
   volume = area * length
   ```

   Here is a sample run:

```
Enter the radius and length of a cylinder: 5.5 12 ↵Enter
The area is 95.0331
The volume is 1140.4
```

3. (*Convert feet into meters*) Write a program that reads a number in feet, converts it to meters, and displays the result. One foot is `0.305` meter. Here is a sample run:

```
Enter a value for feet: 16.5 ↵Enter
16.5 feet is 5.0325 meters
```

4. (*Convert pounds into kilograms*) Write a program that converts pounds into kilograms. The program prompts the user to enter a number in pounds, converts it to kilograms, and displays the result. One pound is `0.454` kilograms. Here is a sample run:

```
Enter a number in pounds: 55.5 ↵Enter
55.5 pounds is 25.197 kilograms
```

5. (*Financial application: calculate tips*) Write a program that reads the subtotal and the gratuity rate, then computes the gratuity and total. For example, if the user enters `10` for subtotal and `15%` for gratuity rate, the program displays `$1.5` as gratuity and `$11.5` as total. Here is a sample run:

```
Enter the subtotal and a gratuity rate: 10 15 ↵Enter
The gratuity is $1.5 and total is $11.5
```

6. (*Physics: acceleration*) Average acceleration is defined as the change of velocity divided by the time taken to make the change, as shown in the following formula:

$$a = \frac{v_1 - v_0}{t}$$

Write a program that prompts the user to enter the starting velocity v_0 in meters/second, the ending velocity v_1 in meters/second, and the time span t in seconds, and displays the average acceleration. Here is a sample run:

```
Enter v0, v1, and t: 5.5 50.9 4.5 ↵Enter
The average acceleration is 10.0889
```

7. (*Science: calculating energy*) Write a program that calculates the energy needed to heat water from an initial temperature to a final temperature. Your program should prompt the user to enter the amount of water in kilograms and the initial and final temperatures of the water. The formula to compute the energy is

```
Q = M * (finalTemperature - initialTemperature) * 4184
```

where `M` is the weight of water in kilograms, temperatures are in degrees Celsius, and energy `Q` is measured in joules. Here is a sample run:

```
Enter the amount of water in kilograms: 55.5 ↵Enter
Enter the initial temperature: 3.5 ↵Enter
Enter the final temperature: 10.5 ↵Enter
The energy needed is 1625484.0
```

8. (*Physics: finding runway length*) Given an airplane's acceleration a and take-off speed v, you can compute the minimum runway length needed for an airplane to take off using the following formula:

$$\text{length} = \frac{v^2}{2a}$$

Write a program that prompts the user to enter v in meters/second (m/s) and the acceleration a in meters/second squared (m/s^2), and displays the minimum runway length. Here is a sample run:

```
Enter speed and acceleration: 60 3.5 ↵Enter
The minimum runway length for this airplane is 514.286
```

CHAPTER 4

USING SELECTION STATEMENTS

Objectives

- Solve problems using structured coding.
- Declare `Boolean` variables and write Boolean expressions using relational operators.
- Design a flowchart to illustrate the logical design of an application.
- Implement selection control using one-way `if` statements.
- Implement selection control using two-way `if-else` statements.
- Implement selection control using nested `if` and multi-way `if` statements.
- Identify common errors and issues when writing `if` statements.
- Generate random numbers using the `Math.random()` method.
- Combine conditions using logical operators (`!`, `&&`, `||`, and `^`).
- Program using selection statements with combined conditions (`LeapYear`, `Lottery`).
- Implement selection control using `switch` statements.
- Write expressions using the conditional expression.
- Examine the rules governing operator precedence and associativity.
- Apply common techniques to debug errors.

4.1 Introduction

The program can decide which statements to execute based on a condition. Selection statements help create structured logical coding to solve problems. Selection statements are sometimes referred to as conditional structures.

problem
conditional structures

If you enter a negative value for `radius` in Listing 3.2, ComputeAreaWithConsoleInput.java, the program displays an invalid result. If the radius is negative, you don't want the program to compute the area. How can you deal with this situation?

selection statements

Like all high-level programming languages, Java provides *selection statements*: statements that let you choose actions with alternative courses. You can use the following selection statement to replace lines 12–17 in Listing 3.2:

```
if (radius < 0) {
  System.out.println("Incorrect input");
}
else {
  area = radius * radius * 3.14159;
  System.out.println("Area is " + area);
}
```

Boolean expression
Boolean value

Selection statements use conditions that are Boolean expressions. A *Boolean expression* is an expression that evaluates to a *Boolean value*: `true` or `false`. We now introduce Boolean types and relational operators.

4.2 boolean Data Type

Key Point

The `boolean` *data type declares a variable with the value either* `true` *or* `false`.

boolean data type
relational operators

How do you compare two values, such as whether a radius is greater than 0, equal to 0, or less than 0? Java provides six *relational operators* (also known as *comparison operators*), shown in Table 4.1, which can be used to compare two values (assume radius is 5 in the table).

TABLE 4.1 Relational Operators

Java Operator	*Mathematics Symbol*	*Name*	*Example (radius is 5)*	*Result*
<	$<$	less than	`radius < 0`	`false`
<=	$\leq$	less than or equal to	`radius <= 0`	`false`
>	$>$	greater than	`radius > 0`	`true`
>=	$\geq$	greater than or equal to	`radius >= 0`	`true`
==	$=$	equal to	`radius == 0`	`false`
!=	$\neq$	not equal to	`radius != 0`	`true`

== vs. =

Caution

The equality testing operator is two equal signs (==), not a single equal sign (=). The latter symbol is for assignment.

The result of the comparison is a Boolean value: `true` or `false`. For example, the following statement displays `true`:

```
double radius = 1;
System.out.println(radius > 0);
```

Boolean variable

A variable that holds a Boolean value is known as a *Boolean variable*. The `boolean` data type is used to declare Boolean variables. A `boolean` variable can hold one of the two values: `true` or `false`. For example, the following statement assigns `true` to the variable `lightsOn`:

```
boolean lightsOn = true;
```

`true` and `false` are treated as reserved words and cannot be used as identifiers in the program.

Program addition quiz

Suppose you want to develop a program to let a first-grader practice addition. The program randomly generates two single-digit integers, `number1` and `number2`, and displays to the student a question such as "What is 1 + 7?," as shown in the sample run in Listing 4.1. After the student types the answer, the program displays a message to indicate whether it is true or false.

There are several ways to generate random numbers. For now, generate the first integer using `System.currentTimeMillis() % 10` and the second using `System.currentTimeMillis() / 7 % 10`. Listing 4.1 gives the program. Lines 5–6 generate two numbers, `number1` and `number2`. Line 14 obtains an answer from the user. The answer is graded in line 18 using a Boolean expression `number1 + number2 == answer`.

LISTING 4.1 AdditionQuiz.java

```
1  import java.util.Scanner;
2
3  public class AdditionQuiz {
4    public static void main(String[] args) {
5      int number1 = (int)(System.currentTimeMillis() % 10);
6      int number2 = (int)(System.currentTimeMillis() / 7 % 10);
7
8      // Create a Scanner
9      Scanner input = new Scanner(System.in);
10
11     System.out.print(
12       "What is " + number1 + " + " + number2 + "? ");
13
14     int answer = input.nextInt();
15
16     System.out.println(
17       number1 + " + " + number2 + " = " + answer + " is " +
18       (number1 + number2 == answer));
19   }
20 }
```

generate number 1

generate number 2

show question

display result

```
What is 1 + 7? 8 ↵Enter
1 + 7 = 8 is true
```

```
What is 4 + 8? 9 ↵Enter
4 + 8 = 9 is false
```

line#	number1	number2	answer	output
5	4			
6		8		
14			9	
16				4 + 8 = 9 is false

✓ Section 4.2 Assessment

1. List six relational operators.
2. Assuming that `x is 1`, show the result of the following Boolean expressions:

```
(x > 0)
(x < 0)
(x != 0)
(x >= 0)
(x != 1)
```

3. Can the following conversions involving casting be allowed? Write a test program to verify your answer.

```
boolean b = true;
i = (int)b;

int i = 1;
boolean b = (boolean)i;
```

4.3 `if` Statements

An `if` statement is a construct that enables a program to specify alternative paths of execution. Flowcharts are often used when designing `if` statements. A flowchart is a tool used to create the logical steps of an application.

why `if` statement?

The preceding program displays a message such as "6 + 2 = 7 is false." If you wish the message to be "6 + 2 = 7 is incorrect," you have to use a selection statement to make this minor change.

Java has several types of selection statements: one-way `if` statements, two-way `if-else` statements, nested `if` statements, multi-way `if-else` statements, `switch` statements, and conditional expressions.

A one-way `if` statement executes an action if and only if the condition is `true`. The syntax for a one-way `if` statement is:

`if` statement

```
if (boolean-expression) {
  statement(s);
}
```

Here, x is not exactly 0.5, but is 0.5000000000000001. You cannot reliably test equality of two floating-point values. However, you can compare whether they are close enough by testing whether the difference of the two numbers is less than some threshold. That is, two numbers x and y are very close if $|x-y| < \epsilon$ for a very small value, ϵ. ϵ, a Greek letter pronounced epsilon, is commonly used to denote a very small value. Normally, you set ϵ to 10^{-14} for comparing two values of the double type and to 10^{-7} for comparing two values of the float type. For example, the following code

```
final double EPSILON = 1E-14;
double x = 1.0 - 0.1 - 0.1 - 0.1 - 0.1 - 0.1;
if (Math.abs(x - 0.5) < EPSILON)
  System.out.println(x + " is approximately 0.5");
```

will display that

```
0.5000000000000001 is approximately 0.5
```

The Math.abs(a) method can be used to return the absolute value of a.

COMMON PITFALL 1: Simplifying Boolean Variable Assignment

Often, new programmers write the code that assigns a test condition to a boolean variable like the code in (a):

```
if (number % 2 == 0)
  even = true;
else
  even = false;
```

(a)

Equivalent

This is shorter

```
boolean even
  = number % 2 == 0;
```

(b)

This is not an error, but it should be better written as shown in (b).

COMMON PITFALL 2: Avoiding Duplicate Code in Different Cases

Often, new programmers write the duplicate code in different cases that should be combined in one place. For example, the highlighted code in the following statement is duplicated.

```
if (inState) {
  tuition = 5000;
  System.out.println("The tuition is " + tuition);
}
else {
  tuition = 15000;
  System.out.println("The tuition is " + tuition);
}
```

This is not an error, but it should be better written as follows:

```
if (inState) {
  tuition = 5000;
}
else {
  tuition = 15000;
}
System.out.println("The tuition is " + tuition);
```

The new code removes the duplication and makes the code easy to maintain, because you only need to change in one place if the print statement is modified.

✓ Section 4.6 Assessment

1. Which of the following statements correctly indents code to add styling, readability, and clarity?

```
if (i > 0) if
(j > 0)
x = 0; else
if (k > 0) y = 0;
else z = 0;
```

(a)

```
if (i > 0) {
  if (j > 0)
    x = 0;
  else if (k > 0)
    y = 0;
}
else
  z = 0;
```

(b)

```
if (i > 0)
  if (j > 0)
    x = 0;
  else if (k > 0)
    y = 0;
  else
    z = 0;
```

(c)

```
if (i > 0)
  if (j > 0)
    x = 0;
  else if (k > 0)
    y = 0;
else
  z = 0;
```

(d)

2. Rewrite the following statement using a Boolean expression and proper indentation and styling:

```
if (count % 10 == 0)
  newLine = true;
else
  newLine = false;
```

3. Are the following statements correct? Which one is better?

```
if (age < 16)
  System.out.println
    ("Cannot get a driver's license");
if (age >= 16)
  System.out.println
    ("Can get a driver's license");
```

(a)

```
if (age < 16)
  System.out.println
    ("Cannot get a driver's license");
else
  System.out.println
    ("Can get a driver's license");
```

(b)

4. What is the output of the following code if `number` is `14`, `15`, or `30`?

```
if (number % 2 == 0)
  System.out.println
    (number + " is even");
if (number % 5 == 0)
  System.out.println
    (number + " is multiple of 5");
```

(a)

```
if (number % 2 == 0)
  System.out.println
    (number + " is even");
else if (number % 5 == 0)
  System.out.println
    (number + " is multiple of 5");
```

(b)

4.7 Generating Random Numbers

You can use `Math.random()` to obtain a random double value between `0.0` and `1.0`, excluding `1.0`.

Program subtraction quiz

Suppose you want to develop a program for a first-grader to practice subtraction. The program randomly generates two single-digit integers, `number1` and `number2`, with `number1 >= number2`, and it displays to the student a question such as "What is 9 – 2?" After the student enters the answer, the program displays a message indicating whether it is correct.

random() method

The previous programs generate random numbers using `System.currentTimeMillis()`. A better approach is to use the `random()` method in the `Math` class. Invoking this method returns a random double value `d` such that $0.0 \leq d < 1.0$. Thus, `(int)(Math.random() * 10)` returns a random single-digit integer (i.e., a number between `0` and `9`).

The program can work as follows:

1. Generate two single-digit integers into `number1` and `number2`.
2. If `number1 < number2`, swap `number1` with `number2`.
3. Prompt the student to answer, `"What is number1 - number2?"`
4. Check the student's answer and display whether the answer is correct.

The complete program is shown in Listing 4.3.

LISTING 4.3 `SubtractionQuiz.java`

```
import java.util.Scanner;

public class SubtractionQuiz {
  public static void main(String[] args) {
    // 1. Generate two random single-digit integers
    int number1 = (int)(Math.random() * 10);
    int number2 = (int)(Math.random() * 10);

    // 2. If number1 < number2, swap number1 with number2
    if (number1 < number2) {
      int temp = number1;
      number1 = number2;
      number2 = temp;
    }

    // 3. Prompt the student to answer "What is number1 - number2?"
    System.out.print
      ("What is " + number1 + " - " + number2 + "? ");
    Scanner input = new Scanner(System.in);
    int answer = input.nextInt();

    // 4. Grade the answer and display the result
    if (number1 - number2 == answer)
      System.out.println("You are correct!");
    else {
      System.out.println("Your answer is wrong.");
      System.out.println(number1 + " - " + number2 +
        " should be " + (number1 - number2));
```

random number

get answer

check the answer

```
29       }
30     }
31   }
```

```
What is 6 - 6?  0 ↵Enter
You are correct!
```

```
What is 9 - 2?  5 ↵Enter
Your answer is wrong
9 - 2 is 7
```

line#	number1	number2	temp	answer	output
6	2				
7		9			
11			2		
12	9				
13		2			
20				5	
26					Your answer is wrong 9 - 2 should be 7

To swap two variables `number1` and `number2`, a temporary variable `temp` (line 11) is used to first hold the value in `number1`. The value in `number2` is assigned to `number1` (line 12), and the value in `temp` is assigned to `number2` (line 13).

✓ Section 4.7 Assessment

1. Which of the following is a possible output from invoking `Math.random()`?

   `323.4, 0.5, 34, 1.0, 0.0, 0.234`

2. **a.** How do you generate a random integer `i` such that $0 \le i < 20$?

   b. How do you generate a random integer `i` such that $10 \le i < 20$?

   c. How do you generate a random integer `i` such that $10 \le i \le 50$?

   d. Write an expression that returns `0` or `1` randomly.

4.8 Case Study: Computing Body Mass Index

You can use nested `if` *statements to write a program that interprets body mass index.*

Body Mass Index (BMI) is a measure of health based on height and weight. It can be calculated by taking your weight in kilograms and dividing it by the square of your height in meters. The interpretation of BMI for people 20 years or older is as follows:

BMI	Interpretation
BMI < 18.5	Underweight
18.5 ≤ BMI < 25.0	Normal
25.0 ≤ BMI < 30.0	Overweight
30.0 ≤ BMI	Obese

Write a program that prompts the user to enter a weight in pounds and height in inches and displays the BMI. Note that one pound is `0.45359237` kilograms and one inch is `0.0254` meters. Listing 4.4 gives the program.

LISTING 4.4 ComputeAndInterpretBMI.java

```
import java.util.Scanner;

public class ComputeAndInterpretBMI {
  public static void main(String[] args) {
    Scanner input = new Scanner(System.in);

    // Prompt the user to enter weight in pounds
    System.out.print("Enter weight in pounds: ");
    double weight = input.nextDouble();

    // Prompt the user to enter height in inches
    System.out.print("Enter height in inches: ");
    double height = input.nextDouble();

    final double KILOGRAMS_PER_POUND = 0.45359237; // Constant
    final double METERS_PER_INCH = 0.0254; // Constant

    // Compute BMI
    double weightInKilograms = weight * KILOGRAMS_PER_POUND;
    double heightInMeters = height * METERS_PER_INCH;
    double bmi = weightInKilograms /
      (heightInMeters * heightInMeters);

    // Display result
    System.out.println("BMI is " + bmi);
    if (bmi < 18.5)
      System.out.println("Underweight");
    else if (bmi < 25)
      System.out.println("Normal");
    else if (bmi < 30)
      System.out.println("Overweight");
    else
      System.out.println("Obese");
  }
}
```

input weight

input height

compute bmi

display output

```
Enter weight in pounds:  146 ↵Enter
Enter height in inches:  70 ↵Enter
BMI is 20.948603801493316
Normal
```

line#	weight	height	weightInKilograms	heightInMeters	bmi	output
9	146					
13		70				
19			66.22448602			
20				1.778		
21					20.9486	
25						BMI is 20.95
31						Normal

The constants KILOGRAMS_PER_POUND and METERS_PER_INCH are defined in lines 15–16. Using constants here makes programs easy to read.

test all cases

You should test the input that covers all possible cases for BMI to ensure that the program works for all cases.

4.9 Case Study: Computing Taxes

You can use nested `if` *statements to write a program for computing taxes.*

Use multi-way `if-else` statements

The United States federal personal income tax is calculated based on filing status and taxable income. There are four filing statuses: single filers, married filing jointly or qualified widow(er), married filing separately, and head of household. The tax rates vary every year. Table 4.2 shows the rates for 2016. If you are, say, single with a taxable income of $10,000, the first $9,275 is taxed at 10% and the other $725 is taxed at 15%, so, your total tax is $1,036.25.

TABLE 4.2 2016 U.S. Federal Personal Tax Rates

Marginal Tax Rate	*Single*	*Married Filing Jointly or Qualifying Widow(er)*	*Married Filing Separately*	*Head of Household*
10%	$0 – $9,275	$0 – $18,550	$0 – $9,275	$0 – $13,250
15%	$9,276 – $37,650	$18,551 – $75,300	$9,276 – $37,650	$13,251 – $50,400
25%	$37,651 – $91,150	$75,301 – $151,900	$37,651 – $75,950	$50,401 – $130,150
28%	$91,151 – $190,150	$151,901 – $231,450	$75,951 – $115,725	$130,151 – $210,800
33%	$190,151 – $413,350	$231,451 – $413,350	$115,726 – $206,675	$210,801 – $413,350
35%	$413,351 – $415,050	$413,351 – $466,950	$206,676 – $233,475	$413,351 – $441,000
39.6%	$415,051+	$466,951+	$233,476+	$441,001+

You are to write a program to compute personal income tax. Your program should prompt the user to enter the filing status and taxable income and compute the tax. Enter 0 for single filers, 1 for married filing jointly or qualified widow(er), 2 for married filing separately, and 3 for head of household.

Your program computes the tax for the taxable income based on the filing status. The filing status can be determined using `if` statements outlined as follows:

```
if (status == 0) {
  // Compute tax for single filers
}
else if (status == 1) {
  // Compute tax for married filing jointly or qualifying
widow(er)
}
else if (status == 2) {
  // Compute tax for married filing separately
}
else if (status == 3) {
  // Compute tax for head of household
}
else {
  // Display wrong status
}
```

For each filing status there are six tax rates. Each rate is applied to a certain amount of taxable income. For example, of a taxable income of $400,000 for single filers, `$9,275` is taxed at 10%, `(37,650 - 9,275)` at 15%, `(91,150 - 37,650)` at 25%, `(190,150 - 91,150)` at 28%, and `(400,000 - 190,150)` at 33%.

Listing 4.5 gives the solution for computing taxes for single filers. The complete solution is left as an exercise.

LISTING 4.5 ComputeTax.java

```
import java.util.Scanner;

public class ComputeTax {
  public static void main(String[] args) {
    // Create a Scanner
    Scanner input = new Scanner(System.in);

    // Prompt the user to enter filing status
    System.out.print("(0-single filer, 1-married jointly or " +
      "qualifying widow(er), 2-married separately, 3-head of " +
      "household) Enter the filing status: ");

    int status = input.nextInt();                          // input status

    // Prompt the user to enter taxable income
    System.out.print("Enter the taxable income: ");
    double income = input.nextDouble();                    // input income

    // Compute tax
    double tax = 0;                                        // compute tax

if (status == 0) { // Compute tax for single filers
  if (income <= 9275)
    tax = income * 0.10;
  else if (income <= 37650)
```

```
26       tax = 9275 * 0.10 + (income - 9275) * 0.15;
27     else if (income <= 91150)
28       tax = 9275 * 0.10 + (37650 - 9275) * 0.15 +
29         (income - 37650) * 0.25;
30     else if (income <= 190150)
31       tax = 9275 * 0.10 + (37650 - 9275) * 0.15 +
32         (91150 - 37650) * 0.25 + (income - 91150) * 0.28;
33     else if (income <= 413350)
34       tax = 9275 * 0.10 + (37650 - 9275) * 0.15 +
35         (91150 - 37650) * 0.25 + (190150 - 91150) * 0.28 +
36         (income - 190150) * 0.33;
37     else if (income <= 415050)
38       tax = 9275 * 0.10 + (37650 - 9275) * 0.15 +
39         (91150 - 37650) * 0.25 + (190150 - 91150) * 0.28 +
40         (413350 - 190150) * 0.33 + (income - 413350) * 0.35;
41     else
42       tax = 9275 * 0.10 + (37650 - 9275) * 0.15 +
43         (91150 - 37650) * 0.25 + (190150 - 91150) * 0.28 +
44         (413350 - 190150) * 0.33 + (415050 - 413350) * 0.35 +
45         (income - 415050) * 0.396;
46   }
47   else if (status == 1) { // Left as an exercise
48     // Compute tax for married file jointly or qualifying widow(er)
49   }
50   else if (status == 2) { // Compute tax for married separately
51     // Left as an exercise
52   }
53   else if (status == 3) { // Compute tax for head of household
54     // Left as an exercise
55   }
56   else {
57     System.out.println("Error: invalid status");
58    System.exit(1);
59   }
60
61   // Display the result
62   System.out.println("Tax is " + (int)(tax * 100) / 100.0);
63   }
64 }
```

exit program

display output

```
(0-single filer, 1-married jointly or qualifying widow(er),
2-married separately, 3-head of household)
Enter the filing status: 0 ↵Enter
Enter the taxable income: 400000 ↵Enter
Tax is 117683.5
```

line#	status	income	tax	output
13	0			
17		400000		
20			0	
38			115529.25	
57				Tax is 115529.25

The program receives the filing status and taxable income. The multi-way `if-else` statements check the filing status and compute the tax based on the filing status.

System.exit(status)

`System.exit(status)` (line 58) is defined in the `System` class. Invoking this method terminates the program. The status `0` indicates that the program is terminated normally. A nonzero status code indicates abnormal termination.

An initial value of `0` is assigned to `tax` (line 20). A compile error would occur if it had no initial value, because all of the other statements that assign values to `tax` are within the `if` statement. The compiler thinks that these statements may not be executed and therefore reports a compile error.

test all cases

To test a program, you should provide the input that covers all cases. For this program, your input should cover all statuses (`0`, `1`, `2`, `3`). For each status, test the tax for each of the six brackets. So, there are a total of 24 cases.

Tip

For all programs, you should write a small amount of code and test it before moving on to add more code. This is called *incremental development and testing*. This approach makes testing easier, because the errors are likely in the new code you just added.

incremental development and testing

✓ Section 4.9 Assessment

1. Are the following two statements equivalent?

```
if (income <= 10000)
  tax = income * 0.1;
else if (income <= 20000)
  tax = 1000 +
    (income - 10000) * 0.15;
```

```
if (income <= 10000)
  tax = income * 0.1;
else if (income > 10000 &&
         income <= 20000)
  tax = 1000 +
    (income - 10000) * 0.15;
```

4.10 Logical Operators

The logical operators `!`, `&&`, `||`, and `^` can be used to create a compound Boolean expression.

logical operators
Boolean operators

Sometimes, whether a statement is executed is determined by a combination of several conditions. You can use logical operators to combine these conditions to form a compound Boolean expression. *Logical operators*, also known as *Boolean operators*, operate on Boolean values to create a new Boolean value. Table 4.3 lists the Boolean operators. Table 4.4 defines the not (`!`) operator, which negates `true` to `false` and `false` to `true`. Table 4.5 defines the and (`&&`) operator. The and (`&&`) of two Boolean operands is `true` if and only if both operands are `true`. Table 4.6 defines the or (`||`) operator. The or (`||`) of two Boolean operands is `true` if at least one of the operands is `true`. Table 4.7 defines the exclusive or (`^`) operator. The exclusive or (`^`) of two Boolean operands is `true` if and only if the two operands have different Boolean values. Note that `p1 ^ p2` is the same as `p1 != p2`.

TABLE 4.3 Boolean Operators

Operator	*Name*	*Description*
!	not	logical negation
&&	and	logical conjunction
||	or	logical disjunction
^	exclusive or	logical exclusion

TABLE 4.4 Truth Table for Operator !

p	!p	*Example (assume* **age = 24, weight = 140***)*
true	false	!(age > 18) is false, because (age > 18) is true.
false	true	!(weight == 150) is true, because (weight == 150) is false.

TABLE 4.5 Truth Table for Operator &&

p_1	p_2	p_1 && p_2	*Example (assume* **age = 24, weight = 140***)*
false	false	false	
false	true	false	(age > 28) && (weight <= 140) is true, because (age > 28) is false.
true	false	false	
true	true	true	(age > 18) && (weight >= 140) is true, because (age > 18) and (weight >= 140) are both true.

TABLE 4.6 Truth Table for Operator ||

p_1	p_2	p_1 || p_2	*Example (assume* **age = 24, weight = 140***)*
false	false	false	(age > 34) || (weight >= 150) is false, because (age > 34) and (weight >= 150) are both false.
false	true	true	
true	false	true	(age > 18) || (weight < 140) is true, because (age > 18) is true.
true	true	true	

TABLE 4.7 Truth Table for Operator ^

p1	p2	p1 ^ p2	*Example (assume* **age = 24, weight = 140***)*
false	false	false	(age > 34) ^ (weight > 140) is false, because (age > 34) and (weight > 140) are both false.
false	true	true	(age > 34) ^ (weight >= 140) is true, because (age > 34) is false but (weight >= 140) is true.
true	false	true	
true	true	false	

Listing 4.6 gives a program that checks whether a number is divisible by 2 and 3, by 2 or 3, and by 2 or 3 but not both:

LISTING 4.6 TestBooleanOperators.java

```
import java.util.Scanner;

public class TestBooleanOperators {
  public static void main(String[] args) {
    // Create a Scanner
    Scanner input = new Scanner(System.in);

    // Receive an input
    System.out.print("Enter an integer: ");
    int number = input.nextInt();

    if (number % 2 == 0 && number % 3 == 0)
      System.out.println(number + " is divisible by 2 and 3.");

    if (number % 2 == 0 || number % 3 == 0)
      System.out.println(number + " is divisible by 2 or 3.");

    if (number % 2 == 0 ^ number % 3 == 0)
      System.out.println(number +
        " is divisible by 2 or 3, but not both.");
  }
}
```

import class

input

and

or

exclusive or

```
Enter an integer: 4 [Enter]
4 is divisible by 2 or 3.
4 is divisible by 2 or 3, but not both.
```

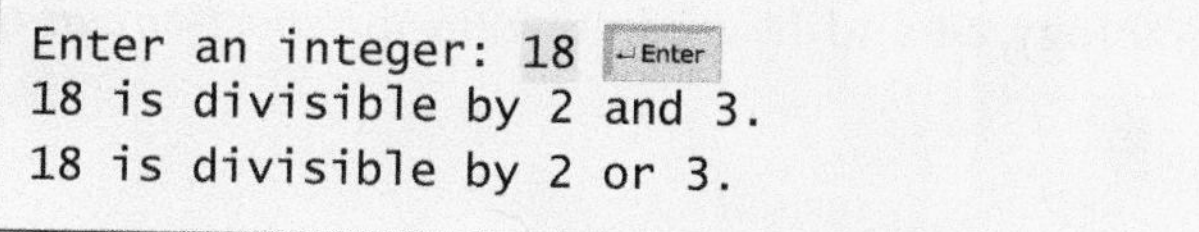

```
Enter an integer: 18 [Enter]
18 is divisible by 2 and 3.
18 is divisible by 2 or 3.
```

`(number % 2 == 0 && number % 3 == 0)` (line 12) checks whether the number is divisible by both 2 and 3. `(number % 2 == 0 || number % 3 == 0)` (line 15) checks whether the number is divisible by 2 or by 3. `(number % 2 == 0 ^ number % 3 == 0)` (line 18) checks whether the number is divisible by 2 or 3, but not both.

Caution

In mathematics, the expression

```
1 <= numberOfDaysInAMonth <= 31
```

incompatible operands

is correct. However, it is incorrect in Java, because `1 <= numberOfDaysInAMonth` is evaluated to a `boolean` value, which cannot be compared with `31`. Here, two operands (a `boolean` value and a numeric value) are *incompatible*. The correct expression in Java is

```
(1 <= numberOfDaysInAMonth) && (numberOfDaysInAMonth <= 31)
```

De Morgan's law

Note

De Morgan's law, named after Indian-born British mathematician and logician Augustus De Morgan (1806–1871), can be used to simplify Boolean expressions. The law states:

```
!(condition1 && condition2) is the same as
  !condition1 || !condition2
!(condition1 || condition2) is the same as
  !condition1 && !condition2
```

For example,

```
! (number % 2 == 0 && number % 3 == 0)
```

can be simplified using an equivalent expression:

```
(number % 2 != 0 || number % 3 != 0)
```

As another example,

```
!(number == 2 || number == 3)
```

is better written as

```
number != 2 && number != 3
```

short-circuit operator
lazy operator

If one of the operands of an `&&` operator is `false`, the expression is `false`; if one of the operands of an `||` operator is `true`, the expression is `true`. Java uses these properties to improve the performance of these operators. When evaluating `p1 && p2`, Java first evaluates `p1` and then, if `p1` is `true`, evaluates `p2`; if `p1` is `false`, it does not evaluate `p2`. When evaluating `p1 || p2`, Java first evaluates `p1` and then, if `p1` is `false`, evaluates `p2`; if `p1` is `true`, it does not evaluate `p2`. In programming language terminology, `&&` and `||` are known as the *short-circuit* or *lazy* operators.

✓ Section 4.10 Assessment

1. Assuming that x is 1, show the result of the following Boolean expressions.

```
(true) && (3 > 4)
!(x > 0) && (x > 0)
(x > 0) || (x < 0)

(x != 0) || (x == 0)
(x >= 0) || (x < 0)
(x != 1) == !(x == 1)
```

2. (a) Write a Boolean expression that evaluates to `true` if a number stored in variable `num` is between `1` and `100`. (b) Write a Boolean expression that evaluates to `true` if a number stored in variable `num` is between `1` and `100` or the number is negative.

3. (a) Write a Boolean expression for $|x - 5| < 4.5$. (b) Write a Boolean expression for $|x - 5| > 4.5$.

4. Assume that `x` and `y` are `int` type. Which of the following are legal Java expressions?

```
x > y > 0
x = y && y
x /= y
x or y
x and y
(x != 0) || (x = 0)
```

5. Are the following two expressions the same?

```
a. x % 2 == 0 && x % 3 == 0
b. x % 6 == 0
```

6. What is the value of the expression `x >= 50 && x <= 100` if `x` is `45`, `67`, or `101`?

7. Suppose, when you run the following program, you enter the input `2 3 6` from the console. What is the output?

```java
public class Test {
  public static void main(String[] args) {
    java.util.Scanner input = new java.util.Scanner(System.in);
    double x = input.nextDouble();
    double y = input.nextDouble();
    double z = input.nextDouble();

    System.out.println("(x < y && y < z) is " + (x < y && y < z));
    System.out.println("(x < y || y < z) is " + (x < y || y < z));
    System.out.println("!(x < y) is " + !(x < y));
    System.out.println("(x + y < z) is " + (x + y < z));
    System.out.println("(x + y > z) is " + (x + y > z));
  }
}
```

8. Write a Boolean expression that evaluates to `true` if `age` is greater than `13` and less than `18`.

9. Write a Boolean expression that evaluates to `true` if `weight` is greater than `50` pounds or height is greater than `60` inches.
10. Write a Boolean expression that evaluates to `true` if `weight` is greater than `50` pounds and height is greater than `60` inches.
11. Write a Boolean expression that evaluates to `true` if either `weight` is greater than `50` pounds or height is greater than `60` inches, but not both.

4.11 Case Study: Determining Leap Year

A year is a leap year if it is divisible by **4** *but not by* **100**, *or if it is divisible by* **400**.

You can use the following Boolean expressions to check whether a year is a leap year:

```
// A leap year is divisible by 4
boolean isLeapYear = (year % 4 == 0);

// A leap year is divisible by 4 but not by 100
isLeapYear = isLeapYear && (year % 100 != 0);

// A leap year is divisible by 4 but not by 100 or divisible by 400
isLeapYear = isLeapYear || (year % 400 == 0);
```

Or you can combine all these expressions into one like this:

```
isLeapYear = (year % 4 == 0 && year % 100 != 0) || (year % 400 == 0);
```

Listing 4.7 gives the program that lets the user enter a year and checks whether it is a leap year.

LISTING 4.7 LeapYear.java

input

leap year?

display result

```
import java.util.Scanner;

public class LeapYear {
  public static void main(String[] args) {
    // Create a Scanner
    Scanner input = new Scanner(System.in);
    System.out.print("Enter a year: ");
    int year = input.nextInt();

    // Check if the year is a leap year
    boolean isLeapYear =
      (year % 4 == 0 && year % 100 != 0) || (year % 400 == 0);

    // Display the result
    System.out.println(year + " is a leap year? " + isLeapYear);
  }
}
```

```
Enter a year: 2008 ↵Enter
2008 is a leap year? true
```

```
Enter a year: 1900 ↵Enter
1900 is a leap year? false
```

```
Enter a year: 2002 ↵Enter
2002 is a leap year? false
```

4.12 Case Study: Lottery

The lottery program involves generating random numbers, comparing digits, and using Boolean operators.

Suppose you want to develop a program to play lottery. The program randomly generates a lottery of a two-digit number, prompts the user to enter a two-digit number, and determines whether the user wins according to the following rules:

1. If the user input matches the lottery number in the exact order, the award is $10,000.
2. If all digits in the user input match all digits in the lottery number, the award is $3,000.
3. If one digit in the user input matches a digit in the lottery number, the award is $1,000.

Note that the digits of a two-digit number may be `0`. If a number is less than `10`, we assume the number is preceded by a `0` to form a two-digit number. For example, number `8` is treated as `08` and number `0` is treated as `00` in the program. Listing 4.8 gives the complete program.

LISTING 4.8 `Lottery.java`

```
import java.util.Scanner;

public class Lottery {
  public static void main(String[] args) {
    // Generate a lottery number
    int lottery = (int)(Math.random() * 100);

    // Prompt the user to enter a guess
    Scanner input = new Scanner(System.in);
    System.out.print("Enter your lottery pick (two digits): ");
    int guess = input.nextInt();

    // Get digits from lottery
    int lotteryDigit1 = lottery / 10;
    int lotteryDigit2 = lottery % 10;

    // Get digits from guess
    int guessDigit1 = guess / 10;
    int guessDigit2 = guess % 10;

    System.out.println("The lottery number is " + lottery);

    // Check the guess
    if (guess == lottery)
      System.out.println("Exact match: you win $10,000");
    else if (guessDigit2 == lotteryDigit1
          && guessDigit1 == lotteryDigit2)
```

generate a lottery number

enter a guess

exact match?

match all digits?

match one digit?

```
28          System.out.println("Match all digits: you win $3,000");
29        else if (guessDigit1 == lotteryDigit1
30                || guessDigit1 == lotteryDigit2
31                || guessDigit2 == lotteryDigit1
32                || guessDigit2 == lotteryDigit2)
33          System.out.println("Match one digit: you win $1,000");
34        else
35          System.out.println("Sorry, no match");
36      }
37    }
```

```
Enter your lottery pick (two digits): 15 ↵Enter
The lottery number is 15
Exact match: you win $10,000
```

```
Enter your lottery pick (two digits): 45 ↵Enter
The lottery number is 54
Match all digits: you win $3,000
```

```
Enter your lottery pick: 23 ↵Enter
The lottery number is 34
Match one digit: you win $1,000
```

```
Enter your lottery pick: 23 ↵Enter
The lottery number is 14
Sorry: no match
```

variable \ line#	6	11	14	15	18	19	33
lottery	34						
guess		23					
lotteryDigit1			3				
lotteryDigit2				4			
guessDigit1					2		
guessDigit2						3	
Output							Match one digit: you win $1,000

The program generates a lottery using the `random()` method (line 6) and prompts the user to enter a guess (line 11). Note that `guess % 10` obtains the last digit from `guess` and `guess / 10` obtains the first digit from `guess`, since `guess` is a two-digit number (lines 18–19).

The program checks the guess against the lottery number in this order:

1. First, check whether the guess matches the lottery exactly (line 24).
2. If not, check whether the reversal of the guess matches the lottery (lines 26–27).
3. If not, check whether one digit is in the lottery (lines 29–32).
4. If not, nothing matches and display `"Sorry, no match"` (lines 34–35).

4.13 `switch` Statements

A `switch` statement executes statements based on the value of a variable or an expression.

switch statement

The `if` statement in Listing 4.5, ComputeTax.java, makes selections based on a single `true` or `false` condition. There are four cases for computing taxes, which depend on the value of `status`. To fully account for all the cases, nested `if` statements were used. Overuse of nested `if` statements makes a program difficult to read. Java provides a `switch` statement to simplify coding for multiple conditions. You can write the following `switch` statement to replace the nested `if` statement in Listing 4.5:

```
switch (status) {
  case 0:  compute tax for single filers;
           break;
  case 1:  compute tax for married jointly or qualifying widow(er);
           break;
  case 2:  compute tax for married filing separately;
           break;
  case 3:  compute tax for head of household;
           break;
  default: System.out.println("Error: invalid status");
           System.exit(1);
}
```

The flowchart of the preceding `switch` statement is shown in Figure 4.5.

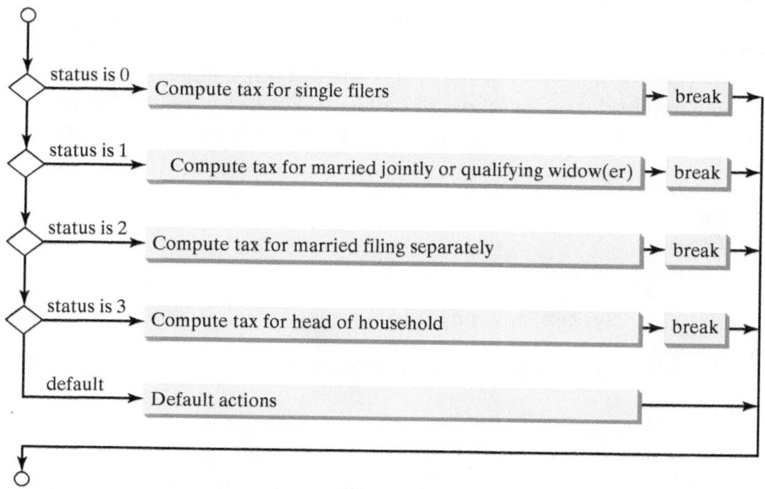

FIGURE 4.5 The `switch` statement checks all cases and executes the statements in the matched case.

This statement checks to see whether the status matches the value 0, 1, 2, or 3, in that order. If matched, the corresponding tax is computed; if not matched, a message is displayed. Here is the full syntax for the switch statement:

```
switch (switch-expression) {
  case value1: statement(s)1;
               break;
  case value2: statement(s)2;
               break;
  ...
  case valueN: statement(s)N;
               break;
  default:     statement(s)-for-default;
}
```

The switch statement observes the following rules:

- The switch-expression must yield a value of char, byte, short, int, or String type and must always be enclosed in parentheses. (The char and String types will be introduced in the next chapter.)
- The value1, . . ., and valueN must have the same data type as the value of the switch-expression. Note that value1, . . ., and valueN are constant expressions, meaning that they cannot contain variables, such as 1 + x.
- When the value in a case statement matches the value of the switch-expression, the statements *starting from this case* are executed until either a break statement or the end of the switch statement is reached.
- The default case, which is optional, can be used to perform actions when none of the specified cases matches the switch-expression.

break

- The keyword break is optional. The break statement immediately ends the switch statement.

without break

fall-through behavior

Caution

Do not forget to use a break statement when one is needed. Once a case is matched, the statements starting from the matched case are executed until a break statement or the end of the switch statement is reached. This is referred to as *fall-through* behavior. For example, the following code displays Weekdays for day of 1 to 5 and Weekends for day 0 and 6.

```
switch (day) {
  case 1:
  case 2:
  case 3:
  case 4:
  case 5: System.out.println("Weekday"); break;
  case 0:
  case 6: System.out.println("Weekend");
}
```

Tip

To avoid programming errors and improve code maintainability, it is a good idea to put a comment in a case clause if break is purposely omitted.

Now let us write a program to find out the Chinese Zodiac sign for a given year. The Chinese Zodiac is based on a twelve-year cycle, with each year represented by an animal—monkey, rooster, dog, pig, rat, ox, tiger, rabbit, dragon, snake, horse, or sheep—in this cycle, as shown in Figure 4.6.

Note that `year % 12` determines the Zodiac sign. 1900 is the year of the rat because `1900 % 12` is `4`. Listing 4.9 gives a program that prompts the user to enter a year and displays the animal for the year.

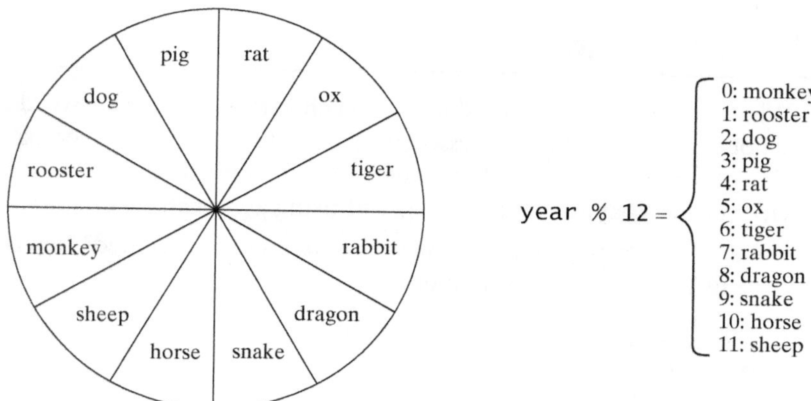

FIGURE 4.6 The Chinese Zodiac is based on a twelve-year cycle.

LISTING 4.9 ChineseZodiac.java

```
import java.util.Scanner;

public class ChineseZodiac {
  public static void main(String[] args) {
    Scanner input = new Scanner(System.in);

    System.out.print("Enter a year: ");
    int year = input.nextInt();

    switch (year % 12) {
      case 0: System.out.println("monkey"); break;
      case 1: System.out.println("rooster"); break;
      case 2: System.out.println("dog"); break;
      case 3: System.out.println("pig"); break;
      case 4: System.out.println("rat"); break;
      case 5: System.out.println("ox"); break;
      case 6: System.out.println("tiger"); break;
      case 7: System.out.println("rabbit"); break;
      case 8: System.out.println("dragon"); break;
      case 9: System.out.println("snake"); break;
      case 10: System.out.println("horse"); break;
      case 11: System.out.println("sheep");
    }
  }
}
```

enter year

determine Zodiac sign

CHAPTER 5

WORKING WITH CHARACTERS AND STRINGS

Objectives

- Use the `char` data type.
- Encode characters using ASCII and Unicode.
- Represent special characters using the escape sequences.
- Compare characters using methods in the `Character` class.
- Introduce objects and instance methods.
- Use the `string` object.
- Return the string length using the `length()` method.
- Return a character in the string using the `charAt(i)` method.
- Use the `+` operator to concatenate strings.
- Use `toUpperCase()` and `toLowerCase()` methods to return uppercase or lowercase strings.
- Use `trim()` method to remove whitespace characters.
- Read a character from the console.
- Compare strings using the `equals()` method and the `compareTo()` methods.
- Find a character or a substring in a string using the `indexOf()` method.
- Identify and document constraints of a software application.
- Format output using the `System.out.printf()` method.

5.1 Introduction

The focus of this chapter is to introduce mathematical functions, characters, and string objects, and use them to develop programs.

Because strings are frequently used in programming, it is beneficial to introduce strings early so that you can begin to use them to develop useful programs. This chapter introduces character and string data types.

method

pre-defined methods

In addition, you will explore the use of methods to perform string manipulation. A *method* is a block of code that performs a specific task. Many methods are pre-written and are available for reuse within your code. These methods are stored in the Java Application Programming Interface (API) and are referred to as *pre-defined methods*. You will use some of these pre-defined methods to perform string manipulation.

This chapter introduces methods. In Chapter 8, you will learn how to modularize code by writing your own custom methods.

5.2 Character Data Type and Operations

Key Point

A character data type represents a single character.

char type

In addition to processing numeric values, you can process characters in Java. The character data type, `char`, is used to represent a single character. A character literal is enclosed in single quotation marks. Consider the following code:

```
char letter = 'A';
char numChar = '4';
```

The first statement assigns character `A` to the `char` variable `letter`. The second statement assigns digit character `4` to the `char` variable `numChar`.

char literal

Caution

A string literal must be enclosed in quotation marks (" "). A character literal is a single character enclosed in single quotation marks (' '). Therefore, `"A"` is a string, but `'A'` is a character.

Unicode and ASCII Code

encoding

Unicode

original Unicode

supplementary Unicode

Computers use binary numbers internally. A character is stored in a computer as a sequence of 0s and 1s. Mapping a character to its binary representation is called *encoding*. There are different ways to encode a character. How characters are encoded is defined by an *encoding scheme*.

Java supports *Unicode*, an encoding scheme established by the Unicode Consortium to support the interchange, processing, and display of written texts in the world's diverse languages. Unicode was originally designed as a 16-bit character encoding. The primitive data type `char` was intended to take advantage of this design by providing a simple data type that could hold any character. However, it turned out that the 65,536 characters possible in a 16-bit encoding are not sufficient to represent all the characters in the world. The Unicode standard therefore has been extended to allow up to 1,112,064 characters. Those characters that go beyond the original 16-bit limit are called *supplementary characters*. Java supports the supplementary characters. The processing and representing of supplementary characters are beyond the scope of this book. For simplicity, this book considers only the original 16-bit Unicode characters. These characters can be stored in a char type variable.

A 16-bit Unicode takes two bytes, preceded by \u, expressed in four hexadecimal digits that run from \u0000 to \uFFFF. Hexadecimal numbers are introduced in Appendix D, Number Systems. For example, the English word welcome is translated into Chinese using two characters, 欢迎. The Unicodes of these two characters are \u6B22\u8FCE. The Unicodes for the Greek letters α β γ are \u03b1 \u03b2 \u03b4.

Most computers use *ASCII* (*American Standard Code for Information Interchange*), an 8-bit encoding scheme for representing all uppercase and lowercase letters, digits, punctuation marks, and control characters. Unicode includes ASCII code, with \u0000 to \u007F corresponding to the 128 ASCII characters. Table 5.1 shows the ASCII code for some commonly used characters. Appendix B, 'The ASCII Character Set,' gives a complete list of ASCII characters and their decimal and hexadecimal codes.

TABLE 5.1 ASCII Code for Commonly Used Characters

Characters	*Code Value in Decimal*	*Unicode Value*
'0' to '9'	48 to 57	\u0030 to \u0039
'A' to 'Z'	65 to 90	\u0041 to \u005A
'a' to 'z'	97 to 122	\u0061 to \u007A

You can use ASCII characters such as 'X', '1', and '$' in a Java program as well as Unicodes. Thus, for example, the following statements are equivalent:

ASCII

```
char letter = 'A';
char letter = '\u0041'; // Character A's Unicode is 0041
```

Both statements assign character A to the char variable letter.

Note

The increment and decrement operators can also be used on char variables to get the next or preceding Unicode character. For example, the following statements display character b.

char increment and decrement

```
char ch = 'a';
System.out.println(++ch);
```

Escape Sequences for Special Characters

Suppose you want to print a message with quotation marks in the output. Can you write a statement like this?

```
System.out.println("He said "Java is fun"");
```

No, this statement has a compile error. The compiler thinks the second quotation character is the end of the string and does not know what to do with the rest of the characters.

escape sequence

To overcome this problem, Java uses a special notation to represent special characters, as shown in Table 5.2. This special notation, called an *escape sequence*, consists of a backslash (\) followed by a character or a combination of digits. For example, \t is an escape sequence for the Tab character and an escape sequence such as \u03b1 is used to represent a Unicode. The symbols in an escape sequence are interpreted as a whole rather than individually. An escape sequence is considered as a single character.

So, now you can print the quoted message using the following statement:

```
System.out.println("He said \"Java is fun\"");
```

The output is

```
He said "Java is fun"
```

Note that the symbols \ and " together represent one character.

TABLE 5.2 Escape Sequences

Escape Sequence	*Name*	*Unicode Code*	*Decimal Value*
\b	Backspace	\u0008	8
\t	Tab	\u0009	9
\n	Linefeed	\u000A	10
\f	Formfeed	\u000C	12
\r	Carriage Return	\u000D	13
\\	Backslash	\u005C	92
\"	Double Quote	\u0022	34

escape character

The backslash \ is called an *escape character*. It is a special character. To display this character, you have to use an escape sequence \\. For example, the following code

```
System.out.println("\\t is a tab character");
```

displays

```
\t is a tab character
```

Comparing and Testing Characters

Two characters can be compared using the relational operators just like comparing two numbers. This is done by comparing the Unicodes of the two characters. For example,

'a' < 'b' is true because the Unicode for 'a' (97) is less than the Unicode for 'b' (98).

'a' < 'A' is false because the Unicode for 'a' (97) is greater than the Unicode for 'A' (65).

'1' < '8' is true because the Unicode for '1' (49) is less than the Unicode for '8' (56).

✓ Section 5.3 Assessment

1. Suppose that `s1`, `s2`, and `s3` are three strings, given as follows:

```
String s1 = "Welcome to Java";
String s2 = "Programming is fun";
String s3 = "Welcome to Java";
```

What are the results of the following expressions?

(a) `s1 == s2`

(b) `s2 == s3`

(c) `s1.equals(s2)`

(d) `s1.equals(s3)`

(e) `s1.compareTo(s2)`

(f) `s2.compareTo(s3)`

(g) `s2.compareTo(s2)`

(h) `s1.charAt(0)`

(i) `s1.indexOf('j')`

(j) `s1.indexOf("to")`

(k) `s1.lastIndexOf('a')`

(l) `s1.lastIndexOf("o", 15)`

(m) `s1.length()`

(n) `s1.substring(5)`

(o) `s1.substring(5, 11)`

(p) `s1.startsWith("Wel")`

(q) `s1.endsWith("Java")`

(r) `s1.toLowerCase()`

(s) `s1.toUpperCase()`

(t) `s1.concat(s2)`

(u) `s1.contains(s2)`

(v) `"\t Wel \t".trim()`

2. Suppose that `s1` and `s2` are two strings. Which of the following statements or expressions are incorrect?

```
String s = "Welcome to Java";
String s3 = s1 + s2;
String s3 = s1 - s2;
s1 == s2;
s1 >= s2;
s1.compareTo(s2);
int i = s1.length();
char c = s1(0);
char c = s1.charAt(s1.length());
```

3. Show the output of the following statements (write a program to verify your results):

```
System.out.println("1" + 1);
System.out.println('1' + 1);
System.out.println("1" + 1 + 1);
System.out.println("1" + (1 + 1));
System.out.println('1' + 1 + 1);
```

4. Evaluate the following expressions (write a program to verify your results):

```
1 + "Welcome " + 1 + 1
1 + "Welcome " + (1 + 1)
1 + "Welcome " + ('\u0001' + 1)
1 + "Welcome " + 'a' + 1
```

5. Let `s1` be `" Welcome "` and `s2` be `" welcome "`. Write the code for the following statements:

   (a) Check whether `s1` is equal to `s2` and assign the result to a Boolean variable `isEqual`.

   (b) Check whether `s1` is equal to `s2`, ignoring case, and assign the result to a Boolean variable `isEqual`.

   (c) Compare `s1` with `s2` and assign the result to an `int` variable `x`.

   (d) Compare `s1` with `s2`, ignoring case, and assign the result to an `int` variable `x`.

   (e) Check whether `s1` has the prefix `AAA` and assign the result to a Boolean variable `b`.

   (f) Check whether `s1` has the suffix `AAA` and assign the result to a Boolean variable `b`.

   (g) Assign the length of `s1` to an `int` variable `x`.

   (h) Assign the first character of `s1` to a `char` variable `x`.

   (i) Create a new string `s3` that combines `s1` with `s2`.

   (j) Create a substring of `s1` starting from index `1`.

   (k) Create a substring of `s1` from index `1` to index `4`.

   (l) Create a new string `s3` that converts `s1` to lowercase.

   (m) Create a new string `s3` that converts `s1` to uppercase.

   (n) Create a new string `s3` that trims whitespace characters on both ends of `s1`.

   (o) Assign the index of the first occurrence of the character `e` in `s1` to an `int` variable `x`.

   (p) Assign the index of the last occurrence of the string `abc` in `s1` to an `int` variable `x`.

5.4 Identifying Software Application Constraints

A constraint is a limit or restriction of your application.

constraints

During the planning and design phase of a software application, project constraints should be identified. Most constraints fall into two categories: a business constraint or a technical constraint.

business constraints

Business constraints often involve project scheduling, budgeting, and security guidelines of the project. For example, if your project has a short deadline, it may prevent the completion of some enhanced features of the application. This is a business constraint.

technical constraints
environmental constraints

Technical constraints are sometimes called *environmental constraints*. They are often beyond the control of the programmer. For instance, a hardware or network configuration may place constraints on the application's performance. Consider an online store application. An example of an environmental constraint is that the application will work only if there is an established connection to the World Wide Web.

Software coding techniques can also impose technical constraints. Section 5.3 introduced the use of the Char data type. Using the Char data type creates a constraint in your application. Code that uses the Char data type is constrained to accept only the 16-bit original Unicode characters.

It is normal for software applications to have constraints. Part of the software design process includes identifying and documenting constraints.

✓ Section 5.4 Assessment

1. What is a constraint? During which phase of the software life cycle should you identify constraints?
2. You are designing an application that retrieves names from a dataset that begin with a particular letter of the alphabet. The user inputs the first letter of the names to be retrieved, and the value is stored in a char data type. Users must have login credentials, and company policy will not allow your application to reset passwords. Applications run slowly during a system backup performed every Sunday.

   List the constraints of the project and identify whether each is a business or a technical constraint.

5.5 Case Studies

Strings are fundamental in programming. The ability to write programs using strings is essential in learning Java programming.

You will frequently use strings to write useful programs. This section presents three examples of solving problems using strings.

Case Study: Converting a Hexadecimal Digit to a Decimal Value

The hexadecimal number system has 16 digits: 0–9, A–F. The letters A, B, C, D, E, and F correspond to the decimal numbers 10, 11, 12, 13, 14, and 15. We now write a program that prompts the user to enter a hex digit and display its corresponding decimal value, as shown in Listing 5.2.

Listing 5.2 HexDigit2Dec.java

convert hex to decimal

```
import java.util.Scanner;

public class HexDigit2Dec {
  public static void main(String[] args) {
    Scanner input = new Scanner(System.in);
    System.out.print("Enter a hex digit: ");
    String hexString = input.nextLine();

    // Check if the hex string has exactly one character
    if (hexString.length() != 1) {
      System.out.println("You must enter exactly one character");
      System.exit(1);
    }
```

input string

check length

```
14
15      // Display decimal value for the hex digit
16      char ch = Character.toUpperCase(hexString.charAt(0));
17      if (ch <= 'F' && ch >= 'A') {
18        int value = ch - 'A' + 10;
19        System.out.println("The decimal value for hex digit "
20          + ch + " is " + value);
21      }
22      else if (Character.isDigit(ch)) {
23        System.out.println("The decimal value for hex digit "
24          + ch + " is " + ch);
25      }
26      else {
27        System.out.println(ch + " is an invalid input");
28      }
29    }
30  }
```

is 0-9?

```
Enter a hex digit: AB7C
You must enter exactly one character
```

```
Enter a hex digit: B
The decimal value for hex digit B is 11
```

```
Enter a hex digit: 8
The decimal value for hex digit 8 is 8
```

```
Enter a hex digit: T
T is an invalid input
```

The program reads a string from the console (line 7) and checks if the string contains a single character (line 10). If not, report an error and exit the program (line 12).

The program invokes the `Character.toUpperCase` method to obtain the character `ch` as an uppercase letter (line 16). If `ch` is between `'A'` and `'F'` (line 17), the corresponding decimal value is `ch - 'A' + 10` (line 18). Note that `ch - 'A'` is `0` if `ch` is `'A'`, `ch - 'A'` is `1` if `ch` is `'B'`, and so on. When two characters perform a numerical operation, the characters' Unicodes are used in the computation.

The program invokes the `Character.isDigit(ch)` method to check if `ch` is between `'0'` and `'9'` (line 22). If so, the corresponding decimal digit is the same as `ch` (lines 23–24).

If `ch` is not between `'A'` and `'F'` nor a digit character, the program displays an error message (line 27).

Case Study: Revising the Lottery Program Using Strings

The lottery program in Chapter 4, Listing 4.8, Lottery.java, generates a random two-digit number, prompts the user to enter a two-digit number, and determines whether the user wins according to the following rule:

1. If the user input matches the lottery number in the exact order, the award is $10,000.
2. If all the digits in the user input match all the digits in the lottery number, the award is $3,000.
3. If one digit in the user input matches a digit in the lottery number, the award is $1,000.

The program in Listing 4.8 uses an integer to store the number. Listing 5.3 gives a new program that generates a random two-digit string instead of a number and receives the user input as a string instead of a number.

LISTING 5.3 LotteryUsingStrings.java

```java
import java.util.Scanner;

public class LotteryUsingStrings {
  public static void main(String[] args) {
    // Generate a lottery as a two-digit string
    String lottery = "" + (int)(Math.random() * 10)
      + (int)(Math.random() * 10);

    // Prompt the user to enter a guess
    Scanner input = new Scanner(System.in);
    System.out.print("Enter your lottery pick (two digits): ");
    String guess = input.nextLine();

    // Get digits from lottery
    char lotteryDigit1 = lottery.charAt(0);
    char lotteryDigit2 = lottery.charAt(1);

    // Get digits from guess
    char guessDigit1 = guess.charAt(0);
    char guessDigit2 = guess.charAt(1);

    System.out.println("The lottery number is " + lottery);

    // Check the guess
    if (guess.equals(lottery))
      System.out.println("Exact match: you win $10,000");
    else if (guessDigit2 == lotteryDigit1
          && guessDigit1 == lotteryDigit2)
      System.out.println("Match all digits: you win $3,000");
    else if (guessDigit1 == lotteryDigit1
          || guessDigit1 == lotteryDigit2
          || guessDigit2 == lotteryDigit1
          || guessDigit2 == lotteryDigit2)
      System.out.println("Match one digit: you win $1,000");
    else
      System.out.println("Sorry, no match");
  }
}
```

generate a lottery

enter a guess

exact match?

match all digits?

match one digit?

```
Enter your lottery pick (two digits): 00 ↵Enter
The lottery number is 00
Exact match: you win $10,000
```

```
Enter your lottery pick (two digits): 45 ↵Enter
The lottery number is 54
Match all digits: you win $3,000
```

```
Enter your lottery pick: 23 ↵Enter
The lottery number is 34
Match one digit: you win $1,000
```

```
Enter your lottery pick: 23 ↵Enter
The lottery number is 14
Sorry: no match
```

The program generates two random digits and concatenates them into the string `lottery` (lines 6–7). After this, `lottery` contains two random digits.

The program prompts the user to enter a guess as a two-digit string (line 12) and checks the guess against the lottery number in this order:

- First check whether the guess matches the lottery exactly (line 25).
- If not, check whether the reversal of the guess matches the lottery (line 27).
- If not, check whether one digit is in the lottery (lines 30–33).
- If not, nothing matches and display "Sorry, no match" (line 36).

Case Study: Guessing Birthdays

You can find out the date of the month when your friend was born by asking five questions. Each question asks whether the day is in one of the five sets of numbers.

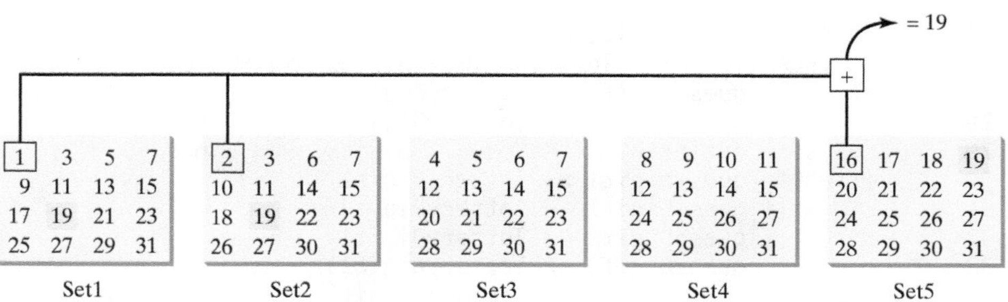

*4. (*Decimal to hex*) Write a program that prompts the user to enter an integer between 0 and 15 and displays its corresponding hex number. Here are some sample runs:

```
Enter a decimal value (0 to 15): 11 ↵Enter
The hex value is B
```

```
Enter a decimal value (0 to 15): 5 ↵Enter
The hex value is 5
```

```
Enter a decimal value (0 to 15): 31 ↵Enter
31 is an invalid input
```

*5. (*Hex to binary*) Write a program that prompts the user to enter a hex digit and displays its corresponding binary number. Here is a sample run:

```
Enter a hex digit: B ↵Enter
The binary value is 1011
```

```
Enter a hex digit: G ↵Enter
G is an invalid input
```

*6. (*Vowel or consonant?*) Write a program that prompts the user to enter a letter and check whether the letter is a vowel or consonant. Here is a sample run:

```
Enter a letter: B ↵Enter
B is a consonant
```

```
Enter a letter grade: a ↵Enter
a is a vowel
```

```
Enter a letter grade: # ↵Enter
# is an invalid input
```

*7. (*Convert letter grade to number*) Write a program that prompts the user to enter a letter grade A, B, C, D, or F and displays its corresponding numeric value 4, 3, 2, 1, or 0. Here is a sample run:

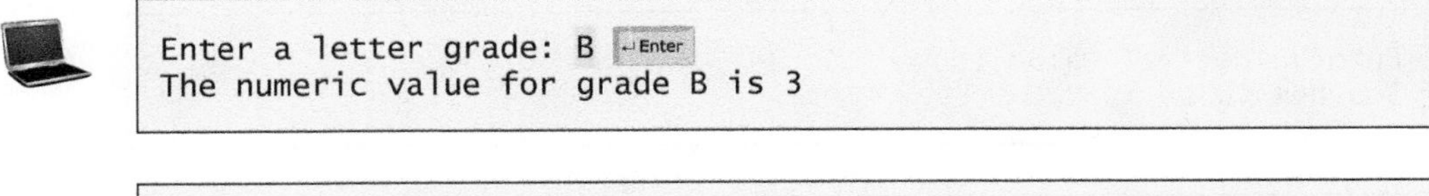

```
Enter a letter grade: B ↵Enter
The numeric value for grade B is 3
```

```
Enter a letter grade: T ↵Enter
T is an invalid grade
```

*8. (*Phone key pads*) The international standard letter/number mapping found on the telephone is shown below:

Write a program that prompts the user to enter a letter and displays its corresponding number.

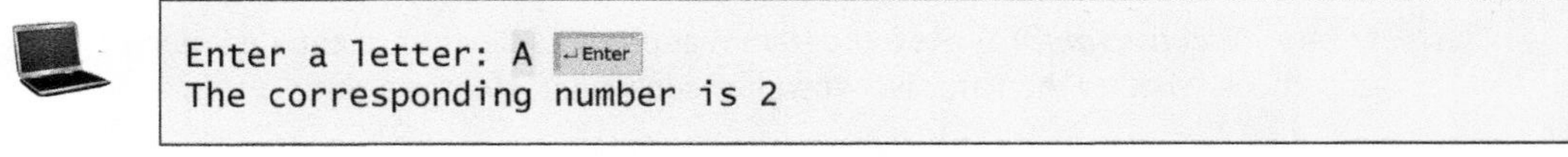

```
Enter a letter: A ↵Enter
The corresponding number is 2
```

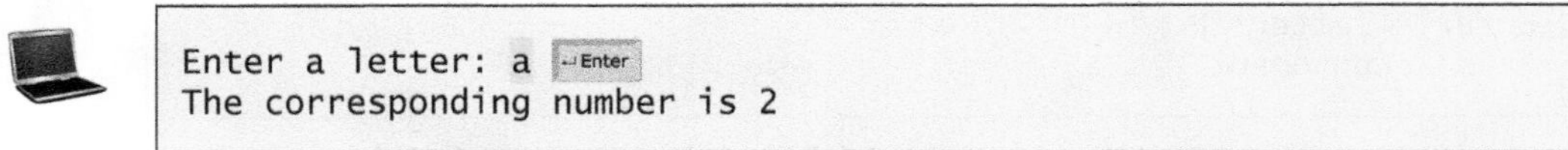

```
Enter a letter: a ↵Enter
The corresponding number is 2
```

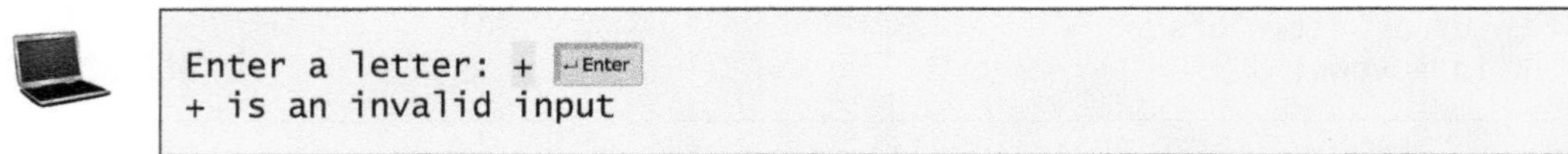

```
Enter a letter: + ↵Enter
+ is an invalid input
```

9. (*Random character*) Write a program that displays a random uppercase letter using the `Math.random()` method.

10. (*Process a string*) Write a program that prompts the user to enter a string and displays its length and its first character.

11. (*Check substring*) Write a program that prompts the user to enter two strings and reports whether the second string is a substring of the first string.

```
Enter string s1: ABCD ↵Enter
Enter string s2: BC ↵Enter
BC is a substring of ABCD
```

```
Enter string s1: ABCD ↵Enter
Enter string s2: BDC ↵Enter
BDC is not a substring of ABCD
```

*12. *(Order three cities)* Write a program that prompts the user to enter three cities and displays them in ascending order. Here is a sample run:

```
Enter the first city: Chicago ↵Enter
Enter the second city: Los Angeles ↵Enter
Enter the third city: Atlanta ↵Enter
The three cities in alphabetical order are Atlanta Chicago Los
Angeles
```

Chapter 6

Using Looping Statements

Objectives

- Write programs for executing statements repeatedly using a `while` loop.
- Apply algorithm strategies to design a loop.
- Control a loop with a sentinel value.
- Write loops using `do-while` statements.
- Write loops using `for` statements.
- Discover the similarities and differences of three types of loop statements.
- Implement program control with `break` and `continue`.

6.1 Introduction

A loop can be used to tell a program to execute statements repeatedly.

problem

Suppose that you need to display a string (e.g., `Welcome to Java!`) a hundred times. It would be tedious to have to write the following statement a hundred times:

```
            ┌ System.out.println("Welcome to Java!");
100 times  ─┤ System.out.println("Welcome to Java!");
            │ ...
            └ System.out.println("Welcome to Java!");
```

So, how do you solve this problem?

loop

Java provides a powerful construct called a *loop* that controls how many times an operation or a sequence of operations is performed in succession. Using a loop statement, you simply tell the computer to display a string a hundred times without having to code the print statement a hundred times, as follows:

```
int count = 0;
while (count < 100) {
  System.out.println("Welcome to Java!");
  count++;
}
```

The variable `count` is initially `0`. The loop checks whether `count < 100` is `true`. If so, it executes the loop body to display the message `Welcome to Java!` and increments `count` by `1`. It repeatedly executes the loop body until `count < 100` becomes `false`. When `count < 100` is `false` (i.e., when `count` reaches `100`), the loop terminates and the next statement after the loop statement is executed.

Loops are constructs that control repeated executions of a block of statements. The concept of looping is fundamental to programming. Java provides three types of loop statements: `while` loops, `do-while` loops, and `for` loops.

6.2 The `while` Loop

A `while` loop executes statements repeatedly while the condition is true.

The syntax for the `while` loop is:

`while` loop

```
while (loop-continuation-condition) {
  // Loop body
  Statement(s);
}
```

loop body
iteration
`loop-continuation-condition`

Figure 6.1a shows the `while`-loop flowchart. The part of the loop that contains the statements to be repeated is called the *loop body*. A one-time execution of a loop body is referred to as an *iteration* (or *repetition*) *of the loop*. Each loop contains a *loop-continuation-condition*, a Boolean expression that controls the execution of the body. It is evaluated each time to determine if the loop body is executed. If its evaluation is `true`, the loop body is executed; if its evaluation is `false`, the entire loop terminates and the program control turns to the statement that follows the `while` loop.

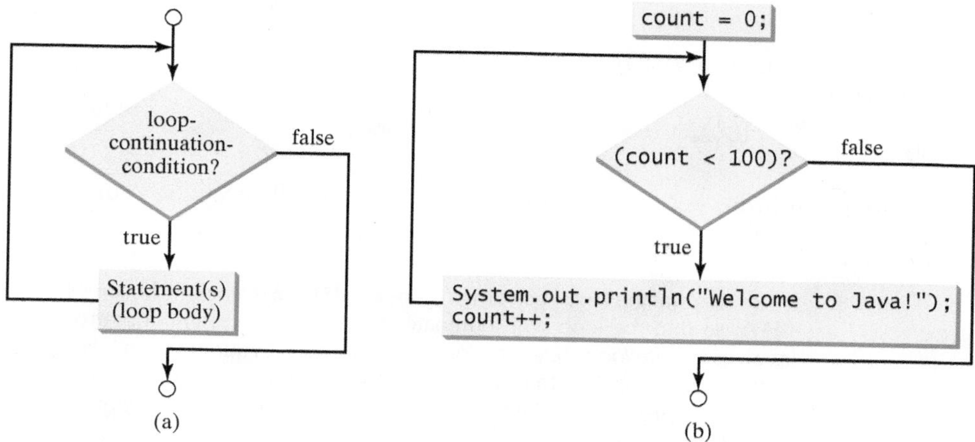

FIGURE 6.1 The `while` loop repeatedly executes the statements in the loop body when the `loop-continuation-condition` evaluates to `true`.

The loop for displaying `Welcome to Java!` a hundred times introduced in the preceding section is an example of a `while` loop. Its flowchart is shown in Figure 6.1b. The `loop-continuation-condition` is `count < 100` and the loop body contains the following two statements:

loop-continuation-condition

```
int count = 0;
while (count < 100) {
  System.out.println("Welcome to Java!");
  count++;
}
```

loop body

In this example, you know exactly how many times the loop body needs to be executed because the control variable `count` is used to count the number of executions. This type of loop is known as a *counter-controlled loop*.

counter-controlled loop

Note

The `loop-continuation-condition` must always appear inside the parentheses. The braces enclosing the loop body can be omitted only if the loop body contains one or no statement.

Here is another example to help understand how a loop works.

```
int sum = 0, i = 1;
while (i < 10) {
  sum = sum + i;
  i++;
}
System.out.println("sum is " + sum); // sum is 45
```

If `i < 10` is `true`, the program adds `i` to `sum`. Variable `i` is initially set to `1`, then is incremented to `2`, `3`, and up to `10`. When `i` is `10`, `i < 10` is `false`, so the loop exits. Therefore, the sum is `1 + 2 + 3 + ... + 9 = 45`.

2. What are the differences between a while loop and a do-while loop? Convert the following while loop into a do-while loop.

```
Scanner input = new Scanner(System.in);
int sum = 0;
System.out.println("Enter an integer " +
  "(the input ends if it is 0)");
int number = input.nextInt();
while (number != 0) {
  sum += number;
  System.out.println("Enter an integer " +
    "(the input ends if it is 0)");
  number = input.nextInt();
}
```

6.4 The for Loop

*A **for** loop has a concise syntax for writing loops.*

Often you write a loop in the following common form:

```
i = initialValue;  // Initialize loop control variable
while (i < endValue)
  // Loop body
  ...
  i++; // Adjust loop control variable
}
```

A for loop can be used to simplify the preceding loop as:

```
for (i = initialValue; i < endValue; i++)
  // Loop body
  ...
}
```

In general, the syntax of a for loop is:

for loop

```
for (initial-action; loop-continuation-condition;
     action-after-each-iteration) {
  // Loop body;
  Statement(s);
}
```

The flowchart of the for loop is shown in Figure 6.3a.

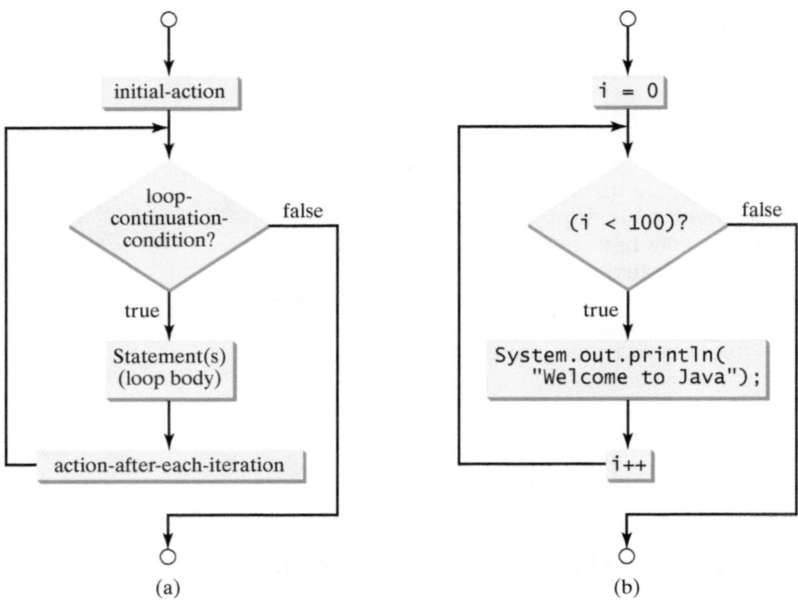

FIGURE 6.3 A `for` loop performs an initial action once, then repeatedly executes the statements in the loop body, and performs an action after an iteration when the `loop-continuation-condition` evaluates to `true`.

The `for` loop statement starts with the keyword `for`, followed by a pair of parentheses enclosing the control structure of the loop. This structure consists of `initial-action`, `loop-continuation-condition`, and `action-after-each-iteration`. The control structure is followed by the loop body enclosed inside braces. The `initial-action`, `loop-continuation-condition`, and `action-after-each-iteration` are separated by semicolons.

control variable

A `for` loop generally uses a variable to control how many times the loop body is executed and when the loop terminates. This variable is referred to as a *control variable.* The `initial-action` often initializes a control variable, the `action-after-each-iteration` usually increments or decrements the control variable, and the `loop-continuation-condition` tests whether the control variable has reached a termination value. For example, the following `for` loop prints `Welcome to Java!` a hundred times:

```
int i;
for (i = 0; i < 100; i++) {
  System.out.println("Welcome to Java!");
}
```

The flowchart of the statement is shown in Figure 6.3b. The `for` loop initializes `i` to `0`, then repeatedly executes the `println` statement and evaluates `i++` while `i` is less than `100`.

initial-action

The `initial-action`, `i = 0`, initializes the control variable, `i`. The `loop-continuation-condition`, `i < 100`, is a Boolean expression. The expression is evaluated right after the initialization and at the beginning of each iteration. If this condition is `true`, the loop body is executed. If it is `false`, the loop terminates and the program control turns to the line following the loop.

The `action-after-each-iteration`, `i++`, is a statement that adjusts the control variable. This statement is executed after each iteration and increments the control variable. Eventually, the value of the control variable should force the `loop-continuation-condition` to become `false`; otherwise, the loop is infinite.

action-after-each-iteration

The loop control variable can be declared and initialized in the `for` loop. Here is an example:

```
for (int i = 0; i < 100; i++) {
  System.out.println("Welcome to Java!");
}
```

If there is only one statement in the loop body, as in this example, the braces can be omitted.

omitting braces

Tip

The control variable must be declared inside the control structure of the loop or before the loop. If the loop control variable is used only in the loop, and not elsewhere, it is a good programming practice to declare it in the `initial-action` of the `for` loop. If the variable is declared inside the loop control structure, it cannot be referenced outside the loop. In the preceding code, for example, you cannot reference `i` outside the `for` loop, because it is declared inside the `for` loop.

declare control variable

Note

The `initial-action` in a `for` loop can be a list of zero or more comma-separated variable declaration statements or assignment expressions. For example:

for loop variations

```
for (int i = 0, j = 0; i + j < 10; i++, j++) {
  // Do something
}
```

The `action-after-each-iteration` in a `for` loop can be a list of zero or more comma-separated statements. For example:

```
for (int i = 1; i < 100; System.out.println(i), i++);
```

This example is correct, but it is a bad example, because it makes the code difficult to read. Normally, you declare and initialize a control variable as an initial action and increment or decrement the control variable as an action after each iteration.

Note

If the `loop-continuation-condition` in a `for` loop is omitted, it is implicitly `true`. Thus the statement given below in (a), which is an infinite loop, is the same as in (b). To avoid confusion, though, it is better to use the equivalent loop in (c).

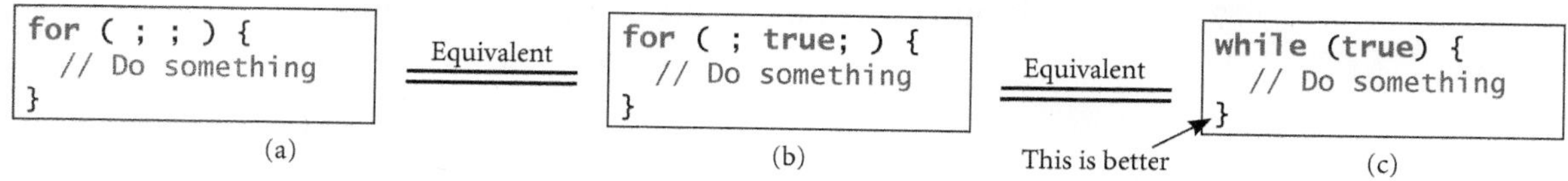

✓ Section 6.4 Assessment

1. Do the following two loops result in the same value in sum?

```
for (int i = 0; i < 10; ++i) {
  sum += i;
}
```

(a)

```
for (int i = 0; i < 10; i++) {
  sum += i;
}
```

(b)

2. What are the three parts of a for loop control? Write a for loop that prints the numbers from 1 to 100.
3. Suppose the input is 2 3 4 5 0. What is the output of the following code?

```
import java.util.Scanner;

public class Test {
  public static void main(String[] args) {
    Scanner input = new Scanner(System.in);

    int number, sum = 0, count;

    for (count = 0; count < 5; count++) {
      number = input.nextInt();
      sum += number;
    }

    System.out.println("sum is " + sum);
    System.out.println("count is " + count);
  }
}
```

4. What does the following statement do?

```
for ( ; ; ) {
  // Do something
}
```

5. If a variable is declared in a for loop control, can it be used after the loop exits?
6. Convert the following for loop statement to a while loop and to a do-while loop:

```
long sum = 0;
for (int i = 0; i <= 1000; i++)
  sum = sum + i;
```

7. Count the number of iterations in the following loops.

```
int count = 0;
while (count < n) {
  count++;
}
```

(a)

```
for (int count = 0;
  count <= n; count++) {
}
```

(b)

```
int count = 5;
while (count < n) {
  count++;
}
```

(c)

```
int count = 5;
while (count < n) {
  count = count + 3;
}
```

(d)

6.5 Which Loop to Use?

You can use a `for` *loop, a* `while` *loop, or a* `do-while` *loop, whichever is convenient.*

pretest loop

posttest loop

The `while` loop and `for` loop are called *pretest loops* because the continuation condition is checked before the loop body is executed. The `do-while` loop is called a *posttest loop* because the condition is checked after the loop body is executed. The three forms of loop statements—`while`, `do-while`, and `for`—are expressively equivalent; that is, you can write a loop in any of these three forms. For example, a `while` loop in (a) in the following figure can always be converted into the `for` loop in (b).

```
while (loop-continuation-condition) {
  // Loop body
}
```

(a)

Equivalent

```
for ( ; loop-continuation-condition; ) {
  // Loop body
}
```

(b)

A `for` loop in (a) in the next figure can generally be converted into the `while` loop in (b) except in certain special cases (see Section 6.7 Assessment Question #2 for such a case).

```
for (initial-action;
     loop-continuation-condition;
     action-after-each-iteration) {
  // Loop body;
}
```

(a)

Equivalent

```
initial-action;
while (loop-continuation-condition) {
  // Loop body;
  action-after-each-iteration;
}
```

(b)

Use the loop statement that is most intuitive and comfortable for you. In general, a `for` loop may be used if the number of repetitions is known in advance, as, for example, when you need to display a message a hundred times. A `while` loop may be used if the number of repetitions is not fixed, as in the case of reading the numbers until the input is `0`. A `do-while` loop can be used to replace a `while` loop if the loop body has to be executed before the continuation condition is tested.

✓ Section 6.7 Assessment

1. What is the keyword `break` for? What is the keyword `continue` for? Will the following programs terminate? If so, give the output.

```
int balance = 10;
while (true) {
  if (balance < 9)
    break;
  balance = balance - 9;
}

System.out.println("Balance is "
  + balance);
```

(a)

```
int balance = 10;
while (true) {
  if (balance < 9)
    continue;
  balance = balance - 9;
}

System.out.println("Balance is "
  + balance);
```

(b)

2. The `for` loop on the left is converted into the `while` loop on the right. What is wrong? Correct it.

```
int sum = 0;
for (int i = 0; i < 4; i++) {
  if (i % 3 == 0) continue;
  sum += i;
}
```

Converted

Wrong conversion

```
int i = 0, sum = 0;
while (i < 4) {
  if (i % 3 == 0) continue;
  sum += i;
  i++;
}
```

3. Rewrite the programs `TestBreak` and `TestContinue` in Listings 6.9 and 6.10 without using `break` and `continue`.
4. After the `break` statement in (a) is executed in the following loop, which statement is executed? Show the output. After the `continue` statement in (b) is executed in the following loop, which statement is executed? Show the output.

```
for (int i = 1; i < 4; i++) {
  for (int j = 1; j < 4; j++) {
    if (i * j > 2)
      break;

    System.out.println(i * j);
  }

  System.out.println(i);
}
```

(a)

```
for (int i = 1; i < 4; i++) {
  for (int j = 1; j < 4; j++) {
    if (i * j > 2)
      continue;

    System.out.println(i * j);
  }

  System.out.println(i);
}
```

(b)

6.8 Case Study: Checking Palindromes

Key Point

This section presents a program that checks whether a string is a palindrome.

A string is a palindrome if it reads the same forward and backward. The words "mom," "dad," and "noon," for instance, are all palindromes.

The problem is to write a program that prompts the user to enter a string and reports whether the string is a palindrome. One solution is to check whether the first character in the string is the same as the last character. If so, check whether the second character is the same as the second-to-last character. This process continues until a mismatch is found or all the characters in the string are checked, except for the middle character if the string has an odd number of characters.

think before you code

Listing 6.11 gives the program.

LISTING 6.11 `Palindrome.java`

input string

low index

high index

update indices

```
import java.util.Scanner;

public class Palindrome {
  /** Main method */
  public static void main(String[] args) {
    // Create a Scanner
    Scanner input = new Scanner(System.in);

    // Prompt the user to enter a string
    System.out.print("Enter a string: ");
    String s = input.nextLine();

    // The index of the first character in the string
    int low = 0;

    // The index of the last character in the string
    int high = s.length() - 1;

    boolean isPalindrome = true;
    while (low < high) {
      if (s.charAt(low) != s.charAt(high)) {
        isPalindrome = false;
        break;
      }

      low++;
      high--;
    }

    if (isPalindrome)
      System.out.println(s + " is a palindrome");
    else
      System.out.println(s + " is not a palindrome");
  }
}
```

```
Enter a string: noon ↵Enter
noon is a palindrome
```

```
Enter a string: moon ↵Enter
moon is not a palindrome
```

The program uses two variables, `low` and `high`, to denote the position of the two characters at the beginning and the end in a string `s` (lines 14, 17). Initially, `low` is `0` and `high` is `s.length() - 1`. If the two characters at these positions match, increment `low` by `1` and decrement `high` by `1` (lines 26–27). This process continues until (`low >= high`) or a mismatch is found (line 21).

The program uses a `boolean` variable `isPalindrome` to denote whether the string `s` is a palindrome. Initially, it is set to `true` (line 19). When a mismatch is discovered (line 21), `isPalindrome` is set to `false` (line 22) and the loop is terminated with a break statement (line 23).

6.9 Case Study: Displaying Prime Numbers

This section presents a program that displays the first fifty prime numbers in five lines, each containing ten numbers.

An integer greater than `1` is *prime* if its only positive divisor is `1` or itself. For example, `2`, `3`, `5`, and `7` are prime numbers, but `4`, `6`, `8`, and `9` are not.

The problem is to display the first 50 prime numbers in five lines, each of which contains ten numbers. The problem can be broken into the following tasks:

- Determine whether a given number is prime.
- For `number` = `2`, `3`, `4`, `5`, `6`, ..., test whether it is prime.
- Count the prime numbers.
- Display each prime number, and display ten numbers per line.

Obviously, you need to write a loop and repeatedly test whether a new `number` is prime. If the `number` is prime, increase the count by `1`. The `count` is `0` initially. When it reaches `50`, the loop terminates.

Here is the algorithm for the problem:

```
Set the number of prime numbers to be printed as
  a constant NUMBER_OF_PRIMES;
Use count to track the number of prime numbers and
  set an initial count to 0;
Set an initial number to 2;

while (count < NUMBER_OF_PRIMES) {
  Test whether number is prime;

  if number is prime {
    Display the prime number and increase the count;
  }

  Increment number by 1;
}
```

To test whether a number is prime, check whether it is divisible by 2, 3, 4, and so on up to number/2. If a divisor is found, the number is not a prime. The algorithm can be described as follows:

```
Use a boolean variable isPrime to denote whether
  the number is prime; Set isPrime to true initially;

for (int divisor = 2; divisor <= number / 2; divisor++) {
  if (number % divisor == 0) {
    Set isPrime to false
    Exit the loop;
  }
}
```

The complete program is given in Listing 6.12.

LISTING 6.12 PrimeNumber.java

count prime numbers

check primeness

exit loop

display if prime

```
public class PrimeNumber {
  public static void main(String[] args) {
    final int NUMBER_OF_PRIMES = 50; // Number of primes to display
    final int NUMBER_OF_PRIMES_PER_LINE = 10; // Display 10 per line
    int count = 0; // Count the number of prime numbers
    int number = 2; // A number to be tested for primeness

    System.out.println("The first 50 prime numbers are \n");

    // Repeatedly find prime numbers
    while (count < NUMBER_OF_PRIMES) {
      // Assume the number is prime
      boolean isPrime = true; // Is the current number prime?

      // Test whether number is prime
      for (int divisor = 2; divisor <= number / 2; divisor++) {
        if (number % divisor == 0) { // If true, number is not prime
          isPrime = false; // Set isPrime to false
          break; // Exit the for loop
        }
      }

      // Display the prime number and increase the count
      if (isPrime) {
        count++; // Increase the count

        if (count % NUMBER_OF_PRIMES_PER_LINE == 0) {
          // Display the number and advance to the new line
          System.out.println(number);
        }
        else
          System.out.print(number + " ");
      }

      // Check if the next number is prime
      number++;
    }
  }
}
```

```
The first 50 prime numbers are
2 3 5 7 11 13 17 19 23 29
31 37 41 43 47 53 59 61 67 71
73 79 83 89 97 101 103 107 109 113
127 131 137 139 149 151 157 163 167 173
179 181 191 193 197 199 211 223 227 229
```

This is a complex program for novice programmers. The key to developing a programmatic solution for this problem, and for many other problems, is to break it into subproblems and develop solutions for each of them in turn. Do not attempt to develop a complete solution in the first trial. Instead, begin by writing the code to determine whether a given number is prime, then expand the program to test whether other numbers are prime in a loop.

subproblem

To determine whether a number is prime, check whether it is divisible by a number between `2` and `number/2` inclusive (lines 16–21). If so, it is not a prime number (line 18); otherwise, it is a prime number. For a prime number, display it. If the count is divisible by `10` (lines 27–30), advance to a new line. The program ends when the count reaches `50`.

The program uses the `break` statement in line 19 to exit the `for` loop as soon as the number is found to be a nonprime. You can rewrite the loop (lines 16–21) without using the `break` statement, as follows:

```
for (int divisor = 2; divisor <= number / 2 && isPrime;
     divisor++) {
  // If true, the number is not prime
  if (number % divisor == 0) {
    // Set isPrime to false, if the number is not prime
    isPrime = false;
  }
}
```

However, using the `break` statement makes the program simpler and easier to read in this case.

Chapter 6 — Review and Assessment

Key Terms

`break` statement 190
`continue` statement 191
`do-while` loop 179
`for` loop 181
infinite loop 170
iteration 168
loop 168
loop body 168
off-by-one error 170
posttest loop 185
pretest loop 185
sentinel value 176
while loop 168

Chapter Summary

1. There are three types of repetition statements: the `while` loop, the `do-while` loop, and the `for` loop.
2. The part of the loop that contains the statements to be repeated is called the *loop body.*
3. A one-time execution of a loop body is referred to as an *iteration of the loop.*
4. An *infinite loop* is a loop statement that executes infinitely.
5. In designing loops, you need to consider both the *loop control structure* and the loop body.
6. The `while` loop checks the `loop-continuation-condition` first. If the condition is `true`, the loop body is executed; if it is `false`, the loop terminates.
7. The `do-while` loop is similar to the `while` loop, except that the `do-while` loop executes the loop body first and then checks the `loop-continuation-condition` to decide whether to continue or to terminate.
8. The `while` loop and the `do-while` loop often are used when the number of repetitions is not predetermined.
9. A *sentinel value* is a special value that signifies the end of the loop.
10. The `for` loop generally is used to execute a loop body a fixed number of times.
11. The `for` loop control has three parts. The first part is an initial action that often initializes a control variable. The second part, the `loop-continuation-condition`, determines whether the loop body is to be executed. The third part is executed after each iteration and is often used to adjust the control variable. Usually, the loop control variables are initialized and changed in the control structure.

12. The `while` loop and `for` loop are called *pretest loops* because the continuation condition is checked before the loop body is executed.

13. The `do-while` loop is called a *posttest loop* because the condition is checked after the loop body is executed.

14. Two keywords, `break` and `continue`, can be used in a loop.

15. The `break` keyword immediately ends the innermost loop, which contains the break.

16. The `continue` keyword only ends the current iteration.

Programming Exercises

Pedagogical Note

Read each problem several times until you understand it. Think how to solve the problem before starting to write code. Translate your logic into a program.

read and think before coding

A problem often can be solved in many different ways. Students are encouraged to explore various solutions.

explore solutions

*1. (*Count positive and negative numbers and compute the average of numbers*) Write a program that reads an unspecified number of integers, determines how many positive and negative values have been read, and computes the total and average of the input values (not counting zeros). Your program ends with the input `0`. Display the average as a floating-point number. Here is a sample run:

```
Enter an integer, the input ends if it is 0: 1 2 -1 3 0 ↵Enter
The number of positives is 3
The number of negatives is 1
The total is 5.0
The average is 1.25
```

```
Enter an integer, the input ends if it is 0: 0 ↵Enter
No numbers are entered except 0
```

2. (*Repeat additions*) Listing 6.4, SubtractionQuizLoop.java, generates five random subtraction questions. Revise the program to generate ten random addition questions for two integers between `1` and `15`. Display the correct count and test time.

3. *(Conversion from kilograms to pounds)* Write a program that displays the following table (note that 1 kilogram is 2.2 pounds):

```
Kilograms       Pounds
1                  2.2
3                  6.6
...
197              433.4
199              437.8
```

4. *(Conversion from miles to kilometers)* Write a program that displays the following table (note that 1 mile is 1.609 kilometers):

```
Miles        Kilometers
1            1.609
2            3.218
...
9            14.481
10           16.090
```

5. *(Conversion from kilograms to pounds and pounds to kilograms)* Write a program that displays the following two tables side by side:

```
Kilograms  Pounds     |        Pounds       Kilograms
1             2.2     |        20                9.09
3             6.6     |        25               11.36
...
197         433.4     |        510             231.82
199         437.8     |        515             234.09
```

6. *(Conversion from miles to kilometers)* Write a program that displays the following two tables side by side:

```
Miles        Kilometers  |  Kilometers        Miles
1            1.609       |  20                12.430
2            3.218       |  25                15.538
...
9            14.481      |  60                37.290
10           16.090      |  65                40.398
```

7. *(Find the highest score)* Write a program that prompts the user to enter the number of students and each student's name and score, and finally displays the name of the student with the highest score.

8. *(Find numbers divisible by 5 and 6)* Write a program that displays all the numbers from 100 to 1,000, ten per line, that are divisible by 5 and 6. Numbers are separated by exactly one space.

9. *(Find numbers divisible by 5 or 6, but not both)* Write a program that displays all the numbers from 100 to 200, ten per line, that are divisible by 5 or 6, but not both. Numbers are separated by exactly one space.

CHAPTER 7

Introduction to Data Structures and Arrays

Objectives

- Describe data structure concepts.
- Explain why data structures are necessary in programming.
- Differentiate between concepts of data represented as a single-dimensional or two-dimensional structure.
- Apply data structure concepts by using arrays to solve problems.
- Access array elements using indexes.
- Declare, create, and initialize an array using an array initializer.
- Simplify programming using a `foreach` loop.
- Apply arrays in application development (`AnalyzeNumbers`, `DeckOfCards`)
- Use the methods in the `java.util.Arrays` class.

7.1 Introduction to Data Structures

A data structure is a grouping of data organized in a particular way and used to store data in computer memory.

data structure

Several types of data structures are used in computer programming. *Arrays* are a common type of data structure. This chapter introduces the concept of data structures by exploring the use of arrays in your programming design.

single-dimensional array

A *single-dimensional array* is a common data structure that organizes data into a single row or column. There are a fixed number of items, or *elements*, in the array. The data is stored sequentially and is retrieved by accessing the particular location in the array. This location is referred to as the *index*.

index

Visualize six names of fruit listed in a row as shown in the following:

```
Fruit [apple, banana, orange, pear, peach, mango]
```

Apple is stored at location 0.
Banana is stored at location 1.
Orange is stored at location 2.
Pear is stored at location 3.
Peach is stored at location 4.
Mango is stored at location 5.

To access banana in the Fruit array, reference the corresponding location, or index. Thus, the value stored in location: Fruit[1] is banana. Notice the index begins at 0, and not at 1.

two-dimensional array

Arrays can also be multi-dimensional. Consider a spreadsheet with columns and rows. This is an example of a two-dimensional array. A *two-dimensional array* is a data structure where information is organized in columns *and* rows. Data in a two-dimensional structure is stored and retrieved by specifying *both* the row and column. As an example, to store data in column A and row 1 of a spreadsheet, you reference the location as [A1]. Detailed information on two-dimensional and multi-dimensional arrays can be found in Supplement G. In this chapter, we will cover single-dimensional arrays.

Arrays are helpful to store a large number of values during the execution of a program. Suppose that you need to read 100 numbers and compute their average. You also need to determine how many numbers are above the average. To solve this problem, your program first reads the numbers and computes their average, then compares each number with the average to determine if it is above the average. In order to accomplish this task, the numbers must all be stored in variables. You have to declare 100 numeric variables and repeatedly write almost identical code 100 times. Writing a program this way would be impractical.

A more efficient way to accomplish this task is by creating a one-dimensional array with a fixed size to hold 100 numeric values. You can store and retrieve values in the array by using looping statements to iterate through the array.

In this chapter, you will learn how to apply data structure concepts by using arrays.

✓ Section 7.1 Assessment

1. What is a data structure? When is it beneficial to use a data structure?
2. Write pseudocode to describe a single-dimensional array that holds the days of the week. Sunday is the first element in the array. Name the array: `weekDays`.
3. Using the `weekDays` array created in question 2, what is the value of x in the following expression? x = `weekDays[4]`;
4. Draw two illustrations, representing data as a single-dimensional and a two-dimensional array. Explain the difference.

7.2 Array Basics

Once an array is created, its size is fixed. An array reference variable is used to access the elements in an array using an index.

An array is used to store a collection of data, but often we find it more useful to think of an array as a collection of variables of the same type. Instead of declaring individual variables, such as `number0`, `number1`, . . . , and `number99`, you declare one array variable such as `numbers` and use `numbers[0]`, `numbers[1]`, . . . , and `numbers[99]` to represent individual variables. This section introduces how to declare array variables, create arrays, and process arrays using indexes.

Declaring Array Variables

To use an array in a program, you must declare a variable to reference the array and specify the array's *element type*. Here is the syntax for declaring an array variable:

element type

```
elementType[] arrayRefVar;
```

The `elementType` can be any data type, and all elements in the array will have the same data type. For example, the following code declares a variable `myList` that references an array of double elements.

```
double[] myList;
```

Note

You can also use `elementType arrayRefVar[]` to declare an array variable. This style comes from the C/C++ language and was adopted in Java to accommodate C/C++ programmers. The style `elementType[] arrayRefVar` is preferred.

Creating Arrays

Unlike declarations for primitive data type variables, the declaration of an array variable does not allocate any space in memory for the array. It creates only a storage location for the reference to an array. If a variable does not contain a reference to an array, the value of the variable is `null`. You cannot assign elements to an array unless it has already been created. After an array variable is declared, you can create an array by using the `new` operator and assign its reference to the variable with the following syntax:

null

```
arrayRefVar = new elementType[arraySize];
```

new operator

This statement does two things:

1. It creates an array using `new elementType[arraySize]`.
2. It assigns the reference of the newly created array to the variable `arrayRefVar`.

Declaring an array variable, creating an array, and assigning the reference of the array to the variable can be combined in one statement as:

```
elementType[] arrayRefVar = new elementType[arraySize];
```

or

```
elementType arrayRefVar[] = new elementType[arraySize];
```

Here is an example of such a statement:

```
double[] myList = new double[10];
```

This statement declares an array variable, `myList`, creates an array of ten elements of `double` type, and assigns its reference to `myList`. To assign values to the elements, use the syntax:

```
arrayRefVar[index] = value;
```

For example, the following code initializes the array.

```
myList[0] = 5.6;
myList[1] = 4.5;
myList[2] = 3.3;
myList[3] = 13.2;
myList[4] = 4.0;
myList[5] = 34.33;
myList[6] = 34.0;
myList[7] = 45.45;
myList[8] = 99.993;
myList[9] = 11123;
```

This array is illustrated in Figure 7.1.

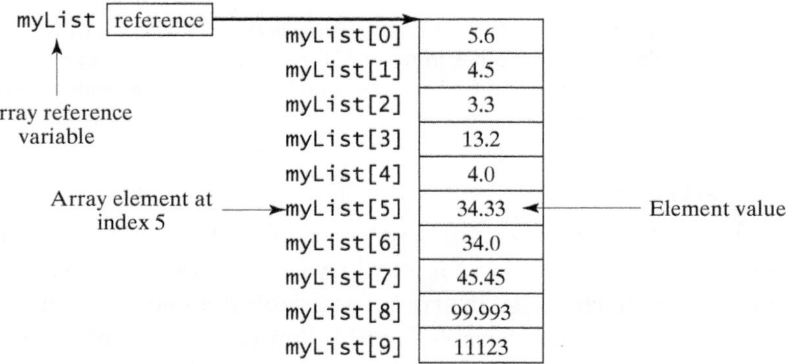

FIGURE 7.1 The array `myList` has ten elements of `double` type and `int` indices from `0` to `9`.

You can use the `equals` method to check whether two arrays are strictly equal. Two arrays are strictly equal if their corresponding elements are the same. In the following code, `list1` and `list2` are equal, but `list2` and `list3` are not.

equals

```
int[] list1 = {2, 4, 7, 10};
int[] list2 = {2, 4, 7, 10};
int[] list3 = {4, 2, 7, 10};
System.out.println(java.util.Arrays.equals(list1, list2)); // true
System.out.println(java.util.Arrays.equals(list2, list3)); // false
```

You can use the `fill` method to fill in all or part of the array. For example, the following code fills `list1` with `5` and fills `8` into elements `list2[1]` through `list2[5-1]`.

fill

```
int[] list1 = {2, 4, 7, 10};
int[] list2 = {2, 4, 7, 7, 7,  10};
java.util.Arrays.fill(list1, 5); // Fill 5 to the whole array
java.util.Arrays.fill(list2, 1, 5, 8); // Fill 8 to a partial array
```

You can also use the `toString` method to return a string that represents all elements in the array. This is a quick and simple way to display all elements in the array. For example, the following code

toString

```
int[] list = {2, 4, 7, 10};
System.out.println(Arrays.toString(list));
```

displays `[2, 4, 7, 10]`.

✓ Section 7.5 Assessment

1. What two methods from the `java.util.Arrays.sort` class can you use to sort a whole or partial array?
2. To apply `java.util.Arrays.binarySearch(array, key)`, should the array be sorted in increasing order, in decreasing order, or neither?
3. Show the output of the following code:

```
int[] list1 = {2, 4, 7, 10};
java.util.Arrays.fill(list1, 7);
System.out.println(java.util.Arrays.toString(list1));

int[] list2 = {2, 4, 7, 10};
System.out.println(java.util.Arrays.toString(list2));
System.out.print(java.util.Arrays.equals(list1, list2));
```

Chapter 7 — Review and Assessment

Key Terms

`0` based 205
data structure 202
index 202
indexed variable 205
`java.util.Arrays.parallelSort` 214
`java.util.Arrays.sort` 214
`new` operator 203
null 203
off-by-one error 209
single-dimensional array 202
two-dimensional array 202

Chapter Summary

1. A *data structure* is a collection of data organized in a particular way, and used to store data in computer memory. An *array* is a commonly used type of data structure.

2. When designing your application, consider using a data structure if you have a large amount of data to store and process during program execution. It is important to note that data structures store data in RAM memory while your program is running.

3. A *single-dimensional array* organizes data into a sequential, single row or column. There are a fixed number of *elements* in an array.

4. An example of a *two-dimensional array* is a spreadsheet where data is stored and retrieved by the location of both a column and a row.

5. Unlike declarations for primitive data type variables, the declaration of an array variable does not allocate any space in memory for the array. An array variable is not a primitive data type variable. An array variable contains a reference to an array.

6. You cannot assign elements to an array unless it has already been created. You can create an array by using the `new` operator with the following syntax: `new elementType[arraySize]`.

7. Each element in the array is represented using the syntax `arrayRefVar[index]`. An *index* must be an integer or an integer expression.

8. After an array is created, its size becomes permanent and can be obtained using `arrayRefVar.length`. Since the index of an array always begins with `0`, the last index is always `arrayRefVar.length - 1`. An *out-of-bounds error* will occur if you attempt to reference elements beyond the bounds of an array.

9. Programmers often mistakenly reference the first element in an array with index `1`, but it should be `0`. This is called the index *off-by-one error*.

10. When an array is created, its elements are assigned the default value of `0` for the numeric primitive data types, `\u0000` for char types, and `false` for `boolean` types.

11. Java has a shorthand notation, known as the *array initializer*, which combines declaring an array, creating an array, and initializing an array in one statement, using the syntax `elementType[] arrayRefVar = {value0, value1, ..., valuek}`.

Programming Exercises

Note
Exercises preceded by a star (*) are more challenging.

*1. (*Assign grades*) Write a program that reads student scores, gets the best score, and then assigns grades based on the following scheme:

Grade is A if score is ≥ best – 10

Grade is B if score is ≥ best – 20;

Grade is C if score is ≥ best – 30;

Grade is D if score is ≥ best – 40;

Grade is F otherwise.

The program prompts the user to enter the total number of students, then prompts the user to enter all of the scores, and concludes by displaying the grades. Here is a sample run:

```
Enter the number of students: 4 [Enter]
Enter 4 scores: 40 55 70 58 [Enter]
Student 0 score is 40 and grade is C
Student 1 score is 55 and grade is B
Student 2 score is 70 and grade is A
Student 3 score is 58 and grade is B
```

2. (*Reverse the numbers entered*) Write a program that reads ten integers and displays them in the reverse of the order in which they were read.

3. (*Analyze scores*) Write a program that reads an unspecified number of scores and determines how many scores are above or equal to the average and how many scores are below the average. Enter a negative number to signify the end of the input. Assume that the maximum number of scores is 100.

*4. (*Revise Listing 6.12, PrimeNumber.java*) Listing 6.12 determines whether a number `n` is prime by checking whether `2`, `3`, `4`, `5`, `6`, ..., `n/2` is a divisor. If a divisor is found, `n` is not prime. A more efficient approach is to check whether any of the prime numbers less than or equal to $\sqrt{n}$ can divide `n` evenly. If not, `n` is prime. Rewrite Listing 6.12 to display the first 50 prime numbers using this approach. You need to use an array to store the prime numbers and later use them to check whether they are possible divisors for `n`.

*5. (*Count single digits*) Write a program that generates 100 random integers between 0 and 9 and displays the count for each number. (*Hint*: Use an array of ten integers, say `counts`, to store the counts for the number of 0s, 1s, ..., 9s.)

CHAPTER 8

USING METHODS TO MODULARIZE CODE

Objectives

- Construct a method definition.
- Explain the principles of *modular* software system design.
- Invoke methods with parameters.
- Define methods with a return value.
- Define methods without a return value.
- Develop reusable code that is modular, easy to read, easy to debug, and easy to maintain.
- Compare a *procedural* vs. a *modular* programming style.
- Design methods using a stepwise refinement (*abstraction*) strategy.
- Identify program *constraints*.
- Identify and track potential issues and resolutions.

8.1 Introduction

Methods can be used to define reusable code and organize and simplify coding. Using methods in the application design is an effective way to modularize code and distribute programming efforts across a team.

Suppose that you need to find the sum of integers from 1 to 10, from 20 to 37, and from 35 to 49, respectively. You may write the code as follows:

```
int sum = 0;
for (int i = 1; i <= 10; i++)
  sum += i;
System.out.println("Sum from 1 to 10 is " + sum);

sum = 0;
for (int i = 20; i <= 37; i++)
  sum += i;
System.out.println("Sum from 20 to 37 is " + sum);

sum = 0;
for (int i = 35; i <= 49; i++)
  sum += i;
System.out.println("Sum from 35 to 49 is " + sum);
```

why methods?

You may have observed that computing these sums from 1 to 10, from 20 to 37, and from 35 to 49 are very similar except that the starting and ending integers are different. Wouldn't it be nice if we could write the common code once and reuse it? We can do so by defining a method and invoking it.

The preceding code can be simplified as follows:

define sum method

main method
invoke sum

```
1  public static int sum(int i1, int i2) {
2    int result = 0;
3    for (int i = i1; i <= i2; i++)
4      result += i;
5
6    return result;
7  }
8
9  public static void main(String[] args) {
10   System.out.println("Sum from 1 to 10 is " + sum(1, 10));
11   System.out.println("Sum from 20 to 37 is " + sum(20, 37));
12   System.out.println("Sum from 35 to 49 is " + sum(35, 49));
13 }
```

Lines 1–7 define the method named sum with two parameters i1 and i2. The statements in the main method invoke sum(1, 10) to compute the sum from 1 to 10, sum(20, 37) to compute the sum from 20 to 37, and sum(35, 49) to compute the sum from 35 to 49.

method

A *method* is a collection of statements grouped together to perform an operation. In earlier chapters you have used predefined methods such as System.out.println, System.exit, and Math.random. These methods are defined in the Java library. In this chapter, you will learn how to define your own methods and apply method abstraction to solve complex problems.

8.2 Defining a Method

A method definition consists of its method name, parameters, return value type, and body.

The syntax for defining a method is as follows:

```
modifier returnValueType methodName(list of parameters) {
  // Method body;
}
```

Let's look at a method defined to find the larger between two integers. This method, named `max`, has two `int` parameters, `num1` and `num2`, the larger of which is returned by the method. Figure 8.1 illustrates the components of this method.

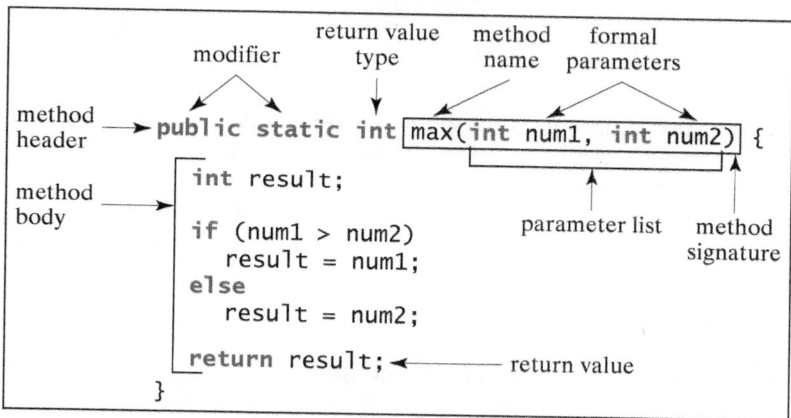

FIGURE 8.1 A method definition consists of a method header and a method body.

The *method header* specifies the *modifiers, return value type, method name*, and *parameters* of the method. The `static` modifier is used for all the methods in this chapter.

method header
modifier

A method may return a value. The `returnValueType` is the data type of the value the method returns. Some methods perform desired operations without returning a value. In this case, the `returnValueType` is the keyword `void`. For example, the `returnValueType` is `void` in the `main` method, as well as in `System.exit`, and `System.out.println`. If a method returns a value, it is called a *value-returning method;* otherwise it is called a *void method.*

value-returning method
void method

The variables defined in the method header are known as *formal parameters* or simply *parameters.* A parameter is like a placeholder: when a method is invoked, you pass a value to the parameter. This value is referred to as an *actual parameter* or *argument.* The *parameter list* refers to the method's type, order, and number of the parameters. The method name and the parameter list together constitute the *method signature.* Parameters are optional; that is, a method may contain no parameters. For example, the `Math.random()` method has no parameters.

parameter
argument
parameter list
method signature

The method body contains a collection of statements that implement the method. The method body of the `max` method uses an `if` statement to determine which number is larger and return the value of that number. In order for a value-returning method to return a result, a return statement using the keyword `return` is *required.* The method terminates when a return statement is executed.

Note

Some programming languages refer to methods as *procedures* and *functions.* In those languages, a value-returning method is called a *function* and a void method is called a *procedure.*

Caution

In the method header, you need to declare each parameter separately. For instance, `max(int num1, int num2)` is correct, but `max(int num1, num2)` is wrong.

define vs. declare

Note

We say "*define* a method" and "*declare* a variable." We are making a subtle distinction here. A definition defines what the defined item is, but a declaration usually involves allocating memory to store data for the declared item.

8.3 Calling a Method

Calling a method executes the code in the method.

In a method definition, you define what the method is to do. To execute the method, you have to *call* or *invoke* it. Figure 8.2 illustrates what the code would look like to invoke the method in Figure 8.1.

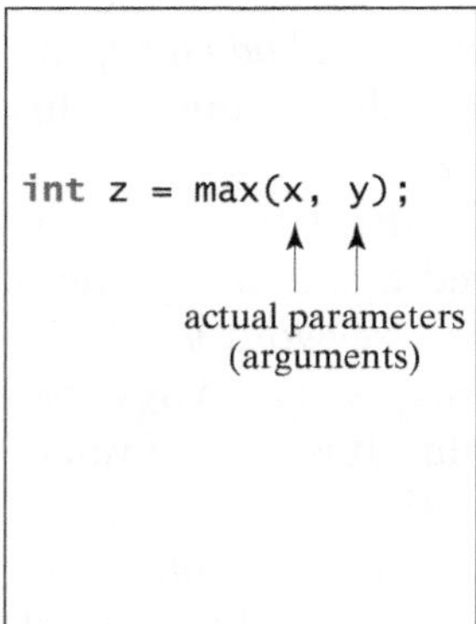

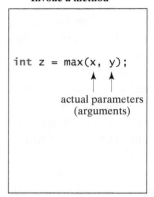

FIGURE 8.2 Example code for invoking a method.

There are two ways to call a method, depending on whether or not the method returns a value.

A value is returned.

If a method returns a value, a call to the method is usually treated as a value. For example,

```
int larger = max(3, 4);
```

calls `max(3, 4)` and assigns the result of the method to the variable `larger`. Another example of a call that is treated as a value is

```
System.out.println(max(3, 4));
```

which prints the return value of the method call `max(3, 4)`.

No value is returned.

A method that does not return a value is called a `void` method. If a method returns `void`, a call to the method must be a statement. For example, the method `println` returns `void`. The following call is a statement:

```
System.out.println("Welcome to Java!");
```

Note

A value-returning method can also be invoked as a statement in Java. In this case, the caller simply ignores the return value. This is not often done, but it is permissible if the caller is not interested in the return value.

When a program calls a method, program control is transferred to the called method. A called method returns control to the caller when its return statement is executed or when its method-ending closing brace is reached.

Listing 8.1 shows a complete program that is used to test the `max` method.

LISTING 8.1 TestMax.java

```
public class TestMax {
  /** Main method */
  public static void main(String[] args) {
    int i = 5;
    int j = 2;
    int k = max(i, j);
    System.out.println("The maximum of " + i +
      " and " + j + " is " + k);
  }

  /** Return the max of two numbers */
  public static int max(int num1, int num2) {
    int result;

    if (num1 > num2)
      result = num1;
    else
      result = num2;

    return result;
  }
}
```

main method

invoke max

define method

```
The maximum of 5 and 2 is 5
```

A brute-force approach is to convert each hex character into a decimal number, multiply it by 16^i for a hex digit at the `i`'s position, and then add all the items together to obtain the equivalent decimal value for the hex number.

Note that

$$h_n \times 16^n + h_{n-1} \times 16^{n-1} + h_{n-2} \times 16^{n-2} + \ldots + h_1 \times 16^1 + h_0 \times 16^0$$
$$= (\ldots((h_n \times 16 + h_n - 1) \times 16 + h_n - 2) \times 16 + \ldots + h_1) \times 16 + h_0$$

This observation, known as the Horner's algorithm, leads to the following efficient code for converting a hex string to a decimal number:

```
int decimalValue = 0;
for (int i = 0; i < hex.length(); i++) {
  char hexChar = hex.charAt(i);
  decimalValue = decimalValue * 16 + hexCharToDecimal(hexChar);
}
```

Here is a trace of the algorithm for hex number `AB8C`:

	i	hexChar	hexCharToDecimal (hexChar)	decimalValue
before the loop				0
after the 1st iteration	0	A	10	10
after the 2nd iteration	1	B	11	10 * 16 + 11
after the 3rd iteration	2	8	8	(10 * 16 + 11) * 16 + 8
after the 4th iteration	3	C	12	((10 * 16 + 11) * 16 + 8) * 16 + 12

Listing 8.7 gives the complete program.

LISTING 8.7 Hex2Dec.java

```
import java.util.Scanner;

public class Hex2Dec {
  /** Main method */
  public static void main(String[] args) {
    // Create a Scanner
    Scanner input = new Scanner(System.in);

    // Prompt the user to enter a string
    System.out.print("Enter a hex number: ");
    String hex = input.nextLine();

    System.out.println("The decimal value for hex number "
      + hex + " is " + hexToDecimal(hex.toUpperCase()));
  }

```

input string

hex to decimal

hex char to decimal
check uppercase

```
17    public static int hexToDecimal(String hex) {
18      int decimalValue = 0;
19      for (int i = 0; i < hex.length(); i++) {
20        char hexChar = hex.charAt(i);
21        decimalValue = decimalValue * 16 + hexCharToDecimal(hexChar);
22      }
23
24      return decimalValue;
25    }
26
27    public static int hexCharToDecimal(char ch) {
28      if (ch >= 'A' && ch <= 'F')
29        return 10 + ch - 'A';
30      else // ch is '0', '1', ..., or '9'
31        return ch - '0';
32    }
33  }
```

```
Enter a hex number: AB8C [Enter]
The decimal value for hex number AB8C is 43916
```

```
Enter a hex number: af71 [Enter]
The decimal value for hex number af71 is 44913
```

The program reads a string from the console (line 11), and invokes the `hexToDecimal` method to convert a hex string to decimal number (line 14). The characters can be in either lowercase or uppercase. They are converted to uppercase before invoking the `hexToDecimal` method.

The `hexToDecimal` method is defined in lines 17–25 to return an integer. The length of the string is determined by invoking `hex.length()` in line 19.

The `hexCharToDecimal` method is defined in lines 27–32 to return a decimal value for a hex character. The character can be in either lowercase or uppercase. Recall that to subtract two characters is to subtract their Unicodes. For example, `'5' - '0'` is `5`.

✓ Section 8.7 Assessment

1. Compare the code design in Listing 5.4 and Listing 8.7. Explain the difference between the two programming styles.

8.8 Software Design Strategies using Abstraction and Stepwise Refinement

The key to developing software is to apply the concept of abstraction.

You will learn many levels of abstraction from this book. *Method abstraction* is achieved by separating the use of a method from its implementation. The client can use a method without knowing how it is implemented. The details of the implementation are encapsulated in the method and hidden from the client who invokes the method. This is also known as *information hiding* or *encapsulation*. If you decide to change the implementation, the client program will not be affected, provided that you do not change the method signature. The implementation of the method is hidden from the client in a "black box," as shown in Figure 8.4.

method abstraction

information hiding

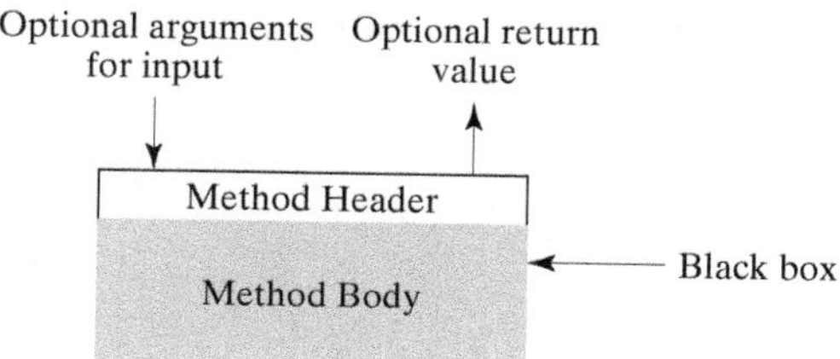

FIGURE 8.4 The method body can be thought of as a black box that contains the detailed implementation for the method.

You have already used the `System.out.print` method to display a string and the `max` method to find the maximum number. You know how to write the code to invoke these methods in your program, but as a user of these methods, you are not required to know how they are implemented.

The concept of method abstraction can be applied to the process of developing programs. When writing a large program, you can use the *divide-and-conquer* strategy, also known as *stepwise refinement*, to decompose it into subproblems. The subproblems can be further decomposed into smaller, more manageable problems.

divide and conquer

stepwise refinement

Suppose you write a program that displays the calendar for a given month of the year. The program prompts the user to enter the year and the month, then displays the entire calendar for the month, as shown in the following sample run.

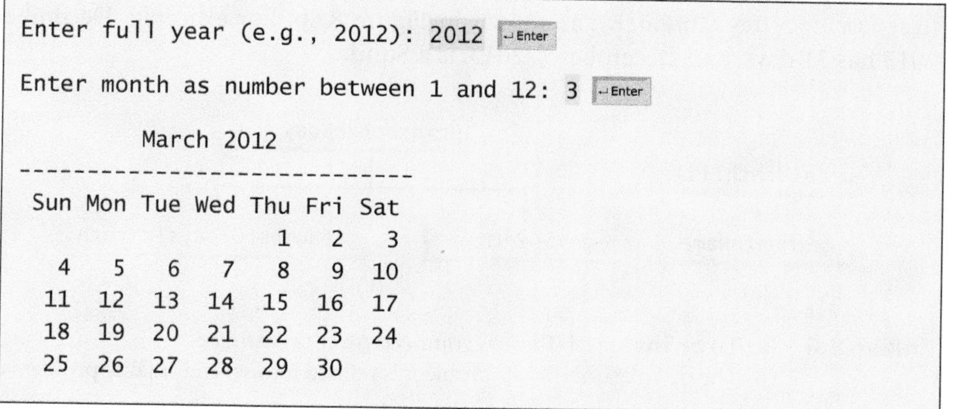

```
Enter full year (e.g., 2012): 2012 ↵Enter

Enter month as number between 1 and 12: 3 ↵Enter

         March 2012
-----------------------------
 Sun Mon Tue Wed Thu Fri Sat
                   1   2   3
   4   5   6   7   8   9  10
  11  12  13  14  15  16  17
  18  19  20  21  22  23  24
  25  26  27  28  29  30
```

Let us use this example to demonstrate the divide-and-conquer approach.

Top-Down Design

How would you get started on such a program? Would you immediately start coding? Beginning programmers often start by trying to work out the solution to every detail. Although details are important in the final program, concern for detail in the early stages may block the problem-solving process. To make problem solving flow as smoothly as possible, this example begins by using method abstraction to isolate details from design and only later implements the details.

For this example, the problem is first broken into two subproblems: get input from the user and print the calendar for the month. At this stage, you should be concerned with what the subproblems will achieve, not with how to get input and print the calendar for the month. You can draw a structure chart to help visualize the decomposition of the problem (see Figure 8.5a).

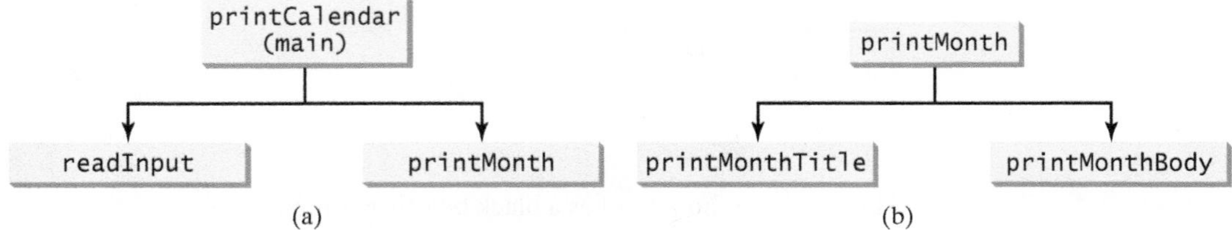

FIGURE 8.5 The structure chart shows that the `printCalendar` problem is divided into two subproblems, `readInput` and `printMonth` in (a), and that `printMonth` is divided into two smaller subproblems, `printMonthTitle` and `printMonthBody` in (b).

You can use `Scanner` to read input for the year and the month. The problem of printing the calendar for a given month can be broken into two subproblems: print the month title and print the month body, as shown in Figure 8.5b. The month title consists of three lines: month and year, a dashed line, and the names of the seven days of the week. You need to get the month name (e.g., January) from the numeric month (e.g., 1). This is accomplished in `getMonthName` (see Figure 8.6a).

In order to print the month body, you need to know which day of the week is the first day of the month (`getStartDay`) and how many days the month has (`getNumberOfDaysInMonth`), as shown in Figure 8.6b. For example, December 2013 has 31 days, and December 1, 2013, is a Sunday.

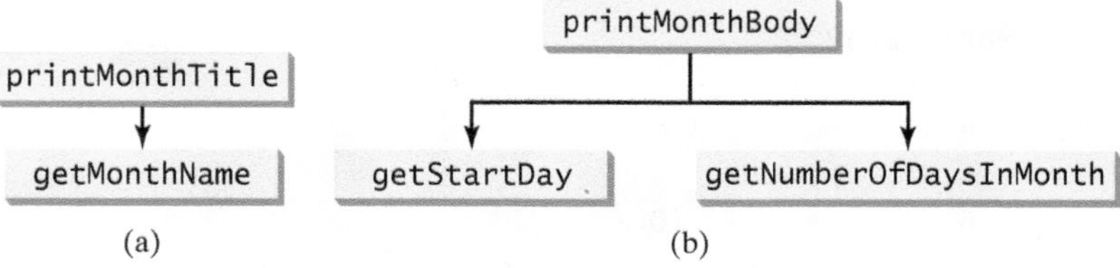

FIGURE 8.6 (a) To `printMonthTitle`, you need `getMonthName`.
(b) The `printMonthBody` problem is refined into several smaller problems.

How would you get the start day for the first date in a month? There are several ways to do so. For now, we'll use an alternative approach. Assume you know that the start day for January 1, 1800, was a Wednesday (`START_DAY_FOR_JAN_1_1800 = 3`). You could compute the total number of days (`totalNumberOfDays`) between January 1, 1800, and the first date of the calendar month. The start day for the calendar month is `(totalNumberOfDays + START_DAY_FOR_JAN_1_1800) % 7`, since every week has seven days. Thus, the `getStartDay` problem can be further refined as `getTotalNumberOfDays`, as shown in Figure 8.7a.

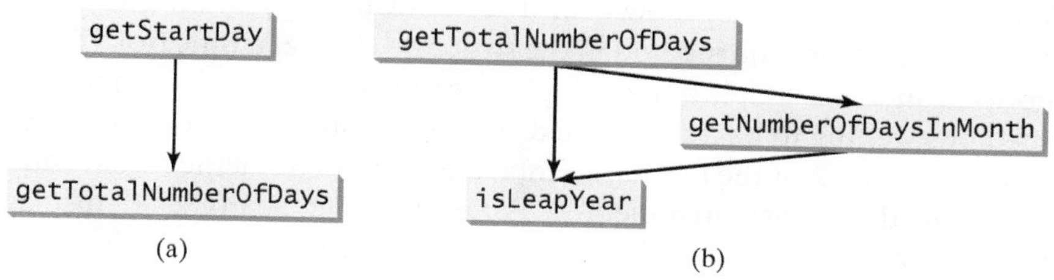

Figure 8.7 (a) To `getStartDay`, you need `getTotalNumberOfDays`. (b) The `getTotalNumberOfDays` problem is refined into two smaller problems.

To get the total number of days, you need to know whether the year is a leap year and the number of days in each month. Thus, `getTotalNumberOfDays` can be further refined into two subproblems: `isLeapYear` and `getNumberOfDaysInMonth`, as shown in Figure 8.7b. The complete structure chart is shown in Figure 8.8.

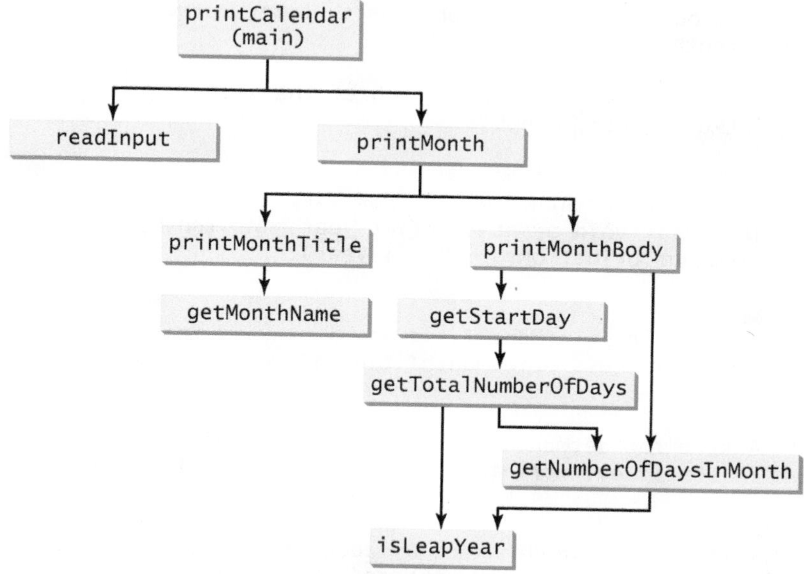

Figure 8.8 The structure chart shows the hierarchical relationship of the subproblems in the program.

Top-Down and/or Bottom-Up Implementation

Now we turn our attention to implementation. In general, a subproblem corresponds to a method in the implementation, although some are so simple that this is unnecessary. You would need to decide which modules to implement as methods and which to combine with other methods. Decisions of this kind should be based on whether the overall program will be easier to read as a result of your choice. In this example, the subproblem `readInput` can be simply implemented in the `main` method.

top-down approach

stub

You can use either a "top-down" or a "bottom-up" approach. The top-down approach implements one method in the structure chart at a time from the top to the bottom. *Stubs*—a simple but incomplete version of a method—can be used for the methods waiting to be implemented. The use of stubs enables you to quickly build the framework of the program. Implement the `main` method first, and then use a stub for the `printMonth` method. For example, let `printMonth` display the year and the month in the stub. Thus, your program may begin like this:

```
public class PrintCalendar {
  /** Main method */
  public static void main(String[] args) {
    Scanner input = new Scanner(System.in);

    // Prompt the user to enter year
    System.out.print("Enter full year (e.g., 2012): ");
    int year = input.nextInt();

    // Prompt the user to enter month
    System.out.print("Enter month as a number between 1 and 12: ");
    int month = input.nextInt();

    // Print calendar for the month of the year
    printMonth(year, month);
  }

  /** A stub for printMonth may look like this */
  public static void printMonth(int year, int month){
    System.out.print(month + " " + year);
  }

  /** A stub for printMonthTitle may look like this */
  public static void printMonthTitle(int year, int month){
  }

  /** A stub for getMonthBody may look like this */
  public static void printMonthBody(int year, int month){
  }

  /** A stub for getMonthName may look like this */
  public static String getMonthName(int month) {
    return "January"; // A dummy value
  }

  /** A stub for getStartDay may look like this */
  public static int getStartDay(int year, int month) {
    return 1; // A dummy value
  }
```

Write a test program that invokes these methods to display the following tables:

Feet	Meters	|	Meters	Feet
1.0	0.305	|	20.0	65.574
2.0	0.610	|	25.0	81.967
...				
9.0	2.745	|	60.0	196.721
10.0	3.050	|	65.0	213.115

7. (*Use the `isPrime` Method*) Listing 8.6, PrimeNumberMethod.java, provides the `isPrime(int number)` method for testing whether a number is prime. Use this method to find the number of prime numbers less than `10000`.

8. (*Display characters*) Write a method that prints characters using the following header:

```
public static void printChars(char ch1, char ch2, int
 numberPerLine)
```

This method prints the characters between `ch1` and `ch2` with the specified numbers per line. Write a test program that prints ten characters per line from `1` to `Z`. Characters are separated by exactly one space.

*9. (*Number of days in a year*) Write a method that returns the number of days in a year using the following header:

```
public static int numberOfDaysInAYear(int year)
```

Write a test program that displays the number of days in year from 2000 to 2020.

*10. (*Display matrix of 0s and 1s*) Write a method that displays an *n*-by-*n* matrix using the following header:

```
public static void printMatrix(int n)
```

Each element is 0 or 1, which is generated randomly. Write a test program that prompts the user to enter `n` and displays an *n*-by-*n* matrix. Here is a sample run:

```
Enter n: 3 ↵Enter
0 1 0
0 0 0
1 1 1
```

*11. (*The* `MyTriangle` *class*) Create a class named `MyTriangle` that contains the following two methods:

```
/** Return true if the sum of any two sides is
 *  greater than the third side. */
public static boolean isValid(
  double side1, double side2, double side3)

/** Return the area of the triangle. */
public static double area(
 double side1, double side2, double side3)
```

Write a test program that reads three sides for a triangle and computes the area if the input is valid. Otherwise, it displays that the input is invalid. The formula for computing the area of a triangle is:

$$s = (\text{side1} + \text{side2} + \text{side3})/2;$$

$$\text{area} = \sqrt{s(s - \text{side1})(s - \text{side2})(s - \text{side3})}$$

*12. (*Count the letters in a string*) Write a method that counts the number of letters in a string using the following header:

```
public static int countLetters(String s)
```

Write a test program that prompts the user to enter a string and displays the number of letters in the string.

*13. (*Phone keypads*) The international standard letter/number mapping for telephones is shown in Chapter 5, Programming Exercise 8. Write a method that returns a number, given an uppercase letter, as follows:

```
int getNumber(char uppercaseLetter)
```

Write a test program that prompts the user to enter a phone number as a string. The input number may contain letters. The program translates a letter (uppercase or lowercase) to a digit and leaves all other characters intact. Here is a sample run of the program:

```
Enter a string: 1-800-Flowers ↵Enter
1-800-3569377
```

```
Enter a string: 1800flowers ↵Enter
18003569377
```

14. (*Geometry: area of a pentagon*) The area of a pentagon can be computed using the following formula:

$$Area = \frac{5 \times s^2}{4 \times \tan\left(\frac{\pi}{5}\right)}$$

Write a method that returns the area of a pentagon using the following header:

```
public static double area(double side)
```

Write a main method that prompts the user to enter the side of a pentagon and displays its area. Here is a sample run:

```
Enter the side: 5.5 ↵Enter
The area of the pentagon is 52.04444136781625
```

15. (*Format an integer*) Write a method with the following header to format the integer with the specified width.

```
public static String format(int number, int width)
```

The method returns a string for the number with one or more prefix `0`s. The size of the string is the width. For example, `format(34, 4)` returns `0034` and `format(34, 5)` returns `00034`. If the number is longer than the width, the method returns the string representation for the number. For example, `format(34, 1)` returns `34`.

Write a test program that prompts the user to enter a number and its width and displays a string returned by invoking `format(number, width)`.

CHAPTER

9

Introduction to Object-Oriented Programming

Objectives

- Explain the principles of *object-oriented programming* (*OOP*).
- Describe the concept of a *class* and an *object* using real-world analogies.
- Create a class design using *Unified Object Modeling* (*UML*) tool.
- Write object-oriented code and use standard programming practices that make your code easy to understand.
- Demonstrate how to define classes and create objects.
- Use the *dot operator* (.) to reference an object's members.
- Use the `Date` and `Random` Java library classes.

9.1 Introduction

Object-oriented programming enables you to develop large-scale software applications. It is the programming paradigm used most often today to build new applications.

Having learned the material in the preceding chapters, you are able to solve many programming problems using selections, loops, and arrays. These are all structured programming constructs used in everyday programming. However, these programming features are not sufficient for large-scale software systems, and for applications developed by a team of programmers.

why oop?

As your project grows in size and complexity, your code should be modular in design and reusable. To create modular, reusable code, you must learn object-oriented programming. Your code should also be well-commented and follow a consistent styling technique. This helps programmers work together in understanding the entire team project.

override

inheritance

extensibility

The basic concept of Object-Oriented Programming (OOP) was introduced in Section 2.3. This chapter will explore OOP in further detail. Consider the classic example of a house. A house is an *object* built from a template, or blueprint. A blueprint provides the foundation to build the house. To build a second, similar house, it is more efficient to use the same blueprint rather than start over from the beginning. Both houses *inherit* all the basic features provided in the template, such as the square footage and floor plan. You, as the developer, can *override* basic features of the template. For instance, the basic design may call for a wood exterior. You can override this feature with a brick exterior. Additionally, the template can be *extended*. For instance, a house can include an additional sunroom. The concepts of *inheritance*, *overriding*, and *extensibility* are all important principles of OOP. It is important to have a basic understanding of these principles as you begin to learn OOP programming. You will explore these concepts further in other advanced computer programming courses.

button class

Suppose you want to develop a graphical user interface (GUI, pronounced *goo-ee*). The design includes two buttons (OK and Cancel) as shown in Figure 9.1. Both buttons are objects. Each button has properties such as size and shape. Buttons recognize certain actions such as a *click* action. Code is written to establish these properties and functionality. Rather than rewriting this code every time a button is added to the GUI, you create a button based upon an existing button template. This template is called a *button class*. When a button is added to the GUI, an instance of the button object is created. The new button inherits basic characteristics and functionality from the base button class. This saves much programming time and effort.

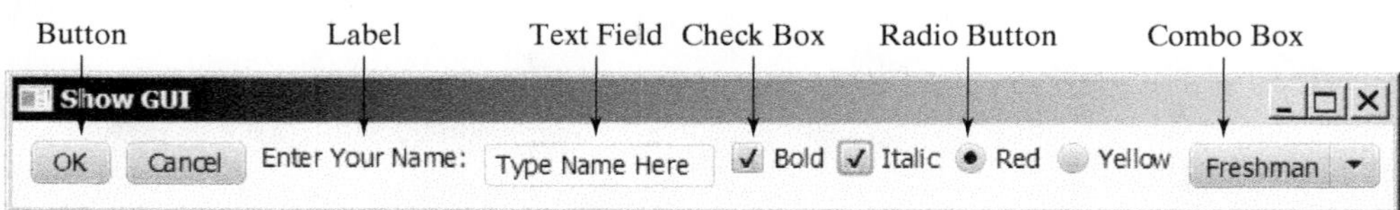

FIGURE 9.1 The GUI objects are created from classes.

In addition to using classes already established, such as the button class, you can create your own classes. These classes can be reused within your application, other applications, or by other programmers.

This chapter explores classes and objects. These are two building blocks for creating modular, object-oriented code.

✓ Section 9.1 Assessment

1. a) Use a pie recipe to explain the principles of object-oriented design. Create a template, or class, for the pie recipe and list four properties or attributes you might include in the class. Name your class `pieRecipe`.

   b) Create a pie object based on the `pieRecipe` class. Identify properties you might inherit, override, and extend from the base class. Articulate the design in a paragraph and draw a picture to illustrate the design.

2. You are required to name your class `pieRecipe` in Question 1. What other names could you have used? Why is it important to follow an appropriate style when naming objects?

9.2 Defining Classes for Objects

A class defines the properties and behaviors for objects.

object-oriented programming (OOP)
object

Object-oriented programming (OOP) involves programming using objects. An *object* represents an entity in the real world that can be distinctly identified. For example, a student, a desk, a circle, a button, and even a loan can all be viewed as objects. An object has a unique identity, state, and behavior.

properties
attributes
data field
actions

- Objects have *properties* or *attributes*. A circle object, for example, has a `radius` property. A rectangle object has a `width` and a `height` property. Properties are stored in a *data field*.
- The *behavior* of an object (also known as its *actions*) is defined by methods. To invoke a method on an object is to ask the object to perform an action. For example, you may define methods named `getArea()` and `getPerimeter()` for circle objects. A circle object may invoke `getArea()` to return its area and `getPerimeter()` to return its perimeter. You may also define the `setRadius(radius)` method. A circle object can invoke this method to change its radius.

class
contract
instantiation
instance

Objects of the same type are defined using a common class. A *class* is a template, blueprint, or *contract* that defines what an object's data fields and methods will be. An object is an instance of a class. You can create many instances of a class. Creating an instance is referred to as *instantiation*. The terms *object* and *instance* are often interchangeable. The relationship between classes and objects is analogous to that between an apple-pie recipe and apple pies: You can make as many apple pies as you want from a single recipe. Figure 9.2 shows a class named `Circle` and its three objects.

```
Random random1 = new Random(3);
System.out.print("From random1: ");
for (int i = 0; i < 10; i++)
  System.out.print(random1.nextInt(1000) + " ");

Random random2 = new Random(3);
System.out.print("\nFrom random2: ");
for (int i = 0; i < 10; i++)
  System.out.print(random2.nextInt(1000) + " ");
```

The code generates the same sequence of random `int` values:

```
From random1: 734 660 210 581 128 202 549 564 459 961
From random2: 734 660 210 581 128 202 549 564 459 961
```

✓ Section 9.6 Assessment

1. What method can you use from the `Date` class to retrieve the current time?

2. Explain the principle of encapsulation in an OOP design. How does it benefit the programmer?

Chapter 9 — Review and Assessment

Key Terms

action 253
attribute 253
class 253
class diagram 255
constructor 254
data field 253
default constructor 261
dot operator 262
encapsulation 263
extensibility 252
inheritance 252
instantiation 253
no-arg constructor 261
object 253
object-oriented programming (OOP) 253
override 252
property 253
reference type 262
Unified Modeling Language (UML) 255
value type 262

Chapter Summary

1. As your project grows in size and complexity, it is important to develop well-commented and structured code that follows a consistent styling technique.

2. *Object-Oriented Programming* (*OOP*) is the most common programming style used today. OOP is particularly helpful in designing large-scale applications requiring a team of programmers.

3. Classes and objects are two basic building blocks in creating object-oriented code.

4. A *class* is a template for objects. One or more objects can be created, or *instantiated*, from a class.

5. The concepts of *inheritance*, *overriding*, *extensibility*, and *encapsulation* are important principles of OOP design. Objects can *inherit* members from a class. The details of the class are hidden, or *encapsulated*. Inherited members can be changed, or *overridden*. You can *extend* an object by adding additional members or functionality.

6. An object is an instance of a class. Use the `new` keyword to create an object, and the dot operator (.) to access members of the object.

7. Objects have *properties* or *attributes*. A circle object, for example, has a `radius` property. A rectangle object has a `width` and a `height` property. Properties are stored in a *data field*.

8. The *behavior* of an object (also known as its *actions*) is defined by methods.

9. Class variables are *reference* types. An object can be very large. Rather than storing the entire object in memory, a reference pointer to the object is stored in memory. When the object is needed during program execution, the pointer is used to retrieve the object. Space must be reserved in memory to store the object reference.

10. *Unified Modeling Language* (*UML*) is a standard tool used to illustrate the design of class templates and objects.

11. There are classes available for re-use in the Java library. Two examples of Java library classes are `Date` class and `Random` class.

Programming Exercises

Note
Exercises preceded by a star (*) are more challenging.

1. (*The `Rectangle` class*) Following the example of the `Circle` class in Section 9.2, design a class named `Rectangle` to represent a rectangle. The class contains:

   - Two `double` data fields named `width` and `height` that specify the width and height of the rectangle. The default values are `1` for both `width` and `height`.
   - A no-arg constructor that creates a default rectangle.
   - A constructor that creates a rectangle with the specified `width` and `height`.
   - A method named `getArea()` that returns the area of this rectangle.
   - A method named `getPerimeter()` that returns the perimeter.

   Draw the UML diagram for the class and then implement the class. Write a test program that creates two `Rectangle` objects—one with width `4` and height `40` and the other with width `3.5` and height `35.9`. Display the width, height, area, and perimeter of each rectangle in this order. Write your code using standard naming convention. Comment your code and use proper spacing and indents for clarity and readability.

2. (*The `Stock` class*) Following the example of the `Circle` class in Section 9.2, design a class named `Stock` that contains:

   - A string data field named `symbol` for the stock's symbol.
   - A string data field named `name` for the stock's name.
   - A `double` data field named `previousClosingPrice` that stores the stock price for the previous day.
   - A `double` data field named `currentPrice` that stores the stock price for the current time.

- A constructor that creates a stock with the specified symbol and name.
- A method named `getChangePercent()` that returns the percentage changed from `previousClosingPrice` to `currentPrice`.

Draw the UML diagram for the class and then implement the class. Write a test program that creates a `Stock` object with the stock symbol `ORCL`, the name `Oracle Corporation`, and the previous closing price of `34.5`. Set a new current price to `34.35` and display the price-change percentage.

*3. (*Use the* `Date` *class*) Write a program that creates a `Date` object, sets its elapsed time to `10000`, `100000`, `1000000`, `10000000`, `100000000`, `1000000000`, `10000000000`, and `100000000000`, and displays the date and time using the `toString()` method, respectively.

*4. (*Use the* `Random` *class*) Write a program that creates a `Random` object with seed `1000` and displays the first 50 random integers between `0` and `100` using the `nextInt(100)` method.

CHAPTER 10

IDENTIFYING SECURITY RISKS AND COMPLYING WITH GOVERNMENT REGULATIONS

Objectives

- Define *risk assessment.*
- Identify the steps to *risk assessment.*
- Identify the computer system components that are subject to *security risks.*
- Describe potential risks to each computer system component.
- Identify and select the correct procedures to reduce security risks.
- Describe ways to recover from a security failure.
- Understand *data encryption.*
- Identify types of *malware* and ways to recover from malware infection.
- Describe the purpose of *cookies.*
- Differentiate between types of *computer crimes.*
- Describe *state and federal laws* that pertain to computer crimes.

10.1 Security Risk Assessment

Maintaining a secure computer system spans a wide range of job roles. Everyone on the team plays a part. The information technology (IT) administrator, database (DB) administrator, software developer, and security analyst all play a role in keeping a computer information system safe. According to the U.S. Bureau of Labor Statistics, demand for jobs in computer security continues to rise.

After an application is developed, the project team's job does not stop there. Software applications require installations, user training, and ongoing support and maintenance. Part of the design and ongoing maintenance of an application includes the evaluation of potential security risks. A *security risk* is a person, object, or situation that poses a threat to the safety of something. Anything that negatively affects your computer system is considered a security risk. Protecting your software system not only includes managing malicious attacks, but also protection from accidental incidents.

security risk

There are three main goals to maintaining a secure computer system:

1. Keeping sensitive data *confidential*.
2. Maintaining the *integrity* of data.
3. Insuring the *availability* of data when and where it is needed.

These three goals of ***Confidentiality***, ***Integrity***, and ***Availability*** are often referred to as the *CIA Triad* principle. To achieve these goals, you must first identify and assess potential risks.

CIA Triad

A *risk assessment* is the process of identifying and planning for factors that can negatively affect the security of a system. A risk assessment includes the following five stages:

risk assessment

Step 1: Identify potential risks.

Identify the potential for both malicious and accidental risks. An example of a malicious attack may be the intrusion of a virus or a burglary of the premises. Examples of accidental risks are damage caused by a natural disaster, or hard drive failure.

Step 2: Quantify the risk.

Quantifying risks is the process of estimating the likelihood of a specific risk. A numerical value or percentage is assigned to each risk reflecting the possibility of the risk occurring. Assigning a value helps rank and prioritize risks. As an example, the likelihood of a hurricane would be far less likely to occur in an interior region of a country. However, the same location may be near a fault-line where earthquakes occur regularly. In this scenario, you would assign a higher risk factor to an earthquake risk than a hurricane risk.

Step 3: Develop a plan.

After identifying and quantifying the risks, create a written plan documenting the findings. There is usually more than one solution to handling security issues. Several factors, such as time and budget, help determine the best plan of action. Management and decision makers use the plan to determine the actions required.

Step 4: Implement a plan.

Once decisions are finalized, the plan is put into place. Prevention is always the "best medicine" when tackling security issues. Implementing the plan involves several members of a team. Those responsible for both hardware and software work together to secure the system.

Step 5: Monitor and evaluate the plan.

A security analyst's job is never done. A good risk assessment plan includes continuous monitoring and evaluation of the plan. Adjustments are made as the project components, usage, and physical location change. Figure 10.1 illustrates the stages involved in a risk assessment. The arrows represent the ongoing process of evaluation.

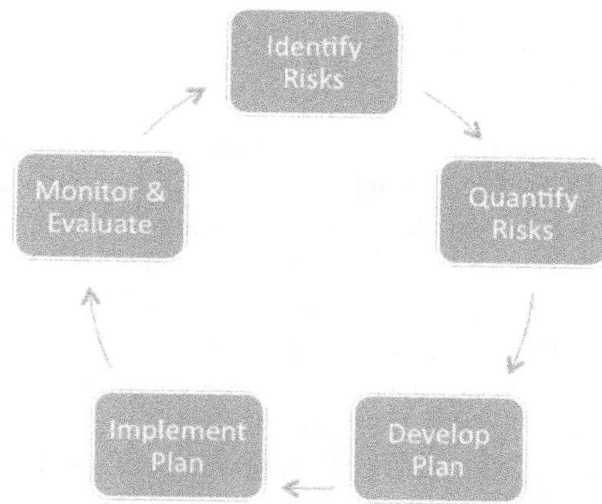

FIGURE 10.1 Steps to security risk assessment.

✓ SECTION 10.1 ASSESSMENT

1. Define risk assessment. List the stages of a risk assessment plan and identify the order in which they should occur.
2. What does the CIA triad principle stand for?
3. Who is responsible for the security of a computer system?
4. Why is a security analyst's job never done?

10.2 Identify Risks to Computer Systems

It is impossible to have 100% assurance that you are protected from a security failure. However, a good risk management plan will identify potential risks, implement tactics to minimize their possibility, and develop a recovery plan in the event of a security breach.

The following components of a computer information system may be at risk:

- Physical facilities of the application servers
- Hardware components of your application
- Network and data communications system
- Software components

Physical Facilities

physical facilities

cloud storage

Physical facilities include the building structure in which the software application servers reside. This may be onsite or in a cloud storage facility. Today many software applications reside in cloud storage. *Cloud storage* is a storage system in which data is stored across multiple servers and various locations. The data can be shared across multiple devices. A third party often hosts the cloud system. Some hosting companies charge a fee, but there are many services available free of charge. Even with cloud storage, a physical location exists and therefore a risk assessment is necessary.

Types of risks that can negatively affect the physical facility are the following:

- Terrorist attack
- Burglary and sabotage
- Acts of nature such as fire, earthquake, lightning strike

After potential risks are identified, the next step is to explore ways to reduce the risk. Installing a security system or hiring security guards are ways to secure your building from burglary, sabotage, or terrorist attacks. Installing proper locks on entryways is a simple but overlooked way to secure a building. Additionally, you need to establish a policy to determine what hours of the day the door should remain locked. Consider the example of your home. Most people have locks on exterior doors, but many robberies occur simply because the door is left unlocked. Even the most sophisticated locking system will be ineffective if it is not used. Requiring proper identification before entering the building insures that only approved personnel are allowed inside.

biometrics

smart chip ID

Security is an ever-increasing concern for both private businesses and government facilities. New technologies such as biometric devices and smart chip ID systems are becoming popular. *Biometrics* is the process of measuring a person's biological features for the purpose of identification. Examples are fingerprint scanners, retina scanners, voice recognition, or facial recognition. *Smart chip ID* cards and badges include a computerized chip that holds credentials and are read by a computer device to determine security clearance.

Q2: When do I need to encrypt my wireless signals?

Most experts will tell you, "Always!", and it *is* good advice, but the coffee shop may not be using encryption, and you *do* want to read your email, which you must log into with your password. Will someone snoop that? Luckily, even if your wireless connection isn't encrypted, your application may be. On the Web, for example, when the URL begins with https, the "s" means secure. This technology is the *secure socket layer (SSL)*, which is often indicated by a lock icon somewhere in the browser window. So, for example, your free email account is likely to use this kind of secure communication. This is probably good enough to read email at the coffee shop even without any better encryption. And finally, our third question:

secure socket layer (SSL)

Q3: If the coffee shop doesn't need secure wireless, do I need it for my wireless router?

Absolutely! First, you will use your own system for more secure transactions like banking. Second, many of us live near others who could piggyback onto your unsecured system. They are happy for you to pay their Internet video streaming charges. Third, even if your neighbors are not going to use your Internet, they can install software that allows them to watch everything you do, like typing passwords. Many applications do not use SSL when asking for your password. So, absolutely, you need to install a security barrier with your router.

Secure wireless technology has been under attack in recent years, with many systems—WEP and WEP2—being completely compromised. Today, WPA2—Wi-Fi Protected Access 2—is solid and recommended

✓ Section 10.3 Assessment

1. Using Julius Caesar's original encryption mode, decrypt the following message.

   `L ORYH SURJUDPPLQJ!`

2. Suppose you reply back to the message sent in the encrypting example where you were asked to "`MEET @ 9`". You reply back:

   `101257 042640 099645 087997`

   What message did you send?

3. Describe the difference between public key and private key encryption.

10.4 Recovering from System Failure and Computer Malware

A risk assessment plan minimizes risk but is not a guarantee against a system failure. Thus, a plan must be in place to recover from a system failure or breach.

Key Point

Recovering from a system failure takes patience and some pre-planning. If the failure involves data loss, the fastest way to recovery is to re-install data and software from a backup. To implement this procedure, you must have a regular back-up plan in place *before* the failure occurs. Once the data is lost or corrupted, it is too late to implement a backup plan. Thinking ahead and documenting the steps in a written plan is best practice for reducing security risks.

If the security breach involves lost or stolen hardware, have a plan in place that allows administrators to disable logons and delete sensitive data from the missing device. Software can be pre-installed on the missing device that allows you to perform these operations from a remote location.

There are millions of known computer viruses and thousands more pop up each day. If you are infected by a virus, use the proper virus removal tool to quarantine or delete the virus. Educating yourself on how to recognize and avoid viruses is the best prevention against them.

Understanding Malware

malware

Malware is an acronym for malicious software. Viruses are a type of malware. Although the term "virus" is often used to categorize all forms of malicious code, there is a distinction between various types. Following are the four categories of malware:

virus

- A *virus* is a program that intends to disrupt or destroy your computer files and data.

worm

- A *worm* is a program that is often embedded in an email attachment. It reproduces itself and can send a copy to everyone on your contact list, thereby propagating and moving on its own.

spyware

- *Spyware* is a program installed on your computer, usually without your permission. It is used to gather personal information and track browsing habits. Spyware is often attached to "free" software.

Trojan

- A *Trojan* is an unasked-for "gift"—like the horse of ancient Greece—that is a malicious program performing unauthorized activities. Trojans arrive with downloads of seemingly benign software, like "sharing" software from sites with "free stuff" such as music or wallpaper.

These are the principle ways malware gets into your computer.

What Does Malware Do?

Malware is a term used to cover a wide variety of threatening software. Some forms of malware simply track your Website browsing habits or download unwanted advertising. Others are more malicious. The three worst activities are the following:

backdoors

- *Backdoors* are software that "pokes a hole" in the computer, creating an access path allowing the attackers who produced the malware to run any program they want on your computer without being stopped by your computer's defenses. Such computers are usually set up to participate in a botnet.
- *Trojans* are software capable of so many unauthorized activities they're classified by type. Trojan keyloggers record every key you type, looking for passwords and other private information; Trojan FakeAVs pretend to be antivirus software, but they extort money from users to "fix" the problem it creates; and Trojan bankers watch for banking and credit card activity to capture account numbers and passwords. These are just a few of the types of Trojans; there are about two dozen others.

- *Rootkits* are software that infects your computer and then fights back against its security systems! If you manage to stop the infection, a rootkit can restart itself, copy itself, or even move itself. Rootkits purposely conceal themselves, which often makes removal nearly impossible. rootkits

The first thing that these malicious systems do is to lower the security defenses of the computer so they don't get detected or caught.

✓ Section 10.4 Assessment

1. If you have a system failure that involves data loss, what should you do?
2. A laptop has been stolen. What should you do to recover from the security breach?
3. A computer has been infected with a virus. What should you do?

10.5 Prevention Strategies

The best line of defense in preventing malicious security attacks is paying attention to what files we open and what Websites and links we visit.

The biggest problem—in fact, almost the only problem—in computer security is us. Using common sense and thinking before we act goes a long way in preventing security issues. There are few things that are truly "free." Consider the experiment done in June 2013 by Coner Myhrvold.

His experiment: Using ten extremely popular search terms, he Googled each. Then he clicked on the first ten search hits with Firefox running on a freshly installed version of Windows for each. When he got to each site, he installed whatever "free stuff" it offered. He then analyzed what was sent and installed on his computer. His results are summarized in Table 10.1.

Table 10.1 Results for search terms from Myhrvold's "Free Stuff" experiment.

Keywords	*Results*	*Infected Files*	*Threats Detected by Lavasoft Ad-Aware*
"free wallpaper"	2/6	11	Adware, Adware Installer, unwanted programs, miscellaneous
"free screensaver"	8/10	191	Hijacker, Adware, Adware Installer, unwanted programs, cookies, miscellaneous
"free games"	2/10	45	Adware, Adware Installer, cookies
"free game cheats"	0/1	0	N/A
"free word unscrambler"	0/10	0	N/A
"free e-cards"	0/10	0	N/A
"free lyrics"	5/10	608	Adware, Adware Installer, toolbar, cookies
"free music downloads"	5/10	835	Trojan, Adware, Adware Installer, toolbar, browser, plug-in, miscellaneous

The first column shows the search terms—definitely popular. Next is the number of links leading to downloads, out of the total landing pages with links. Third is the count of infected files received, and the final column tells what they were infected with. Notice he got 835 infected files from 5 free music sites! Also, two malware files were installed: a backdoor (Hijacker) and a Trojan. But Myrhvold summarized the real problem:

"Adware such as iLivid wreaked havoc on my PC speed and performance despite the fact that I installed several free programs [. . .] that promised the exact opposite. *Post install, my computer was effectively unusable.* Just opening the Web browser took several minutes because of the slate of adware running startup and background processes."

Safe Computing Checklist

Among the points security specialists continually make is that we will be safe if we just pay attention to what we're doing and understand the risks that go with it. Here are their most important bits of advice:

- **Turn off Bluetooth when not in use.** Bluetooth wireless is subject to many vulnerabilities, including nearby parties listening to calls and placing calls through your device. If you must use it, turn it *completely* off—not just "invisible" mode—when you're not in a conversation.
- **Keep your phone and other computers locked.** It may seem like you are always holding your phone, but you do put it down occasionally, making it possible for someone else to pick it up. Keeping it locked is a tiny hassle considering the personal data you have stored on it. . . or, considering the chance of loss or theft, do you want your sensitive information stored there in the first place?
- **Do not automatically click on email attachments.** Email attachments such as .jpg files are basically data and are generally safe, but many other files also contain program code. Malware can be embedded in the file's program code. When you open such files, the code runs and a worm or virus can be released. Table 10.2 is a list of file types that could potentially contain malware or viruses. Make sure they come from a reliable source before opening.
- **Never enter sensitive information in a pop-up.** Pop-ups are the main way malware gathers information. Most pop-ups are a nuisance, so turning them off entirely isn't a bad idea; that setting can be found in your Internet browser's Tools > Settings.
- **Thinking of getting something for nothing? Think again. . . .** As the story about Coner Myhrvold's experiment indicates, downloading free stuff can be extremely risky. But, we all like freebees. The security advice: Don't download until you've done your homework and have convinced yourself you're getting something of value from a legitimate site.
- **Know where you're going.** When you're surfing, it's always possible for Web links to appear to be connecting you to one place, when they're actually sending you somewhere else. Clicking a link provided to you in an email or in social media may actually link you to another site. If you are unfamiliar with the source, rather than clicking the link, copy/paste the blue anchor text into your Web browser. This avoids you being surreptitiously redirected to another site.

- **Be somewhat skeptical.** Social engineering (phishing) takes many forms, but there is just one goal: to get you to voluntarily give up your private information. This can be a form of data or identity theft. Be aware and pay attention to the Website you are actually on by viewing the URL of the site.
- **Use extreme care when visiting notorious sites.** Music sharing, sports gambling, and pornography sites are notorious as sources of "electronic infection." Minimizing visits minimizes risk.

TABLE 10.2 File extensions that can carry malware, primarily for Windows OS.

The file extension is the letter sequence following the last dot in the file name. Beware of files that have two extensions such as **data.txt.exe**. The two extensions are oftentimes a way to make a malicious file look safe. The last extension is the actual file type that the operating system will recognize.

Extension	Description
.386	Virtual Device Driver (Windows 386 enhanced mode)
.3gr	VGA Graphics Driver/configuration files
.add	Adapter Driver file
.ade	Microsoft Access project extension
.asp	Active Server Page
.bas	Microsoft Visual Basic class module
.bat	Batch file
.chm	Compiled HTML Help file
.cmd	Microsoft Windows NT command script
.com	Microsoft MS-DOS program
.cpl	Control Panel extension
.crt	Security certificate
.dbx	Database Index
.dll	Dynamic Link Library
.exe	Program file
.fon	Font file
.hlp	Help file
.hta	HTML program
.inf	Setup information
.ins	Internet Naming Service
.isp	Internet communication settings
.js	JavaScript file
.jse	JavaScript encoded-script file
.lnk	Shortcut
.mdb	Microsoft Access program
.mde	Microsoft Access MDE database
.msc	Microsoft Common Console document
.msi	Microsoft Windows Installer package
.msp	Microsoft Windows Installer patch
.mst	Microsoft Windows Installer Transform file
.ocx	Microsoft Object Linking
.pcd	Corel Adaptec CD Creator image file
.pif	Shortcut to MS-DOS program
.reg	Registration entries
.scr	Screen saver
.sct	Windows Script Component
.shb	Shell Scrap object
.shs	Shell Scrap object
.url	Internet shortcut
.vb	Visual Basic Script file
.vbe	Visual Basic Script-encoded file
.vbs	Visual Basic Script file
.vxd	Microsoft Windows Virtual Device Driver
.wsc	Windows Script Component
.wsf	Windows Script File
.wsh	Windows Script Host Settings file

10.6 Computer Crimes and the Law

Computer crime is on the rise. There are many laws at both the state and federal level to punish those who commit computer crimes. As technology continually changes, these laws are also ever changing.

A *computer crime* is any act that either maliciously targets a computer system, or uses a computer to commit a crime. Computer crimes are punishable by probation, fines, or jail sentencing. Following are five categories of computer crimes:

computer crime

- Computer hacking
- Identity theft
- Child pornography
- Cyber bullying
- Data theft

Types of Crimes

computer hacking

- *Computer hacking* is the unauthorized entry into a computer system for malicious reasons. Hacking may involve the stealing of sensitive data, altering or deleting data, or causing harm to the computer infrastructure. Most states have laws that prohibit computer hacking. Hacking is also prohibited under the Federal Computer Fraud and Abuse Act (CFAA).

  The largest retail hacking incident took place in 2013 when hackers infiltrated Target's system and stole credit card information and personal data from over 40 million loyal customers. The challenge for law enforcement is that it is usually dealing across international boundaries. The Target incident, for example, was linked to hackers in Russia.

identify theft

computer fraud

- *Identify theft* is the act of posing as someone else for fraudulent reasons. If identity theft is committed with the use of a computer, it is a computer fraud. Today, companies and Internet sites track large quantities of data about persons who use their products or visit their Websites. The security breaches of large companies which store consumer data, social media, Internet shopping, and storage of personal data all contribute to the rise of identity theft.

child pornography

- Possessing *child pornography* on a computer is a felony under federal law. Additionally, all 50 states have laws against child pornography. Child pornography is sexually explicit photos or videos of persons under the age of eighteen years old.

cyber bullying

computer abuse

- *Cyber bullying* is the act of threatening, stalking, or harassing someone through social media or over the Internet. Bullying someone with the use of a computer is a form of computer abuse. More and more states are adopting laws against cyber bullying. These laws are geared towards protecting minors and have gained widespread attention. A notorious incident was that of Rebecca Sedwick of Florida. In 2013, Rebecca committed suicide at the age of 12 after classmates harassed her on social media. Some students even urged her to commit suicide.

data theft

- *Data theft* is the stealing or collection of personal data from someone without his or her consent. While developing an application, one of your tasks may be to collect, manage, and store user data. It is important to understand the laws based around privacy. Privacy is the right of people to freely choose what data and under what circumstances they choose to share with others. It is good practice to ask for and document users' consent before collecting and storing personal information. Many sites and apps require acknowledgement of the company privacy policy. To protect your privacy, it is important to take the time to read and understand the policy. You can explore the privacy policy of U.S. government Websites at www.usa.gov/policies.

Tip

If you believe you have been a victim of identity theft, go to the Federal Trade Commission's Web site for instructions on what to do. *www.consumer.ftc.gov/features/feature-0014-identity-theft*

While there are many state and federal laws that are aimed at prosecuting computer crimes and fraud, the *Computer Fraud and Abuse Act* (*CFAA*) covers a wide variety of crimes. The CFAA is a federal law and carries a penalty of up to $250,000 and 20 years in jail. If the crime involves illegal transfer of money or property and the Internet is used across state boundaries, a person can be convicted under the federal Wire Fraud Act.

Computer Fraud and Abuse Act (CFAA)

Note

You can listen to an interview concerning the alarming rate of cybercrime and the Target security breach at http://www.npr.org/2014/01/13/262185937/how-the-hackers-did-it-a-discussion-about-targets-data-breach.

IT Careers

According to the U.S. Bureau of Labor Statistics, demand for security analysts is expected to grow by 18 percent through the year 2024. You can learn more about computer jobs and jobs in security at http://www.bls.gov/ooh/computer-and-information-technology/home.htm.

✓ Section 10.6 Assessment

1. Define computer crime and cite some examples.
2. What federal law prohibits computer hacking?
3. What law prohibits illegal interstate transfer of money or property over the Internet?
4. What factors influence the rise of computer crime?

10.7 Privacy Rights

Privacy is the right of people to choose freely under what circumstances and to what extent they will reveal themselves and their behavior to others.

This definition emphasizes first that it is the person who decides the "circumstances" and the "extent" to which information is revealed, not anyone else. The person has the control. Second, it emphasizes that the range of features over which the person controls the information embodies every aspect of the person—themselves and their behaviors. Adopting such an inclusive definition is essential for covering situations of importance.

Enjoying the Benefits of Privacy

Now that we have the definition, what are the threats to privacy? There are only two basic threats: government and business. Historically, the governmental threat—a regime spying on its citizens— worries people the most, probably because when it happens the consequences are very serious. The business threat is a more recent worry, and its IT aspects even newer still. There are two types of business threats: surveillance of employees and the use of business-related information, including transaction information, for other purposes.

governmental threat

business threat

Voluntary Disclosure

In principle, a person can enjoy perfect privacy by simply deciding not to reveal anything to anyone; that is, to be a hermit, though that probably would mean living alone on a remote island, surviving on coconuts and clams. But most of us interact with many people and organizations—businesses, employers, and governments—to whom it is in our interest to reveal private information. That is, we freely choose to reveal information in exchange for real benefits.

- We tell our doctors many personal facts about ourselves so they can help us stay healthy.
- We allow credit card companies to check our credit record in exchange for the convenience of paying with a card.
- We permit our employer to read email we send at work, understanding that we are using the employer's computer, Internet connection, and time; that the email system is there for us to use on the job; and that we have no need or intent to send personal email.
- We reveal to the government our religion—though not in the United States —our parents' names and birthplaces, our race and ethnicity, and so on for the purposes of enjoying the rights of citizenship.

How private can we be when we reveal so much about ourselves, our attitudes, and our behavior? There must be clear guidelines adopted for handling private information, so that we have standards by which to judge whether the trust is warranted. For that, we have the Fair Information Practices principles.

Organization for Economic Cooperation and Development (OECD)

Fair Information Practices

In 1980 the Organization for Economic Cooperation and Development (OECD)—an organization of (currently) 34 countries concerned with international trade—developed an eight-point list of privacy principles that became known as the Fair Information Practices. They have become a widely accepted standard, forming a reasonably complete solution to the problem of keeping information private while at the same time revealing appropriate information to businesses and governments. We all have an interest in these principles becoming law. The principles also give a standard that businesses and governments can meet as a "due diligence test" for protecting citizens' rights of privacy, thereby protecting themselves from criticism or legal action. The OECD principles, listed in Table 10.3, are a practical implementation of privacy protection in the presence of computer technology.

Who Is Protected?

In 1995, in a landmark advancement for privacy, the European Union (EU) issued the European Data Protection Directive, a benchmark law incorporating the OECD principles. In the next few years, the member countries adopted it. Many non-EU countries, such as Australia, Canada, Hong Kong, and New Zealand, have also adopted laws based on OECD principles.

Europe's adoption of these standards is important because one provision in the EU directive requires that data about EU citizens be protected by the standards of the law even when it leaves their country. Non-EU countries that want information on EU citizens must show that they have privacy laws consistent with the OECD principles.

TABLE 10.3 A brief explanation of the OECD's Fair Information Practices guidelines.

Guideline	*Explanation*
Limited Collection	There should be limits to the personal data collected; data should be collected by fair and lawful means, and with the knowledge and consent of the person whenever possible.
Purpose	The purposes for collecting personal data should be stated when it is collected; the uses should be limited to those purposes.
Quality	The data should be relevant to the purpose of collection; it should be accurate, complete, and up-to-date.
Use Limitation	Personal data should not be disclosed or used for purposes other than stated in the Purpose Principle, except with the consent of the individual or by the authority of law.
Security	Personal data should be protected by reasonable security measures against risks of disclosure, unauthorized access, misuse, modification, destruction, or loss.
Openness	There should be general openness of policies and practices about personal data collection, making it possible to know of its existence, kind, and purpose of use, as well as the contact information for the data controller.
Participation	An individual should be able to (a) determine if the data controller has information about him or her, and (b) discover what it is. If the request is denied, the individual should be allowed to challenge the denial.
Accountability	The data controller should be accountable for complying with these principles.

Switzerland, a non-EU country, applied and was approved. The United States applied and was not. What sorts of laws protect U.S. privacy?

The United States has no OECD-like law. Its few privacy laws speak to specific situations. This is a hit-or-miss approach that is known as sectoral, meaning that it applies to different sectors of society. For example, the Health Insurance Portability and Accountability Act (HIPAA) protects an American's personally identifiable health information. Automobile registration information is also private by a specific law, as is the privacy of video rental titles by another specific law.

Health Insurance Portability and Accountability Act (HIPAA)

Most sectors—social media, to pick one—are not covered by privacy laws, and without broad OECD-like coverage, the EU isn't likely to approve the United States. This is a huge headache for multinational companies doing business with OECD countries. In order to accommodate the laws of other countries, they must establish a *safe harbor*, meaning that the company complies with OECD standards for citizens of EU countries.

A famous case concerning the right to privacy centered around the public exposure of the collection of data by the U.S. National Security Agency (NSA).

In June 2013 Edward Snowden—an analyst for the U.S. National Security Agency (NSA)—revealed that the U.S. government was collecting complete metadata records from telephone carriers. (Metadata is data about data, such as when a call was made, the number it was to, and so on; it doesn't include the content.) Further, using a surveillance program called PRISM, Snowden said the NSA was gathering data of Americans' online activity from Facebook, Microsoft, Google, and other large tech companies. This development took Americans by surprise, but it was also a shock overseas, because the records included calls and data from countries with OECD privacy laws, such as Germany.

U.S. National Security Agency (NSA)

Edward Snowden

Patriot Act

The Patriot Act was signed into law after the September 11, 2001 (9/11) terrorist attack on the World Trade Center Towers in New York City. The intent was to provide government with access to information that could lead to the capture of terrorists or prevention of future attacks.

Snowden's exposure of government activities has created much controversy over the Patriot Act.

USA Freedom Act

In June 2015, The Patriot Act was extended into law. However, a section of the law was changed stopping the NSA from collecting phone records from citizens not involved in a terrorist crime. This section of the law, known as The USA Freedom Act, was signed into law by President Obama.

This is an area of the law that continues to be scrutinized. You can follow the latest developments at the Electronic Privacy Information Center (www.epic.org/privacy/) and the Electronic Freedom Foundation (www.eff.org).

✓ Section 10.7 Assessment

1. Define privacy.
2. Explain the purpose of the Organization for Economic Cooperation and Development (OECD).
3. What is the Patriot Act?
4. What is the USA Freedom Act?
5. If you are writing a software application that collects and stores private user data, what should you do to comply with privacy laws?

10.8 Understanding Cookies

While most cookies are not harmful to your computer, understanding what cookies are and learning how to control the use of cookies helps reduce security risks.

Cookies are a standard computer science concept originally used by Netscape engineers to connect the identity of a client across a series of independent client/server events. Here's the problem cookies solve.

cookies

Figure 10.5 illustrates the Web server's view of the client/server relationship. Imagine this is your bank's server and that you are paying bills online, which makes you a client. The server is helping many clients at once, and to know who's who, the server stores a cookie—a record containing seven fields of information that uniquely identify a customer's session—on your computer. *Cookies* are exchanged between the client and the server on each transmission of information, allowing the server to know which of the many client computers is sending information.

Though cookies serve a useful purpose—and most of us want to enable cookies so we can bank online—*third-party cookies* are a key way Web surfing behavior is tracked. The first two parties are you and the Web site you're visiting; the third party is a company—often an ad agency hired by the server company to place ads—that records where you've visited, based on the history you left as recorded in their database built with third-party cookies.

Generally, accepting cookies makes for more effective use of the Web, but it is wise to block third-party cookies (in your browser's privacy settings) if you haven't set the Do Not Track flag.

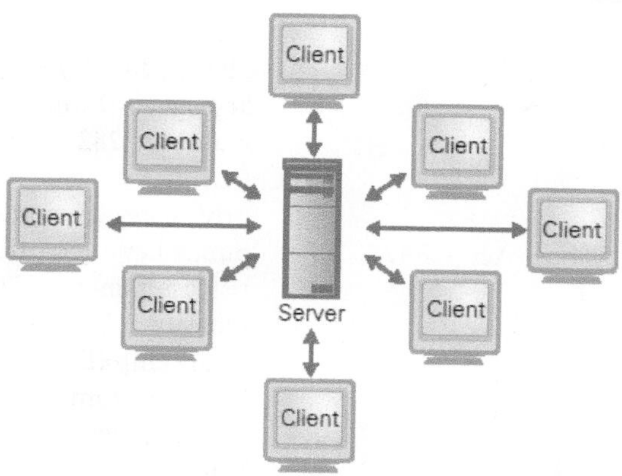

FIGURE 10.5 Server's view of the client/server relationship.

✓ SECTION 10.8 ASSESSMENT

1. Explain how cookies can be helpful.
2. For added security, what types of cookies should you block?

Chapter 10 — Review and Assessment

Key Terms

biometrics 272
CIA triad 270
cloud storage 272
computer abuse 290
computer crime 285
computer fraud 286
Computer Fraud and Abuse Act (CFAA) 287
computer hacking 286
cookie 290
cyber bullying 286
data communication system 274
data theft 286
encryption 275
Ethernet 273
fiber optics 273
firewall 274
identify theft 286
keylogger 276
malware 282
Patriot Act 290
private key encryption 278
public key encryption 279
risk assessment 270
security risk 270
smart chip ID 272
USA Freedom Act 290
Wi-Fi Protected Access (WPA) 275
Wi-Fi Protected Access II (WPA2) 275
Wired Equivalent Privacy (WEP) 275

Chapter Summary

1. *Risk assessment* is the process of defining potential risks, identifying and implementing ways to reduce risks, and planning for security failures.
2. The three goals of a security plan are to keep sensitive data *confidential*, maintain data *integrity*, and insure the *availability* of the computer system.
3. The *physical facilities*, *hardware*, *software*, and *data communication system* are all components of a computer information system that are susceptible to security risks.
4. *Encryption* and *authentication* are two methods used to secure computer information systems.
5. *Malware* stands for malicious software and can be in the form of a *virus*, *Trojan*, *worm*, or *spyware*.
6. Install anti-virus software as a preventative measure. In the event of a malware security breach, install additional software to remove the malware.
7. *Computer hacking*, *identity theft*, *child pornography*, *cyber bullying*, and *data theft* are forms of computer crimes.
8. Computer crimes, fraud, and abuse are prohibited under both federal and state laws. Persons convicted of a crime involving a computer may serve probation, jail time, or be charged a penalty fee.

9. Follow *privacy laws* when collecting user information. Make company privacy policy available to software system users. Obtain consent to collect data.

Chapter Assessment

For each of the next four questions, create a two-column table. Use the following template.

Type of security risk	Ways to reduce the risk

1. Identify three security risks for the *physical facility* component of a computer system. Identify a way to control or minimize each risk.
2. Identify three security risks for the *hardware* component of a computer system. Identify a way to control or minimize each risk.
3. Identify three security risks for the *data communications* component of a computer system. Identify a way to control or minimize each risk.
4. Identify three security risks for the *software* component of a computer system. Identify a way to control or minimize each risk.
5. Identify and define five categories of computer crimes. Explain the state and federal laws, and penalties associated with each.
6. Define four categories of malware. What procedures would you use to recover from a malware infection?

Applied Learning

1. The process of identifying risks and creating an assessment plan can be applied to many things in life. Identify an activity or scenario in your life that has potential risks. It may help you by brainstorming possible "*what if*" questions. Here are two examples. *What if* a fire broke out in my home? *What if* my car broke down on an isolated road? There are many possible outcomes to these questions. Estimating the likelihood of, or quantifying, the risk helps put things in perspective, and helps you plan ahead.

   Identify a scenario in your life that has risks. Using the five-stage process in Figure 10.1, create a written assessment plan.

2. You are working on a team project to develop an airline ticketing application. The application allows passengers to book airplane flights over the Internet. The data is stored at the main headquarters on internal servers. Working in small teams, identify four computer components that may be susceptible to a security risk and create an action plan to minimize the risks.

3. Many companies offer free cloud storage such as Apple, Google, and Microsoft. Research the various services. Write a set of logical instructions describing how to open a cloud storage account. Exchange instructions with a team partner. Following each other's instructions, open a cloud storage account. Provide verbal feedback to your team partner on the set of instructions. (Are they easy to follow? Are there any missing steps?) Revise your instructions based upon the feedback.

NetBeans Tutorial

Supplement A

Objectives

- Learn how to install NetBeans.
- Write a program using NetBeans Integrated Development Environment (IDE).

A.1 Installing NetBeans

NetBeans is a free Integrated Development Environment (IDE) supported by Oracle. It is available for download at Oracle's Website.

You need to install both the **NetBeans IDE** and the **Java Development Kit (JDK)** to complete the exercises in this book. You can find both applications at this Website: http://www.oracle.com/technetwork/java/javase/downloads/index.html.

Download the *Standard Edition* and choose the operating system that matches your computer. You can download them separately as shown in Figure A.1.

Java SE Downloads

Figure A.1 Java Standard Edition and NetBeans IDE Download Interface.

Alternatively, you can download and install them together in a bundle as shown in Figure A.2.

Java SE and NetBeans Cobundle (JDK 8u73 and NB 8.1)		
Product / File Description	File Size	Download
Linux x86	281.84 MB	jdk-8u73-nb-8_1-linux-i586.sh
Linux x64	277.82 MB	jdk-8u73-nb-8_1-linux-x64.sh
Mac OS X	340.95 MB	jdk-8u73-nb-8_1-macosx-x64.dmg
Windows x86	298.3 MB	jdk-8u73-nb-8_1-windows-i586.exe
Windows x64	305.27 MB	jdk-8u73-nb-8_1-windows-x64.exe

Figure A.2 Bundle download of JDK and NetBeans.

Once you have downloaded and installed these two programs, you will be ready to create your first application in Java using NetBeans.

A.2 Writing a Program Using NetBeans

This application will display "Hello World!" to the user screen. Following are the steps to create a program:

1. **Create a project using NetBeans IDE.**

   In the NetBeans IDE, you can write, test, build, and run your code.

   The first step is to create a project to store your code.

2. **Compile your code and save it into a class file.**

   Once you have written your code, you can compile it. Java uses a programming language compiler called javac. Javac translates your English-like code into machine language.

3. **Run the program.**

   Run your application to test.

Create a project using NetBeans IDE

1. Locate the **NetBeans IDE program** on your operating system and start it.
2. Choose **New Project...Java Application** as illustrated in Figure A.3.

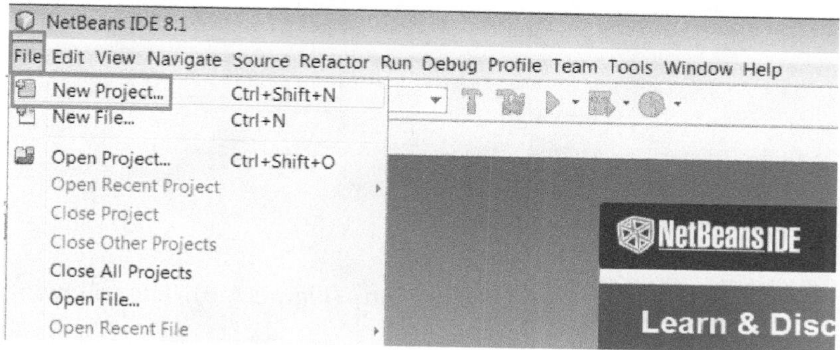

FIGURE A.3 Choose: File, New Project.

3. Choose **Java...Java Application Project**. Choose **Next>** as shown in Figure A.4.

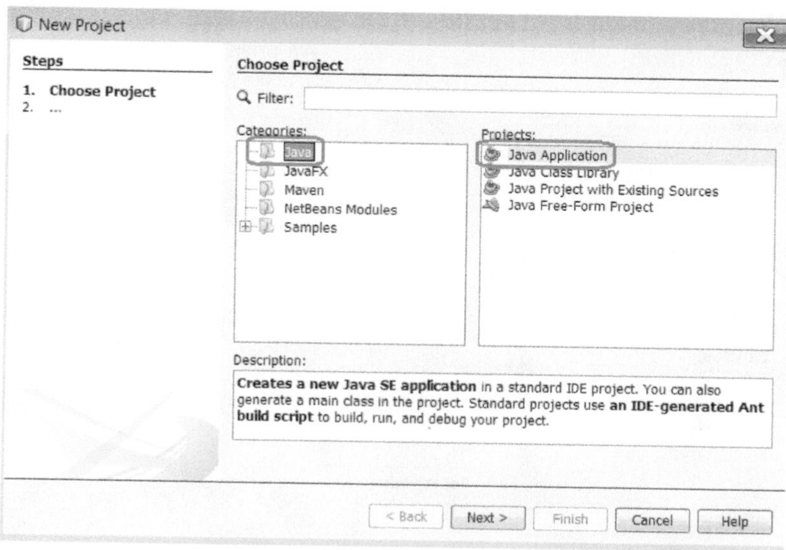

FIGURE A.4 Choose: Java, Java Application Project window.

4. Name your project `Hello World App` and make all selections exactly as shown in Figure A.5. Click **Finish**.

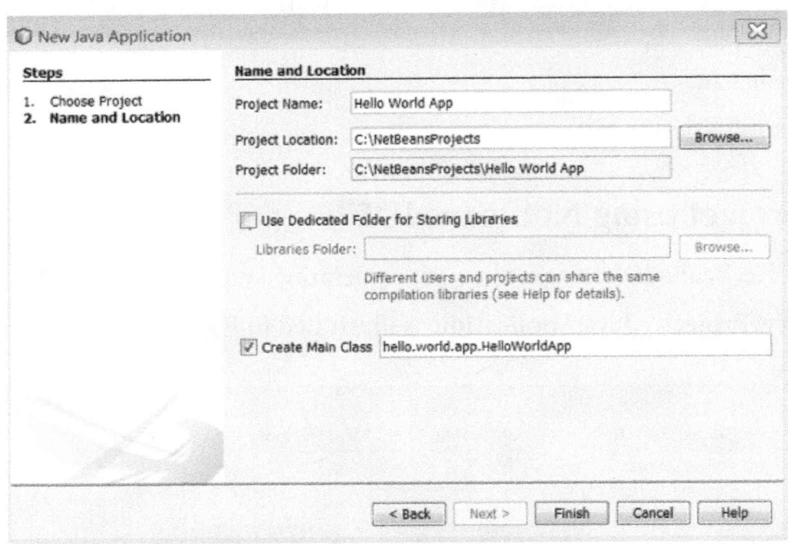

FIGURE A.5 Project Name and Location window.

5. The IDE window is divided into three sections (Figure A.6). The following describes the three sections:

   - The *Projects window* is where you can navigate through all the components of your project. The components can be expanded or contracted by clicking on the '+' or '-' symbols.
   - The *Source Editor window* is where you will write your code.
   - The *Navigator window* is where you can navigate between elements within a class.

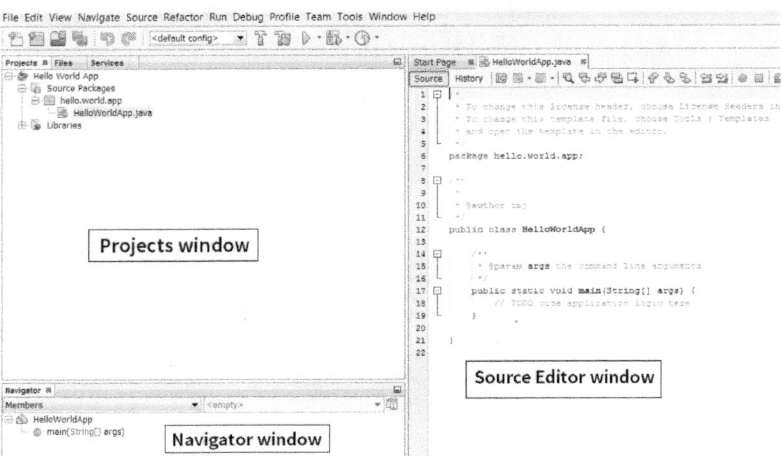

FIGURE A.6 IDE Window Sections.

6. Choose **Tools | Java Platforms.** The **JDK (default)** should be listed on the left-hand side of the platform manager window, as shown in Figure A.7. If you do not see it, click **Add Platform,** navigate to your JDK install directory, and click **Finish.** You will know if it was added correctly if it appears in the platform manager window.

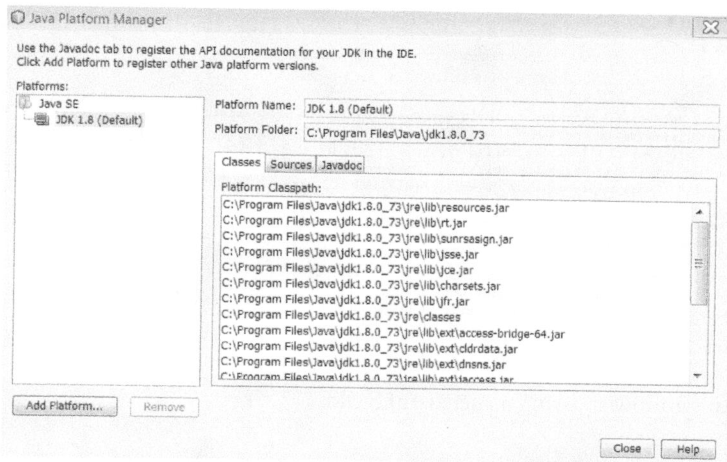

FIGURE A.7 Java Platform Manager window.

7. Write the code. Refer back to Figure A.5 and note that the **Create Main Class** checkbox is selected. This default option creates some basic code for you that is common to most classes.

   - Find the program comment section at the beginning of the code. Add a comment by changing the existing comment section.

   ```
   /**
   * Hello World program using Java
   * @author your name goes here
   */
   ```

   - Replace the line of code:

   ```
   // TODO code application logic here
   ```

   with

   ```
   System.out.println("Hello World!");
   ```

   Java is 'case sensitive' so type the code in as shown. In other words, "A" and "a" are not the same in Java. `System.out.printLn` is not the same as `system.out.println`.

8. Choose **File | Save.**

USING PACKAGES

Objectives

- Understand the value of using packages.
- Add program code to create a package.

SUPPLEMENT

C

C.1 Packages are Used to Organize and Group Classes

As an example, you can group together the classes and programming exercises in this textbook in a series of packages named chapter1, chapter2, chapter3, etc.

To use packages, include the following line of code:

```
package packagename;
```

Place this line of code directly after the initial comment block.

Chapter 2, Listing 2.1 creates a Welcome class. To organize the Welcome class into a package named Chapter1, use the following code.

```
/** Use package for the class */
package chapter1;
  public class Welcome {
public static void main(String[] args) {
System.out.println("Welcome to Java!");
  }
}
```

A package corresponds to a file folder. If you are using NetBeans or Eclipse, the folder is automatically created for you when you run the code. In other words, after running the code above, a folder named chapter1 is created on your storage device. Having all related classes grouped together in a file package makes it easy to locate files.

If you are not using an IDE such as NetBeans or Eclipse, you may have to manually create a directory and name it chapter1.

Supplement D

Algorithmic Thinking

Objectives

- Explain similarities and differences among algorithms, programs, and heuristic solutions.
- List the five essential properties of an algorithm.
- Use the *Intersecting Alphabetized List* algorithm to:
  - Follow the flow of the instruction execution
  - Follow an analysis explaining why an algorithm works
- Demonstrate algorithmic thinking by being able to:
  - Explain the importance of alphabetical ordering for solutions
  - Explain the importance of the barrier abstraction for correctness

D.1 Algorithm Basics

An algorithm is a precise, systematic method for producing a specified result.

algorithm

As we've learned, computers must be given instructions for everything they do, so all they do is run algorithms. We normally call them programs, which are algorithms customized to do a specific task. Naturally, programmers and software developers care a lot about algorithms. But, they matter to the rest of us, too. Many of the problems we must solve personally are solved by algorithms, from describing how to achieve a clever effect in video editing to correcting mistakes in a term paper. Algorithms are solutions. And the best part is that by writing out the method carefully, some other agent—another person or a computer—can do the work. Of course, that is the reason computers are such powerful and useful tools.

Jean-Dominique Bauby

In this supplementary chapter, we familiarize ourselves with algorithms and become more adept at reading them, writing them, and evaluating them. We start by learning about Jean-Dominique Bauby, a man whose hospital care required the use of algorithms. Next, we review algorithms we already know—how we learn them and how we use them. After that, we consider some defining characteristics of algorithms. Then, we study an algorithm we use every day; because it is an "industrial-strength" algorithm, it illustrates how an algorithm can exist in different forms, and why we prefer some algorithms over others. Finally, we consider how we know an algorithm does what it claims. Again, a simple illustration makes the point.

Algorithms

In this section, we begin with simple, intuitive examples to continue our earlier discussion of algorithms. You already know that algorithms are important in our study. Now you'll find out they're even more familiar than you might have realized.

Writing One Letter at a Time

The book (and movie) *The Diving Bell and the Butterfly* tells the true story of a French man who became paralyzed from his chin down. He couldn't write. He couldn't talk. He couldn't even swallow. All he could do was turn his head a few degrees and blink his left eyelid. But he could think. And amazingly, he wrote the book about himself just by blinking his left eyelid!

The man, Jean-Dominique Bauby, wrote in *The Diving Bell and the Butterfly* that to be so paralyzed was like wearing the heavy suit and metal helmet deep sea divers wore in the days before SCUBA gear. He suffered from a condition called Locked-In Syndrome: His body was useless but his mind was active. He compared his thoughts to a butterfly, flitting quickly from one topic to the next. The idea became the title of his book.

Before he was paralyzed, Bauby was editor-in-chief at the fashion magazine *Elle* and an accomplished writer. So, it is not surprising that he wrote a book. What is surprising is that simply by blinking his left eye, he was able to communicate well enough to write at all. His problem—writing by blinking—will give us a situation to study algorithms.

Homemade Algorithms

Whenever Bauby wanted to say something, he had to spell it out letter by letter. To assist him, his nurses and visitors would say the alphabet, or point to the letters of the alphabet listed on a card in the order shown in Figure D.1. When they got to the right letter, he blinked. Then, they would go on to the next letter, starting over with the alphabet (see Figure D.1). It is a slow process. Try it!

E	S	A	R	I	N	T	U	L
O	M	D	P	C	F	B	V	
H	G	J	Q	Z	Y	X	K	W

FIGURE D.1 Alphabet listing shown to Jean-Dominque Bauby. When the nurse points to the correct letter, he blinks his left eyelid.

This process is an algorithm invented by his nurses. It illustrates important points about algorithms:

- We use and invent algorithms all the time to solve our problems; it doesn't take a degree in computer science to create algorithms.
- Although the algorithm doesn't seem to compute in the popular imagination of computing—where are the numbers, the mathematical formulas? —it does; it creates the content for a document, namely Bauby's book.
- The agent running the algorithm is not a computer. It's a nurse, and Bauby is the user. Often the agent that "runs" the algorithm is a person rather than a computer.
- As we are about to see, there are better and worse variations of this algorithm.

These observations emphasize the point that an algorithm is not an exotic creation requiring years of study and deep scientific knowledge, but rather a familiar concept that we use all the time without realizing it or thinking about it.

Many Questions; Fewer Questions

One way that the process was sped up was "word completion," in which the attendant said the word she guessed Bauby was trying to spell. This familiar autocomplete technique—for example, URL completion on the Web and word completion when texting—can save a lot of effort if you're blinking letters. However, there is an additional way to speed up blink-communication.

Supplement D — Review and Assessment

Chapter Summary

1. We use algorithms daily, and we continually create them as we instruct other people in how to do a task.
2. Everyday algorithms can sometimes be unclear because natural language is imprecise.
3. Algorithms have five fundamental properties.
4. Algorithms can be given at different levels of detail depending on the abilities of the agent.
5. Problems can be solved by different algorithms in different ways.
6. Algorithms always work—either they give the answer or say no answer is possible—and they are evaluated on their use of resources such as space and time.
7. The *Intersecting Alphabetized Lists* (IAL) algorithm is used in Web searching and is preferred over other solutions.
8. Properties of the *Intersecting Alphabetized Lists* algorithm are used to explain why it works.

Review Questions

1. An algorithm is a(n)

   a. list of general nonspecific steps to produce an output.

   b. logarithm.

   c. systematic method for producing a specified result.

   d. math problem.

2. Algorithms are used by

   a. only computers.

   b. only humans.

   c. various agents.

   d. no one, they are not real.

3. Algorithms must always

   a. produce output.

   b. produce output or state that there is no solution.

   c. produce input or state that there is no solution.

   d. state that there is no solution.

4. Algorithms are guaranteed to work

   a. 99.9 percent of the time.

   b. 100 percent of the time.

   c. depends on the computers they are running on.

   d. 50 percent of the time.

5. When writing an algorithm in a natural language it is helpful to use ________ instead of ________.

   a. programming language, natural language

   b. nouns, pronouns

   c. abbreviations, actual words

   d. nouns, adjectives

6. If an algorithm is performed with the same data, at different times with different agents the output will be

   a. the same.

   b. different.

   c. sometimes different and sometimes the same.

   d. impossible to tell.

7. How many algorithms can solve one specific problem?

   a. only one

   b. many

   c. It depends on the type of algorithm.

Short Answer

1. Programs containing ________ cannot be verified exhaustively.
2. A program is an algorithm that has been ________.
3. Algorithms must be ________; they eventually stop with the right output or a statement that no solution is possible.
4. Algorithms must be definite. They must specify ordered steps, including details on how to ________________.
5. The steps in algorithms must be ________ so that the agent is able to follow them.

Exercises

1. This chapter describes how Jean-Dominique Bauby wrote a book by blinking. Explain what he was doing in terms of PandA concepts as he is being presented the alphabet.
2. What is the Web searching process called if not an algorithm?
3. State whether the following properties hold for the placeholder technique. Be sure to include details to support your answer.

   a. input

   b. output

   c. definiteness

   d. effectiveness
4. Explain how detailed an algorithm needs to be.
5. The IAL requires the agent to advance the arrow for the alphabetically earliest URL. Show that the IAL is effective by explaining how an agent would know which list has the "alphabetically earliest" URL, and so must have its arrow advanced.
6. What makes IAL (intersect an alphabetized list) faster than NAL (no alphabetized lists)?
7. Give the steps for checking your email inbox.
8. Explain the five proprieties of your algorithm for Exercise 7 (input specified, output specified, definiteness, effectiveness, and finiteness).

9. Develop an algorithm for brushing your teeth. Then explain the correctness of your algorithm, detailing why it works.

10. Why is it not enough to make sure an algorithm works by running it on a few inputs? How can you ensure that an algorithm will always produce the correct output or state that there is no solution for the given input?

Supplement E

Understanding Variable Scope

Objectives

- Explain variable scope.
- Understand local variable scope.
- Determine the scope of variables within a loop.

E.1 The Scope of Variables

The scope of a variable is the part of the program where the variable can be referenced.

scope of variables
local variable

Chapter 3 introduced the scope of a variable. This section discusses the scope of variables in detail. A variable defined inside a method is referred to as a *local variable.* The scope of a local variable starts from its declaration and continues to the end of the block that contains that variable. A local variable must be declared and assigned a value before it can be used.

A parameter is actually a local variable. The scope of a method parameter covers the entire method. A variable declared in the initial-action part of a `for`-loop header has its scope in the entire loop. However, a variable declared inside a `for`-loop body has its scope limited in the loop body from its declaration to the end of the block that contains the variable, as shown in Figure E.1.

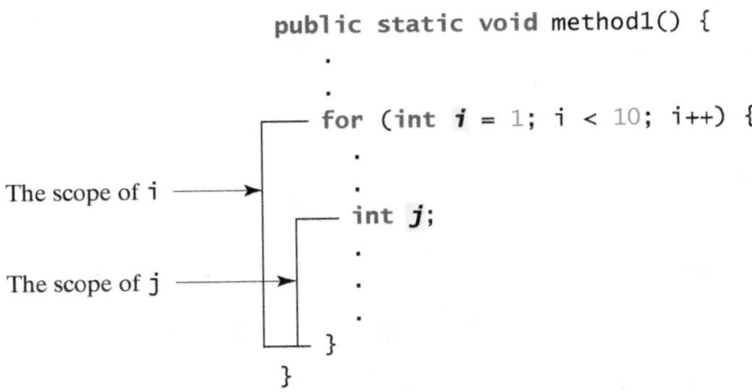

FIGURE E.1 A variable declared in the initial action part of a `for`-loop header has its scope in the entire loop.

You can declare a local variable with the same name in different blocks in a method, but you cannot declare a local variable twice in the same block or in nested blocks, as shown in Figure E.2.

It is fine to declare `i` in two nonnested blocks.

```
public static void method1() {
  int x = 1;
  int y = 1;

  for (int i = 1; i < 10; i++) {
    x += i;
  }

  for (int i = 1; i < 10; i++) {
    y += i;
  }
}
```

It is wrong to declare `i` in two nested blocks.

```
public static void method2() {

  int i = 1;
  int sum = 0;

  for (int i = 1; i < 10; i++)
    sum += i;
  }

}
```

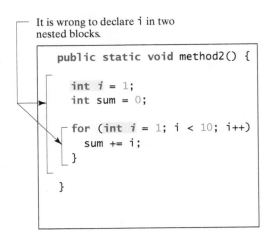

FIGURE E.2 A variable can be declared multiple times in nonnested blocks, but only once in nested blocks.

Caution

Do not declare a variable inside a block and then attempt to use it outside the block. Here is an example of a common mistake:

```
for (int i = 0; i < 10; i++) {
}

System.out.println(i);
```

The last statement would cause a syntax error, because variable `i` is not defined outside of the `for` loop.

✓ Section E.1 Assessment

1. Define variable scope.
2. What is a local variable?
3. What is the scope of a local variable?
4. Fix the code below so the value of `i` is printed to the console.

```
for (int i = 0; i < 10; i++) {
}

System.out.println(i);
```

The method `getArray` prompts the user to enter values for the array (lines 11–24) and returns the array (line 23).

The method `sum` (lines 26–35) has a two-dimensional array argument. You can obtain the number of rows using `m.length` (line 28) and the number of columns in a specified row using `m[row].length` (line 29).

✓ Section G.4 Assessment

1. Show the output of the following code:

```
public class Test {
  public static void main(String[] args) {
    int[][] array = {{1, 2, 3, 4}, {5, 6, 7, 8}};
    System.out.println(m1(array)[0]);
    System.out.println(m1(array)[1]);
  }

  public static int[] m1(int[][] m) {
    int[] result = new int[2];
    result[0] = m.length;
    result[1] = m[0].length;
    return result;
  }
}
```

G.5 Case Study: Grading a Multiple-Choice Test

The problem is to write a program that will grade multiple-choice tests.

Grade multiple-choice test

Suppose you need to write a program that grades multiple-choice tests. Assume there are eight students and ten questions, and the answers are stored in a two-dimensional array. Each row records a student's answers to the questions, as shown in the following array.

Students' Answers to the Questions:

	0	1	2	3	4	5	6	7	8	9
Student 0	A	B	A	C	C	D	E	E	A	D
Student 1	D	B	A	B	C	A	E	E	A	D
Student 2	E	D	D	A	C	B	E	E	A	D
Student 3	C	B	A	E	D	C	E	E	A	D
Student 4	A	B	D	C	C	D	E	E	A	D
Student 5	B	B	E	C	C	D	E	E	A	D
Student 6	B	B	A	C	C	D	E	E	A	D
Student 7	E	B	E	C	C	D	E	E	A	D

The key is stored in a one-dimensional array:

Key to the Questions:

	0	1	2	3	4	5	6	7	8	9
Key	D	B	D	C	C	D	A	E	A	D

Your program grades the test and displays the result. It compares each student's answers with the key, counts the number of correct answers, and displays it. Listing G.2 gives the program.

LISTING G.2 GradeExam.java

2-D array

1-D array

compare with key

```
1  public class GradeExam {
2    /** Main method */
3    public static void main(String[] args) {
4      // Students' answers to the questions
5      char[][] answers = {
6        {'A', 'B', 'A', 'C', 'C', 'D', 'E', 'E', 'A', 'D'},
7        {'D', 'B', 'A', 'B', 'C', 'A', 'E', 'E', 'A', 'D'},
8        {'E', 'D', 'D', 'A', 'C', 'B', 'E', 'E', 'A', 'D'},
9        {'C', 'B', 'A', 'E', 'D', 'C', 'E', 'E', 'A', 'D'},
10       {'A', 'B', 'D', 'C', 'C', 'D', 'E', 'E', 'A', 'D'},
11       {'B', 'B', 'E', 'C', 'C', 'D', 'E', 'E', 'A', 'D'},
12       {'B', 'B', 'A', 'C', 'C', 'D', 'E', 'E', 'A', 'D'},
13       {'E', 'B', 'E', 'C', 'C', 'D', 'E', 'E', 'A', 'D'}};
14
15     // Key to the questions
16     char[] keys = {'D', 'B', 'D', 'C', 'C', 'D', 'A', 'E', 'A', 'D'};
17
18     // Grade all answers
19     for (int i = 0; i < answers.length; i++) {
20       // Grade one student
21       int correctCount = 0;
22       for (int j = 0; j < answers[i].length; j++) {
23         if (answers[i][j] == keys[j])
24           correctCount++;
25       }
26
27       System.out.println("Student " + i + "'s correct count is " +
28         correctCount);
29     }
30   }
31 }
```

```
Student 0's correct count is 7
Student 1's correct count is 6
Student 2's correct count is 5
Student 3's correct count is 4
Student 4's correct count is 8
Student 5's correct count is 7
Student 6's correct count is 7
Student 7's correct count is 7
```

The statement in lines 5–13 declares, creates, and initializes a two-dimensional array of characters and assigns the reference to `answers` of the `char[][]` type.

The statement in line 16 declares, creates, and initializes an array of `char` values and assigns the reference to `keys` of the `char[]` type.

Each row in the array `answers` stores a student's answer, which is graded by comparing it with the key in the array `keys`. The result is displayed immediately after a student's answer is graded.

G.6 Case Study: Finding the Closest Pair

This section presents a geometric problem for finding the closest pair of points.

Given a set of points, the closest-pair problem is to find the two points that are nearest to each other. In Figure G.3, for example, points `(1, 1)` and `(2, 0.5)` are closest to each other. There are several ways to solve this problem. An intuitive approach is to compute the distances between all pairs of points and find the one with the minimum distance, as implemented in Listing G.3.

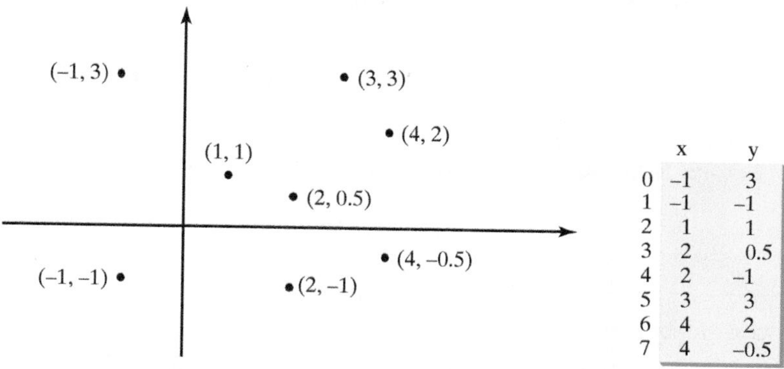

FIGURE G.3 Points can be represented in a two-dimensional array.

LISTING G.3 `FindNearestPoints.java`

```
import java.util.Scanner;

public class FindNearestPoints {
  public static void main(String[] args) {
    Scanner input = new Scanner(System.in);
    System.out.print("Enter the number of points: ");
    int numberOfPoints = input.nextInt();

    // Create an array to store points
    double[][] points = new double[numberOfPoints][2];
    System.out.print("Enter " + numberOfPoints + " points: ");
    for (int i = 0; i < points.length; i++) {
      points[i][0] = input.nextDouble();
      points[i][1] = input.nextDouble();
    }

    // p1 and p2 are the indices in the points' array
    int p1 = 0, p2 = 1; // Initial two points
    double shortestDistance = distance(points[p1][0], points[p1][1],
      points[p2][0], points[p2][1]); // Initialize shortestDistance

    // Compute distance for every two points
    for (int i = 0; i < points.length; i++) {
      for (int j = i + 1; j < points.length; j++) {
        double distance = distance(points[i][0], points[i][1],
          points[j][0], points[j][1]); // Find distance

```

number of points
2-D array
read points
track two points
track shortestDistance
for each point i
for each point j
distance between i and j
distance between two points

update shortestDistance

```
28          if (shortestDistance > distance) {
29            p1 = i; // Update p1
30            p2 = j; // Update p2
31            shortestDistance = distance; // Update shortestDistance
32          }
33        }
34      }
35
36      // Display result
37      System.out.println("The closest two points are " +
38        "(" + points[p1][0] + ", " + points[p1][1] + ") and (" +
39        points[p2][0] + ", " + points[p2][1] + ")");
40    }
41
42    /** Compute the distance between two points (x1, y1) and (x2, y2)*/
43    public static double distance(
44        double x1, double y1, double x2, double y2) {
45      return Math.sqrt((x2 - x1) * (x2 - x1) + (y2 - y1) * (y2 - y1));
46    }
47  }
```

```
Enter the number of points: 8 ↵Enter
Enter 8 points: -1 3  -1 -1  1 1  2 0.5  2 -1  3 3  4 2 4 -0.5 ↵Enter
The closest two points are (1, 1) and (2, 0.5)
```

The program prompts the user to enter the number of points (lines 6–7). The points are read from the console and stored in a two-dimensional array named points (lines 12–15). The program uses the variable shortestDistance (line 19) to store the distance between the two nearest points, and the indices of these two points in the points array are stored in p1 and p2 (line 18).

For each point at index i, the program computes the distance between points[i] and points[j] for all j > i (lines 23–34). Whenever a shorter distance is found, the variable shortestDistance and p1 and p2 are updated (lines 28–32).

The distance between two points (x1, y1) and (x2, y2) can be computed using the formula $\sqrt{(x_2 - x_1)^2 + (y_2 - y_1)^2}$ (lines 43–46).

The program assumes that the plane has at least two points. You can easily modify the program to handle the case if the plane has zero or one point.

multiple closest pairs

Note that there might be more than one closest pair of points with the same minimum distance. The program finds one such pair. You may modify the program to find all closest pairs in Programming Exercise G.8.

input file

Tip

It is cumbersome to enter all points from the keyboard. You may store the input in a file, say **FindNearestPoints.txt**, and compile and run the program using the following command:

```
java FindNearestPoints < FindNearestPoints.txt
```

G.7 Case Study: Sudoku

The problem is to check whether a given Sudoku solution is correct.

Sudoku

This section presents an interesting problem of a sort that appears in the newspaper every day. It is a number-placement puzzle, commonly known as *Sudoku*. This is a very challenging problem. To make it accessible to the novice, this section presents a simplified version of the Sudoku problem, which is to verify whether a Sudoku solution is correct.

fixed cells
free cells

Sudoku is a 9 × 9 grid divided into smaller 3 × 3 boxes (also called *regions* or *blocks*), as shown in Figure G.4a. Some cells, called *fixed cells*, are populated with numbers from 1 to 9. The objective is to fill the empty cells, also called *free cells*, with the numbers 1 to 9 so that every row, every column, and every 3 × 3 box contains the numbers 1 to 9, as shown in Figure G.4b.

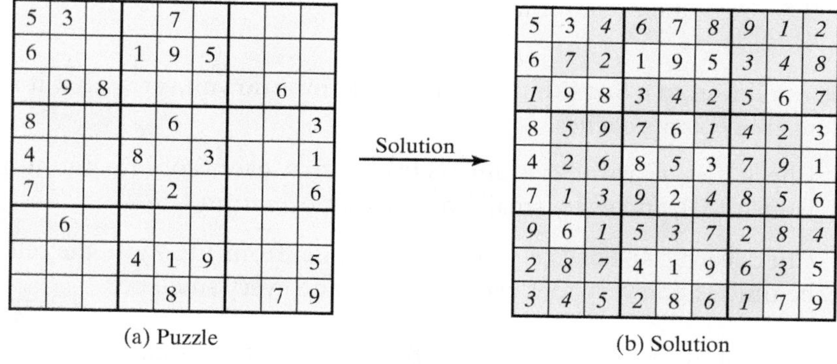

5	3			7				
6			1	9	5			
	9	8					6	
8				6				3
4			8		3			1
7				2				6
	6							
			4	1	9			5
				8			7	9

(a) Puzzle

5	3	4	6	7	8	9	1	2
6	7	2	1	9	5	3	4	8
1	9	8	3	4	2	5	6	7
8	5	9	7	6	1	4	2	3
4	2	6	8	5	3	7	9	1
7	1	3	9	2	4	8	5	6
9	6	1	5	3	7	2	8	4
2	8	7	4	1	9	6	3	5
3	4	5	2	8	6	1	7	9

(b) Solution

FIGURE G.4 The Sudoku puzzle in (a) is solved in (b).

representing a grid

For convenience, we use value 0 to indicate a free cell, as shown in Figure G.5a. The grid can be naturally represented using a two-dimensional array, as shown in Figure G.5b.

5	3	0	0	7	0	0	0	0
6	0	0	1	9	5	0	0	0
0	9	8	0	0	0	0	6	0
8	0	0	0	6	0	0	0	3
4	0	0	8	0	3	0	0	1
7	0	0	0	2	0	0	0	6
0	6	0	0	0	0	0	0	0
0	0	0	4	1	9	0	0	5
0	0	0	0	8	0	0	7	9

(a)

```
int[][] grid =
  {{5, 3, 0, 0, 7, 0, 0, 0, 0},
   {6, 0, 0, 1, 9, 5, 0, 0, 0},
   {0, 9, 8, 0, 0, 0, 0, 6, 0},
   {8, 0, 0, 0, 6, 0, 0, 0, 3},
   {4, 0, 0, 8, 0, 3, 0, 0, 1},
   {7, 0, 0, 0, 2, 0, 0, 0, 6},
   {0, 6, 0, 0, 0, 0, 2, 8, 0},
   {0, 0, 0, 4, 1, 9, 0, 0, 5},
   {0, 0, 0, 0, 8, 0, 0, 7, 9}
  };
```

(b)

FIGURE G.5 A grid can be represented using a two-dimensional array.

To find a solution for the puzzle, we must replace each 0 in the grid with an appropriate number from 1 to 9. For the solution to the puzzle in Figure G.5, the grid should be as shown in Figure G.6.

```
A solution grid is
 {{5, 3, 4, 6, 7, 8, 9, 1, 2},
  {6, 7, 2, 1, 9, 5, 3, 4, 8},
  {1, 9, 8, 3, 4, 2, 5, 6, 7},
  {8, 5, 9, 7, 6, 1, 4, 2, 3},
  {4, 2, 6, 8, 5, 3, 7, 9, 1},
  {7, 1, 3, 9, 2, 4, 8, 5, 6},
  {9, 6, 1, 5, 3, 7, 2, 8, 4},
  {2, 8, 7, 4, 1, 9, 6, 3, 5},
  {3, 4, 5, 2, 8, 6, 1, 7, 9}
 };
```

FIGURE G.6 A solution is stored in grid.

Once a solution to a Sudoku puzzle is found, how do you verify that it is correct? Here are two approaches:

- Check if every row has numbers from 1 to 9, every column has numbers from 1 to 9, and every small box has numbers from 1 to 9.
- Check each cell. Each cell must be a number from 1 to 9 and the cell must be unique on every row, every column, and every small box.

The program in Listing G.4 prompts the user to enter a solution and reports whether it is valid. We use the second approach in the program to check whether the solution is correct.

LISTING G.4 CheckSudokuSolution.java

read input

solution valid?

read solution

```java
import java.util.Scanner;

public class CheckSudokuSolution {
  public static void main(String[] args) {
    // Read a Sudoku solution
    int[][] grid = readASolution();

    System.out.println(isValid(grid) ? "Valid solution" :
      "Invalid solution");
  }

  /** Read a Sudoku solution from the console */
  public static int[][] readASolution() {
    // Create a Scanner
    Scanner input = new Scanner(System.in);

    System.out.println("Enter a Sudoku puzzle solution:");
    int[][] grid = new int[9][9];
    for (int i = 0; i < 9; i++)
      for (int j = 0; j < 9; j++)
        grid[i][j] = input.nextInt();

```

```
23       return grid;
24     }
25
26     /** Check whether a solution is valid */
27     public static boolean isValid(int[][] grid) {
28       for (int i = 0; i < 9; i++)
29         for (int j = 0; j < 9; j++)
30           if (grid[i][j] < 1 || grid[i][j] > 9
31               || !isValid(i, j, grid))
32             return false;
33         return true; // The solution is valid
34     }
35
36     /** Check whether grid[i][j] is valid in the grid */
37     public static boolean isValid(int i, int j, int[][] grid) {
38       // Check whether grid[i][j] is unique in i's row
39       for (int column = 0; column < 9; column++)
40         if (column != j && grid[i][column] == grid[i][j])
41           return false;
42
43       // Check whether grid[i][j] is unique in j's column
44       for (int row = 0; row < 9; row++)
45         if (row != i && grid[row][j] == grid[i][j])
46           return false;
47
48       // Check whether grid[i][j] is unique in the 3-by-3 box
49       for (int row = (i / 3) * 3; row < (i / 3) * 3 + 3; row++)
50         for (int col = (j / 3) * 3; col < (j / 3) * 3 + 3; col++)
51           if (row != i && col != j && grid[row][col] == grid[i][j])
52             return false;
53
54       return true; // The current value at grid[i][j] is valid
55     }
56   }
```

check solution

check rows

check columns

check small boxes

```
Enter a Sudoku puzzle solution:
9 6 3 1 7 4 2 5 8 [Enter]
1 7 8 3 2 5 6 4 9 [Enter]
2 5 4 6 8 9 7 3 1 [Enter]
8 2 1 4 3 7 5 9 6 [Enter]
4 9 6 8 5 2 3 1 7 [Enter]
7 3 5 9 6 1 8 2 4 [Enter]
5 8 9 7 1 3 4 6 2 [Enter]
3 1 7 2 4 6 9 8 5 [Enter]
6 4 2 5 9 8 1 7 3 [Enter]
Valid solution
```

The program invokes the `readASolution()` method (line 6) to read a Sudoku solution and return a two-dimensional array representing a Sudoku grid.

The `isValid(grid)` method checks whether the values in the grid are valid by verifying that each value is between `1` and `9` and that each value is valid in the grid (lines 27–34).

`isValid` method

isValid method

The `isValid(i, j, grid)` method checks whether the value at `grid[i][j]` is valid. It checks whether `grid[i][j]` appears more than once in row `i` (lines 39–41), in column `j` (lines 44–46), and in the 3 × 3 box (lines 49–52).

How do you locate all the cells in the same box? For any `grid[i][j]`, the starting cell of the 3 × 3 box that contains it is `grid[(i / 3) * 3][(j / 3) * 3]`, as illustrated in Figure G.7.

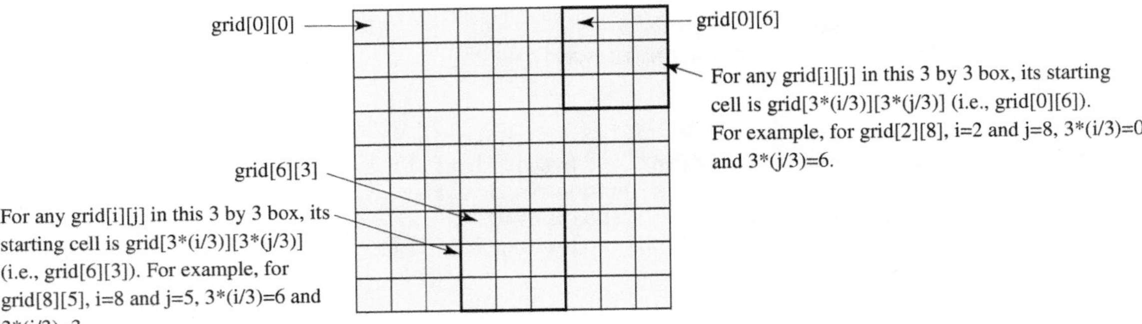

FIGURE G.7 The location of the first cell in a 3 × 3 box determines the locations of other cells in the box.

With this observation, you can easily identify all the cells in the box. For instance, if `grid[r][c]` is the starting cell of a 3 × 3 box, the cells in the box can be traversed in a nested loop as follows:

```
// Get all cells in a 3-by-3 box starting at grid[r][c]
for (int row = r; row < r + 3; row++)
  for (int col = c; col < c + 3; col++)
    // grid[row][col] is in the box
```

input file

It is cumbersome to enter 81 numbers from the console. When you test the program, you may store the input in a file, say **CheckSudokuSolution.txt**, and run the program using the following command:

```
java CheckSudokuSolution < CheckSudokuSolution.txt
```

G.8 Multidimensional Arrays

A two-dimensional array consists of an array of one-dimensional arrays and a three-dimensional array consists of an array of two-dimensional arrays.

In the preceding section, you used a two-dimensional array to represent a matrix or a table. Occasionally, you will need to represent n-dimensional data structures. In Java, you can create n-dimensional arrays for any integer n.

The way to declare two-dimensional array variables and create two-dimensional arrays can be generalized to declare n-dimensional array variables and create n-dimensional arrays for $n >= 3$. For example, you may use a three-dimensional array to store exam scores for a class of six students with five exams, and each exam has two parts (multiple-choice and essay). The following syntax declares a three-dimensional array variable `scores`, creates an array, and assigns its reference to `scores`.

```
double[][][] scores = new double[6][5][2];
```

You can also use the short-hand notation to create and initialize the array as follows:

```
double[][][] scores = {
  {{7.5, 20.5}, {9.0, 22.5}, {15, 33.5}, {13, 21.5}, {15, 2.5}},
  {{4.5, 21.5}, {9.0, 22.5}, {15, 34.5}, {12, 20.5}, {14, 9.5}},
  {{6.5, 30.5}, {9.4, 10.5}, {11, 33.5}, {11, 23.5}, {10, 2.5}},
  {{6.5, 23.5}, {9.4, 32.5}, {13, 34.5}, {11, 20.5}, {16, 7.5}},
  {{8.5, 26.5}, {9.4, 52.5}, {13, 36.5}, {13, 24.5}, {16, 2.5}},
  {{9.5, 20.5}, {9.4, 42.5}, {13, 31.5}, {12, 20.5}, {16, 6.5}}};
```

`scores[0][1][0]` refers to the multiple-choice score for the first student's second exam, which is `9.0`. `scores[0][1][1]` refers to the essay score for the first student's second exam, which is `22.5`. This is depicted in the following figure:

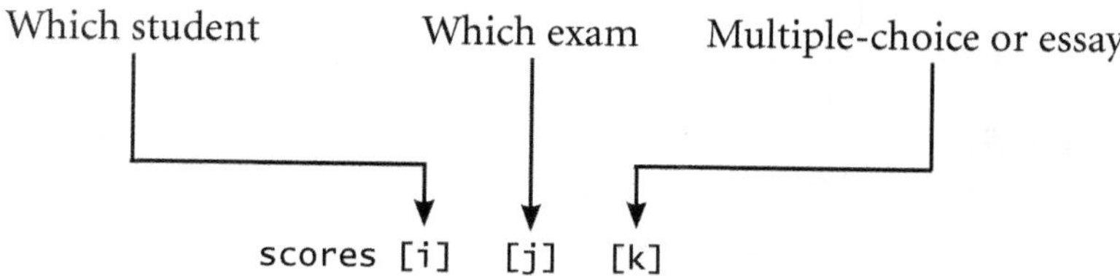

A multidimensional array is actually an array in which each element is another array. A three-dimensional array consists of an array of two-dimensional arrays. A two-dimensional array consists of an array of one-dimensional arrays. For example, suppose `x = new int[2][2][5]`, and `x[0]` and `x[1]` are two-dimensional arrays. `X[0][0]`, `x[0][1]`, `x[1][0]`, and `x[1][1]` are one-dimensional arrays and each contains five elements. `x.length` is `2`, `x[0].length` and `x[1].length` are `2`, and `X[0][0].length`, `x[0][1].length`, `x[1][0].length`, and `x[1][1].length` are `5`.

G.9 Case Study: Guessing Birthdays

You may recall from Chapter 5 that you can find out the date of the month when your friend was born by asking five questions. Each question asks whether the day is in one of the five sets of numbers. Expanding on the Chapter 5 example, Listing G.6 GuessBirthdayUsingArray.java stores the five sets of numbers in a three-dimensional array.

The birthday is the sum of the first numbers in the sets where the day appears. For example, if the birthday is `19`, it appears in Set1, Set2, and Set5. The first numbers in these three sets are `1`, `2`, and `16`. Their sum is `19`.

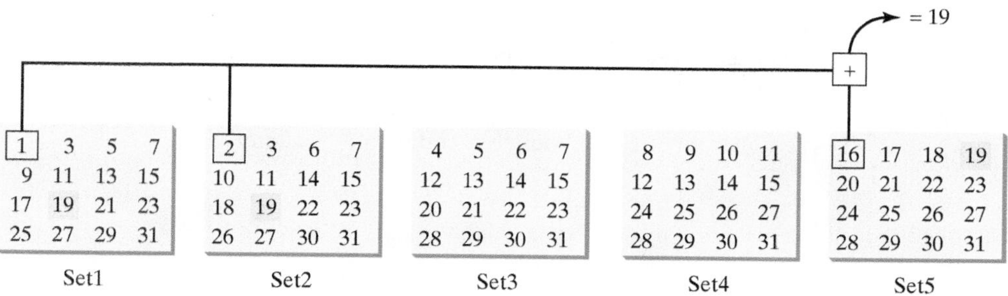

Listing G.6 shows the code, followed by a sample run using the birthday of 19. A for loop is used to retrieve the user's five answers. Refer back to Chapter 5 for a discussion on the mathematics behind the game.

LISTING G.6 GuessBirthdayUsingArray.java

```
import java.util.Scanner;

public class GuessBirthdayUsingArray {
  public static void main(String[] args) {
    int day = 0; // Day to be determined
    int answer;

    int[][][] dates = {
      {{ 1,  3,  5,  7},
       { 9, 11, 13, 15},
       {17, 19, 21, 23},
       {25, 27, 29, 31}},
      {{ 2,  3,  6,  7},
       {10, 11, 14, 15},
       {18, 19, 22, 23},
       {26, 27, 30, 31}},
      {{ 4,  5,  6,  7},
       {12, 13, 14, 15},
       {20, 21, 22, 23},
       {28, 29, 30, 31}},
      {{ 8,  9, 10, 11},
       {12, 13, 14, 15},
       {24, 25, 26, 27},
       {28, 29, 30, 31}},
      {{16, 17, 18, 19},
       {20, 21, 22, 23},
       {24, 25, 26, 27},
       {28, 29, 30, 31}}};

    // Create a Scanner
    Scanner input = new Scanner(System.in);

    for (int i = 0; i < 5; i++) {
      System.out.println("Is your birthday in Set" + (i + 1) + "?");
      for (int j = 0; j < 4; j++) {
        for (int k = 0; k < 4; k++)
          System.out.printf("%4d", dates[i][j][k]);
        System.out.println();
      }

      System.out.print("\nEnter 0 for No and 1 for Yes: ");
      answer = input.nextInt();

      if (answer == 1)
        day += dates[i][0][0];
    }

    System.out.println("Your birthday is " + day);
  }
}
```

three-dimensional array

Set i

add to day

A three-dimensional array `dates` is created in Lines 8–28. This array stores five sets of numbers. Each set is a 4-by-4 two-dimensional array.

The loop starting from line 33 displays the numbers in each set and prompts the user to answer whether the birthday is in the set (lines 41–42). If the day is in the set, the first number (`dates[i][0][0]`) in the set is added to variable `day` (line 45).

Following is a sample run of Listing G.6:

line#	day	answer	output
35	0		
44		1	
47	1		
53		1	
56	3		
62		0	
71		0	
80		1	
83	19		
85			Your birthday is 19!

✓ Section G.9 Assessment

1. Declare an array variable for a three-dimensional array, create a $4 \times 6 \times 5$ `int` array, and assign its reference to the variable.
2. Assume `int[][][] x = new char[12][5][2]`, how many elements are in the array? What are `x.length`, `x[2].length`, and `x[0][0].length`?
3. Show the output of the following code:

```
int[][][] array = {{{1, 2}, {3, 4}}, {{5, 6},{7, 8}}};
System.out.println(array[0][0][0]);
System.out.println(array[1][1][1]);
```

Supplement G — Review and Assessment

Chapter Summary

1. A two-dimensional array can be used to store a table.
2. A variable for two-dimensional arrays can be declared using the syntax: `elementType[][] arrayVar`.
3. A two-dimensional array can be created using the syntax: `new elementType[ROW_SIZE][COLUMN_SIZE]`.
4. Each element in a two-dimensional array is represented using the syntax: `arrayVar[rowIndex][columnIndex]`.
5. You can create and initialize a two-dimensional array using an array initializer with the syntax: `elementType[][] arrayVar = {{row values}, . . . , {row values}}`.
6. You can use arrays of arrays to form multidimensional arrays. For example, a variable for three-dimensional arrays can be declared as `elementType[][][] arrayVar`, and a three-dimensional array can be created using `new elementType[size1][size2][size3]`.

Programming Exercises

Note

Exercises preceded by a star (*) are challenging.
Exercises preceded by two stars (**) are more challenging.
Exercises preceded by three stars (***) are most challenging.

*1. (*Sum elements column by column*) Write a method that returns the sum of all the elements in a specified column in a matrix using the following header:

```
public static double sumColumn(double[][] m, int columnIndex)
```

Write a test program that reads a 3-by-4 matrix and displays the sum of each column. Here is a sample run:

```
Enter a 3-by-4 matrix row by row:
1.5 2 3 4 [Enter]
5.5 6 7 8 [Enter]
9.5 1 3 1 [Enter]
Sum of the elements at column 0 is 16.5
Sum of the elements at column 1 is 9.0
Sum of the elements at column 2 is 13.0
Sum of the elements at column 3 is 13.0
```

*2. (*Sum the major diagonal in a matrix*) Write a method that sums all the numbers in the major diagonal in an $n \times n$ matrix of `double` values using the following header:

```
public static double sumMajorDiagonal(double[][] m)
```

Write a test program that reads a 4-by-4 matrix and displays the sum of all its elements on the major diagonal. Here is a sample run:

```
Enter a 4-by-4 matrix row by row:
1 2 3 4.0 [Enter]
5 6.5 7 8 [Enter]
9 10 11 12 [Enter]
13 14 15 16 [Enter]
Sum of the elements in the major diagonal is 34.5
```

*3. (*Sort students on grades*) Rewrite Listing G.2, GradeExam.java, to display the students in increasing order of the number of correct answers.

**4. (*Compute the weekly hours for each employee*) Suppose the weekly hours for all employees are stored in a two-dimensional array. Each row records an employee's seven-day work hours with seven columns. For example, the following array stores the work hours for eight employees. Write a program that displays employees and their total hours in decreasing order of the total hours.

	Su	M	T	W	Th	F	Sa
Employee 0	2	4	3	4	5	8	8
Employee 1	7	3	4	3	3	4	4
Employee 2	3	3	4	3	3	2	2
Employee 3	9	3	4	7	3	4	1
Employee 4	3	5	4	3	6	3	8
Employee 5	3	4	4	6	3	4	4
Employee 6	3	7	4	8	3	8	4
Employee 7	6	3	5	9	2	7	9

5. (*Algebra: add two matrices*) Write a method to add two matrices. The header of the method is as follows:

```
public static double[][] addMatrix(double[][] a, double[][] b)
```

In order to be added, the two matrices must have the same dimensions and the same or compatible types of elements. Let c be the resulting matrix. Each element c_{ij} is $a_{ij} + b_{ij}$. For example, for two 3×3 matrices a and b, c is

$$\begin{pmatrix} a_{11} & a_{12} & a_{13} \\ a_{21} & a_{22} & a_{23} \\ a_{31} & a_{32} & a_{33} \end{pmatrix} + \begin{pmatrix} b_{11} & b_{12} & b_{13} \\ b_{21} & b_{22} & b_{23} \\ b_{31} & b_{32} & b_{33} \end{pmatrix} = \begin{pmatrix} a_{11} + b_{11} & a_{12} + b_{12} & a_{13} + b_{13} \\ a_{21} + b_{21} & a_{22} + b_{22} & a_{23} + b_{23} \\ a_{31} + b_{31} & a_{32} + b_{32} & a_{33} + b_{33} \end{pmatrix}$$

Write a test program that prompts the user to enter two 3×3 matrices and displays their sum. Here is a sample run:

```
Enter matrix1: 1 2 3 4 5 6 7 8 9 [Enter]
Enter matrix2: 0 2 4 1 4.5 2.2 1.1 4.3 5.2 [Enter]
The matrices are added as follows
 1.0 2.0 3.0        0.0 2.0 4.0        1.0 4.0 7.0
 4.0 5.0 6.0   +    1.0 4.5 2.2   =    5.0 9.5 8.2
 7.0 8.0 9.0        1.1 4.3 5.2        8.1 12.3 14.2
```

**6. (*Algebra: multiply two matrices*) Write a method to multiply two matrices. The header of the method is:

```
public static double[][]
    multiplyMatrix(double[][] a, double[][] b)
```

To multiply matrix a by matrix b, the number of columns in a must be the same as the number of rows in b, and the two matrices must have elements of the same or compatible types. Let c be the result of the multiplication. Assume the column size of matrix a is n. Each element c_{ij} is $a_{i1} \times b_{1j} + a_{i2} \times b_{2j} + \ldots + a_{in} \times b_{nj}$. For example, for two 3×3 matrices a and b, c is

$$\begin{pmatrix} a_{11} & a_{12} & a_{13} \\ a_{21} & a_{22} & a_{23} \\ a_{31} & a_{32} & a_{33} \end{pmatrix} \times \begin{pmatrix} b_{11} & b_{12} & b_{13} \\ b_{21} & b_{22} & b_{23} \\ b_{31} & b_{32} & b_{33} \end{pmatrix} = \begin{pmatrix} c_{11} & c_{12} & c_{13} \\ c_{21} & c_{22} & c_{23} \\ c_{31} & c_{32} & c_{33} \end{pmatrix}$$

where $c_{ij} = a_{i1} \times b_{1j} + a_{i2} \times b_{2j} + a_{i3} \times b_{3j}$.

Write a test program that prompts the user to enter two 3×3 matrices and displays their product. Here is a sample run:

```
Enter matrix1: 1 2 3 4 5 6 7 8 9 ↵Enter
Enter matrix2: 0 2 4 1 4.5 2.2 1.1 4.3 5.2 ↵Enter
The multiplication of the matrices is
 1 2 3      0 2.0 4.0        5.3 23.9 24
 4 5 6   *  1 4.5 2.2   =    11.6 56.3 58.2
 7 8 9      1.1 4.3 5.2      17.9 88.7 92.4
```

*7. (*Points nearest to each other*) Listing G.3 gives a program that finds two points in a two-dimensional space nearest to each other. Revise the program so that it finds two points in a three-dimensional space nearest to each other. Use a two-dimensional array to represent the points. Test the program using the following points:

```
double[][] points = {{-1, 0, 3}, {-1, -1, -1}, {4, 1, 1},
  {2, 0.5, 9}, {3.5, 2, -1}, {3, 1.5, 3}, {-1.5, 4, 2},
  {5.5, 4, -0.5}};
```

The formula for computing the distance between two points `(x1, y1, z1)` and `(x2, y2, z2)` is $\sqrt{(x_2 - x_1)^2 + (y_2 - y_1)^2 + (z_2 - z_1)^2}$.

**8. (*All closest pairs of points*) Revise Listing G.3, FindNearestPoints.java, to display all closest pairs of points with the same minimum distance. Here is a sample run:

```
Enter the number of points: 8 ↵Enter
Enter 8 points: 0 0 1 1 -1 -1  2 2 -2 -2 -3 -3 -4 -4 5 5
↵Enter
The closest two points are (0.0, 0.0) and (1.0, 1.0)
The closest two points are (0.0, 0.0) and (-1.0, -1.0)
The closest two points are (1.0, 1.0) and (2.0, 2.0)
The closest two points are (-1.0, -1.0) and (-2.0, -2.0)
The closest two points are (-2.0, -2.0) and (-3.0, -3.0)
The closest two points are (-3.0, -3.0) and (-4.0, -4.0)
Their distance is 1.4142135623730951
```

***9. (*Game: play a tic-tac-toe game*) In a game of tic-tac-toe, two players take turns marking an available cell in a 3 × 3 grid with their respective tokens (either X or O). When one player has placed three tokens in a horizontal, vertical, or diagonal row on the grid, the game is over and that player has won. A draw (no winner) occurs when all the cells on the grid have been filled with tokens and neither player has achieved a win. Create a program for playing tic-tac-toe.

The program prompts two players to enter an X token and O token alternately. Whenever a token is entered, the program redisplays the board on the console and determines the status of the game (win, draw, or continue). Here is a sample run:

```
-------------
|   |   |   |
-------------
|   |   |   |
-------------
|   |   |   |
-------------
Enter a row (0, 1, or 2) for player X: 1 ↵Enter
Enter a column (0, 1, or 2) for player X: 1 ↵Enter

-------------
|   |   |   |
-------------
|   | X |   |
-------------
|   |   |   |
-------------
Enter a row (0, 1, or 2) for player O: 1 ↵Enter
Enter a column (0, 1, or 2) for player O: 2 ↵Enter

-------------
|   |   |   |
-------------
|   | X | O |
-------------
|   |   |   |
-------------
Enter a row (0, 1, or 2) for player X:

  . . .

-------------
| X |   |   |
-------------
| O | X | O |
-------------
|   |   | X |
-------------
X player won
```

*10. (*Largest row and column*) Write a program that randomly fills in 0s and 1s into a 4-by-4 matrix, prints the matrix, and finds the first row and column with the most 1s. Here is a sample run of the program:

```
0011
0011
1101
1010
The largest row index: 2
The largest column index: 2
```

**11. (*Game: nine heads and tails*) Nine coins are placed in a 3-by-3 matrix with some face up and some face down. You can represent the state of the coins using a 3-by-3 matrix with values 0 (heads) and 1 (tails).

Here are some examples:

```
0 0 0    1 0 1    1 1 0    1 0 1    1 0 0
0 1 0    0 0 1    1 0 0    1 1 0    1 1 1
0 0 0    1 0 0    0 0 1    1 0 0    1 1 0
```

Each state can also be represented using a binary number. For example, the preceding matrices correspond to the numbers

```
000010000 101001100 110100001 101110100 100111110
```

There are a total of 512 possibilities, so you can use decimal numbers 0, 1, 2, 3, . . . , and 511 to represent all states of the matrix. Write a program that prompts the user to enter a number between 0 and 511 and displays the corresponding matrix with the characters `H` and `T`. Here is a sample run:

```
Enter a number between 0 and 511: 7 [Enter]
H H H
H H H
T T T
```

The user entered `7`, which corresponds to `000000111`. Since `0` stands for `H` and `1` for `T`, the output is correct.

*12. (*Locate the largest element*) Write the following method that returns the location of the largest element in a two-dimensional array.

```
public static int[] locateLargest(double[][] a)
```

The return value is a one-dimensional array that contains two elements. These two elements indicate the row and column indices of the largest element in the two-dimensional array. Write a test program that prompts the user to enter a two-dimensional array and displays the location of the largest element in the array. Here is a sample run:

```
Enter the number of rows and columns of the array: 3 4 [Enter]
Enter the array:
23.5 35 2 10 [Enter]
4.5 3 45 3.5 [Enter]
35 44 5.5 9.6 [Enter]
The location of the largest element is at (1, 2)
```

**13. (*Explore matrix*) Write a program that prompts the user to enter the length of a square matrix, randomly fills in `0`s and `1`s into the matrix, prints the matrix, and finds the rows, columns, and diagonals with all `0`s or `1`s. Here is a sample run of the program:

```
Enter the size for the matrix: 4 ↵Enter
0111
0000
0100
1111
All 0s on row 1
All 1s on row 3
No same numbers on a column
No same numbers on the major diagonal
No same numbers on the sub-diagonal
```

***14.** (*Sort two-dimensional array*) Write a method to sort a two-dimensional array using the following header:

```
public static void sort(int m[][])
```

The method performs a primary sort on rows and a secondary sort on columns. For example, the following array

```
{{4, 2},{1, 7},{4, 5},{1, 2},{1, 1},{4, 1}}
```

will be sorted to

```
{{1, 1},{1, 2},{1, 7},{4, 1},{4, 2},{4, 5}}.
```

***15.** (*Shuffle rows*) Write a method that shuffles the rows in a two-dimensional `int` array using the following header:

```
public static void shuffle(int[][] m)
```

Write a test program that shuffles the following matrix:

```
int[][] m = {{1, 2}, {3, 4}, {5, 6}, {7, 8}, {9, 10}};
```

***16.** (*Central city*) Given a set of cities, the central city is the city that has the shortest total distance to all other cities. Write a program that prompts the user to enter the number of the cities and the locations of the cities (coordinates), and finds the central city and its total distance to all other cities. Here is a sample run:

```
Enter the number of cities: 5 ↵Enter
Enter the coordinates of the cities:
  2.5 5 5.1 3 1 9 5.4 54 5.5 2.1 ↵Enter
The central city is at (2.5, 5.0)
The total distance to all other cities is 60.81
```

***17.** (*Even number of 1s*) Write a program that generates a 6-by-6 two-dimensional matrix filled with 0s and 1s, displays the matrix, and checks if every row and every column have an even number of 1s.

*18. (*Game: find the flipped cell*) Suppose you are given a 6-by-6 matrix filled with 0s and 1s. All rows and all columns have an even number of 1s. Let the user flip one cell (i.e., flip from 1 to 0 or from 0 to 1) and write a program to find which cell was flipped. Your program should prompt the user to enter a 6-by-6 array with 0s and 1s and find the first row *r* and first column *c* where the even number of the 1s property is violated (i.e., the number of 1s is not even). The flipped cell is at (*r*, *c*). Here is a sample run:

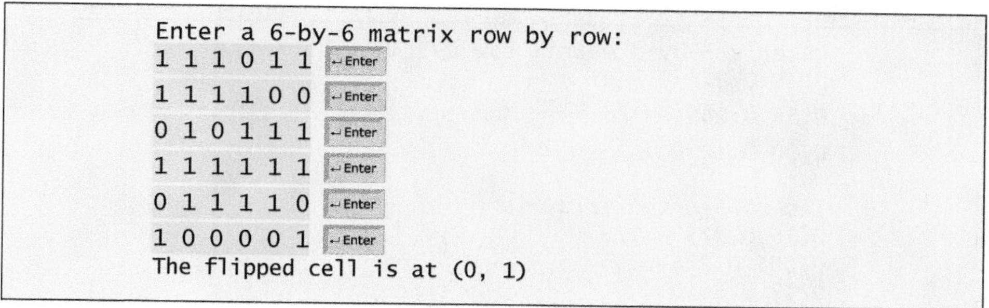

```
Enter a 6-by-6 matrix row by row:
1 1 1 0 1 1 ↵Enter
1 1 1 1 0 0 ↵Enter
0 1 0 1 1 1 ↵Enter
1 1 1 1 1 1 ↵Enter
0 1 1 1 1 0 ↵Enter
1 0 0 0 0 1 ↵Enter
The flipped cell is at (0, 1)
```

*19. (*Check Sudoku solution*) Listing G.4 checks whether a solution is valid by checking whether every number is valid in the board. Rewrite the program by checking whether every row, every column, and every small box has the numbers 1 to 9.

*20. (*Markov matrix*) An $n \times n$ matrix is called a *positive Markov matrix* if each element is positive and the sum of the elements in each column is 1. Write the following method to check whether a matrix is a Markov matrix.

```
public static boolean isMarkovMatrix(double[][] m)
```

Write a test program that prompts the user to enter a 3×3 matrix of double values and tests whether it is a Markov matrix. Here are the sample runs:

```
Enter a 3-by-3 matrix row by row:
0.15 0.875 0.375 ↵Enter
0.55 0.005 0.225 ↵Enter
0.30 0.12 0.4 ↵Enter
It is a Markov matrix
```

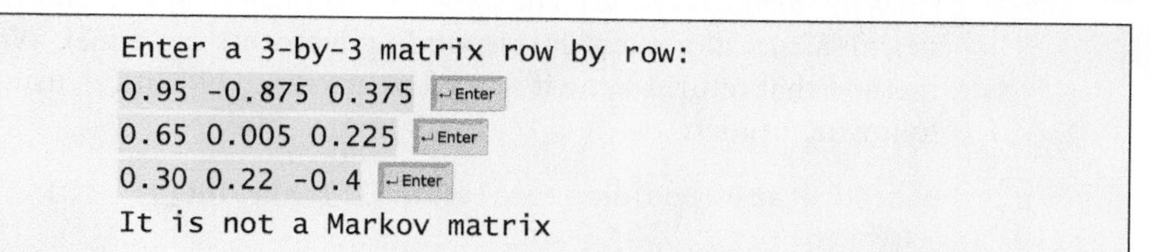

```
Enter a 3-by-3 matrix row by row:
0.95 -0.875 0.375 ↵Enter
0.65 0.005 0.225 ↵Enter
0.30 0.22 -0.4 ↵Enter
It is not a Markov matrix
```

*21. (*Row sorting*) Implement the following method to sort the rows in a two-dimensional array. A new array is returned and the original array is intact.

```
public static double[][] sortRows(double[][] m)
```

Write a test program that prompts the user to enter a 3 × 3 matrix of double values and displays a new row-sorted matrix. Here is a sample run:

```
Enter a 3-by-3 matrix row by row:
0.15 0.875 0.375 [Enter]
0.55 0.005 0.225 [Enter]
0.30 0.12 0.4 [Enter]

The row-sorted array is
0.15 0.375 0.875
0.005 0.225 0.55
0.12 0.30 0.4
```

*22. (*Column sorting*) Implement the following method to sort the columns in a two-dimensional array. A new array is returned and the original array is intact.

```
public static double[][] sortColumns(double[][] m)
```

Write a test program that prompts the user to enter a 3 × 3 matrix of double values and displays a new column-sorted matrix. Here is a sample run:

```
Enter a 3-by-3 matrix row by row:
0.15 0.875 0.375 [Enter]
0.55 0.005 0.225 [Enter]
0.30 0.12 0.4 [Enter]

The column-sorted array is
0.15 0.0050 0.225
0.3  0.12   0.375
0.55 0.875  0.4
```

23. (*Strictly identical arrays*) The two-dimensional arrays `m1` and `m2` are *strictly identical* if their corresponding elements are equal. Write a method that returns `true` if `m1` and `m2` are strictly identical, using the following header:

```
public static boolean equals(int[][] m1, int[][] m2)
```

Write a test program that prompts the user to enter two 3 × 3 arrays of integers and displays whether the two are strictly identical. Here are the sample runs:

```
Enter list1: 51 22 25 6 1 4 24 54 6 ↵Enter
Enter list2: 51 22 25 6 1 4 24 54 6 ↵Enter
The two arrays are strictly identical
```

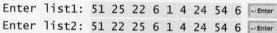

```
Enter list1: 51 25 22 6 1 4 24 54 6 ↵Enter
Enter list2: 51 22 25 6 1 4 24 54 6 ↵Enter
The two arrays are not strictly identical
```

24. (*Identical arrays*) The two-dimensional arrays `m1` and `m2` are *identical* if they have the same contents. Write a method that returns `true` if `m1` and `m2` are identical, using the following header:

```
public static boolean equals(int[][] m1, int[][] m2)
```

Write a test program that prompts the user to enter two 3 × 3 arrays of integers and displays whether the two are identical. Here are the sample runs:

```
Enter list1: 51 25 22 6 1 4 24 54 6 ↵Enter
Enter list2: 51 22 25 6 1 4 24 54 6 ↵Enter
The two arrays are identical
```

```
Enter list1: 51 5 22 6 1 4 24 54 6 ↵Enter
Enter list2: 51 22 25 6 1 4 24 54 6 ↵Enter
The two arrays are not identical
```

*25. (*Algebra: solve linear equations*) Write a method that solves the following 2 × 2 system of linear equations:

$$a_{00}x + a_{01}y = b_0 \qquad x = \frac{b_0a_{11} - b_1a_{01}}{a_{00}a_{11} - a_{01}a_{10}} \qquad y = \frac{b_1a_{00} - b_0a_{10}}{a_{00}a_{11} - a_{01}a_{10}}$$
$$a_{10}x + a_{11}y = b_1$$

The method header is

```
public static double[] linearEquation(double[][] a, dou-
ble[] b)
```

The method returns `null` if $a_{00}a_{11} - a_{01}a_{10}$ is `0`. Write a test program that prompts the user to enter a_{00}, a_{01}, a_{10}, a_{11}, b_0, and b_1, and displays the result. If $a_{00}a_{11} - a_{01}a_{10}$ is `0`, report that "The equation has no solution."

*26. (*Geometry: area of a triangle*) Write a method that returns the area of a triangle using the following header:

```
public static double getTriangleArea(double[][] points)
```

APPENDIX C

OPERATOR PRECEDENCE CHART

The operators are shown in decreasing order of precedence from top to bottom. Operators in the same group have the same precedence, and their associativity is shown in the table.

Operator	*Name*	*Associativity*
()	Parentheses	Left to right
()	Function call	Left to right
[]	Array subscript	Left to right
.	Object member access	Left to right
++	Postincrement	Left to right
--	Postdecrement	Left to right
++	Preincrement	Right to left
--	Predecrement	Right to left
+	Unary plus	Right to left
-	Unary minus	Right to left
!	Unary logical negation	Right to left
(type)	Unary casting	Right to left
new	Creating object	Right to left
*	Multiplication	Left to right
/	Division	Left to right
%	Remainder	Left to right
+	Addition	Left to right
-	Subtraction	Left to right
<<	Left shift	Left to right
>>	Right shift with sign extension	Left to right
>>>	Right shift with zero extension	Left to right
<	Less than	Left to right
<=	Less than or equal to	Left to right
>	Greater than	Left to right
>=	Greater than or equal to	Left to right

Operator	*Name*	*Associativity*
instanceof	Checking object type	Left to right
==	Equal comparison	Left to right
!=	Not equal	Left to right
&	(Unconditional AND)	Left to right
^	(Exclusive OR)	Left to right
|	(Unconditional OR)	Left to right
&&	Conditional AND	Left to right
||	Conditional OR	Left to right
?:	Ternary condition	Right to left
=	Assignment	Right to left
+=	Addition assignment	Right to left
-=	Subtraction assignment	Right to left
*=	Multiplication assignment	Right to left
/=	Division assignment	Right to left
%=	Remainder assignment	Right to left

APPENDIX D

NUMBER SYSTEMS

Introduction

Computers use binary numbers internally, because computers are made naturally to store and process 0s and 1s. The binary number system has two digits, 0 and 1. A number or character is stored as a sequence of 0s and 1s. Each 0 or 1 is called a *bit* (binary digit).

binary numbers

In our daily life we use decimal numbers. When we write a number such as 20 in a program, it is assumed to be a decimal number. Internally, computer software is used to convert decimal numbers into binary numbers, and vice versa.

decimal numbers

We write computer programs using decimal numbers. However, to deal with an operating system, we need to reach down to the "machine level" by using binary numbers. Binary numbers tend to be very long and cumbersome. Often hexadecimal numbers are used to abbreviate them, with each hexadecimal digit representing four binary digits. The hexadecimal number system has 16 digits: 0–9 and A–F. The letters A, B, C, D, E, and F correspond to the decimal numbers 10, 11, 12, 13, 14, and 15.

hexadecimal number

The digits in the decimal number system are 0, 1, 2, 3, 4, 5, 6, 7, 8, and 9. A decimal number is represented by a sequence of one or more of these digits. The value that each digit represents depends on its position, which denotes an integral power of 10. For example, the digits 7, 4, 2, and 3 in decimal number 7423 represent 7000, 400, 20, and 3, respectively, as shown below:

$$\boxed{7\,|\,4\,|\,2\,|\,3} = 7 \times 10^3 + 4 \times 10^2 + 2 \times 10^1 + 3 \times 10^0$$

$$10^3 \; 10^2 \; 10^1 \; 10^0 = 7000 + 400 + 20 + 3 = 7423$$

The decimal number system has ten digits, and the position values are integral powers of 10. We say that 10 is the *base* or *radix* of the decimal number system. Similarly, since the binary number system has two digits, its base is 2, and since the hex number system has 16 digits, its base is 16.

base

radix

If 1101 is a binary number, the digits 1, 1, 0, and 1 represent 1×2^3, 1×2^2, 0×2^1, and 1×2^0, respectively:

$$\boxed{1\,|\,1\,|\,0\,|\,1} = 1 \times 2^3 + 1 \times 2^2 + 0 \times 2^1 + 1 \times 2^0$$

$$2^3 \; 2^2 \; 2^1 \; 2^0 = 8 + 4 + 0 + 1 = 13$$

If 7423 is a hex number, the digits 7, 4, 2, and 3 represent 7×16^3, 4×16^2, 2×16^1, and 3×16^0, respectively:

7	4	2	3

$$= 7 \times 16^3 + 4 \times 16^2 + 2 \times 16^1 + 3 \times 16^0$$

$$16^3 \; 16^2 \; 16^1 \; 16^0 = 28672 + 1024 + 32 + 3 = 29731$$

Conversions Between Binary and Decimal Numbers

binary to decimal

Given a binary number $b_n b_{n-1} b_{n-2} \ldots b_2 b_1 b_0$, the equivalent decimal value is

$$b_n \times 2^n + b_{n-1} \times 2^{n-1} + b_{n-2} \times 2^{n-2} + \ldots + b_2 \times 2^2 + b_1 \times 2^1 + b_0 \times 2^0$$

Here are some examples of converting binary numbers to decimals:

Binary	*Conversion Formula*	*Decimal*
10	$1 \times 2^1 + 0 \times 2^0$	2
1000	$1 \times 2^3 + 0 \times 2^2 + 0 \times 2^1 + 0 \times 2^0$	8
10101011	$1 \times 2^7 + 0 \times 2^6 + 1 \times 2^5 + 0 \times 2^4 + 1 \times 2^3 + 0 \times 2^2 + 1 \times 2^1 + 1 \times 2^0$	171

decimal to binary

To convert a decimal number d to a binary number is to find the bits b_n, b_{n-1}, $b_{n-2}, \ldots, b_2$, b_1 and b_0 such that

$$d = b_n \times 2^n + b_{n-1} \times 2^{n-1} + b_{n-2} \times 2^{n-2} + \ldots + b_2 \times 2^2 + b_1 \times 2^1 + b_0 \times 2^0$$

These bits can be found by successively dividing d by 2 until the quotient is 0. The remainders are $b_0, b_1, b_2, \ldots, b_{n-2}, b_{n-1}$, and b_n.

For example, the decimal number 123 is 1111011 in binary. The conversion is done as follows:

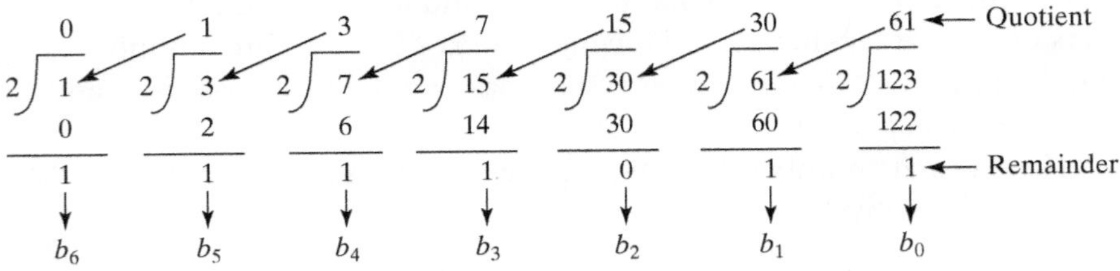

Tip
The Windows Calculator, as shown in Figure D.1, is a useful tool for performing number conversions. To run it, search for *Calculator* from the *Start* button and launch Calculator, then under *View* select *Scientific*.

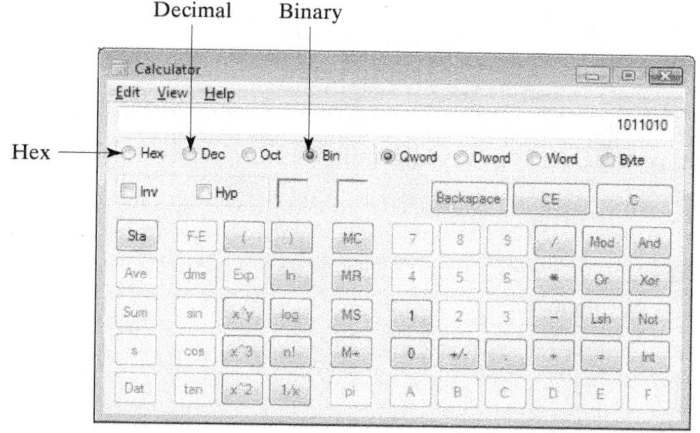

FIGURE D.1 You can perform number conversions using the Windows Calculator.

Conversions Between Hexadecimal and Decimal Numbers

Given a hexadecimal number $h_n h_{n-1} h_{n-2} \ldots h_2 h_1 h_0$, the equivalent decimal value is

hex to decimal

$$h_n \times 16^n + h_{n-1} \times 16^{n-1} + h_{n-2} \times 16^{n-2} + \ldots + h_2 \times 16^2 + h_1 \times 16^1 + h_0 \times 16^0$$

Here are some examples of converting hexadecimal numbers to decimals:

Hexadecimal	*Conversion Formula*	*Decimal*
7F	$7 \times 16^1 + 15 \times 16^0$	127
FFFF	$15 \times 16^3 + 15 \times 16^2 + 15 \times 16^1 + 15 \times 16^0$	65535
431	$4 \times 16^2 + 3 \times 16^1 + 1 \times 16^0$	1073

To convert a decimal number d to a hexadecimal number is to find the hexadecimal digits $h_n, h_{n-1}, h_{n-2}, \ldots, h_2, h_1$, and h_0 such that

decimal to hex

$$d = h_n \times 16^n + h_{n-1} \times 16^{n-1} + h_{n-2} \times 16^{n-2} + \ldots + h_2 \times 16^2 + h_1 \times 16^1 + h_0 \times 16^0$$

These numbers can be found by successively dividing d by 16 until the quotient is 0. The remainders are $h_0, h_1, h_2, \ldots, h_{n-2}, h_{n-1}$, and h_n.

For example, the decimal number 123 is 7B in hexadecimal. The conversion is done as follows:

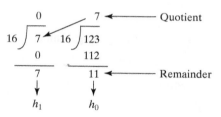

```
         0            7  <------- Quotient
    16 ) 7  <--  16 ) 123
         0            112
       ----          -----
         7            11  <------- Remainder
         |            |
         v            v
        h1            h0
```

Conversions Between Binary and Hexadecimal Numbers

hex to binary

To convert a hexadecimal to a binary number, simply convert each digit in the hexadecimal number into a four-digit binary number, using Table D.1.

TABLE D.1 Converting Hexadecimal to Binary

Hexadecimal	*Binary*	*Decimal*
0	0000	0
1	0001	1
2	0010	2
3	0011	3
4	0100	4
5	0101	5
6	0110	6
7	0111	7
8	1000	8
9	1001	9
A	1010	10
B	1011	11
C	1100	12
D	1101	13
E	1110	14
F	1111	15

For example, the hexadecimal number 7B is 1111011, where 7 is 111 in binary, and B is 1011 in binary.

To convert a binary number to a hexadecimal, convert every four binary digits from right to left in the binary number into a hexadecimal number.

binary to hex

For example, the binary number 1110001101 is 38D, since 1101 is D, 1000 is 8, and 11 is 3, as shown below.

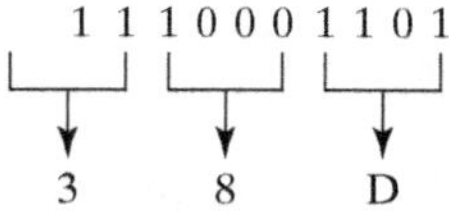

Note

Octal numbers are also useful. The octal number system has eight digits, 0 to 7. A decimal number 8 is represented in the octal system as 10.

Here are some good online resources for practicing number conversions:

- http://forums.cisco.com/CertCom/game/binary_game_page.htm
- http://people.sinclair.edu/nickreeder/Flash/binDec.htm
- http://people.sinclair.edu/nickreeder/Flash/binHex.htm

✓ Appendix D Assessment

1. Convert the following decimal numbers into hexadecimal and binary numbers:

   `100; 4340; 2000`

2. Convert the following binary numbers into hexadecimal and decimal numbers:

   `1000011001; 100000000; 100111`

3. Convert the following hexadecimal numbers into binary and decimal numbers:

   `FEFA9; 93; 2000`

Appendix E

Java Quick Reference

Console Input

```
Scanner input = new Scanner(System.in);
int intValue = input.nextInt();
long longValue = input.nextLong();
double doubleValue = input.nextDouble();
float floatValue = input.nextFloat();
String string = input.next();
String line = input.nextLine();
```

Console Output

```
System.out.println(anyValue);
```

Conditional Expression

```
boolean-expression ? expression1 :
  expression2

y = (x > 0) ? 1 : -1

System.out.println(number % 2 == 0 ?
  "number is even" : "number is odd");
```

Primitive Data Types

byte	8 bits
short	16 bits
int	32 bits
long	64 bits
float	32 bits
double	64 bits
char	16 bits
boolean	true/false

Arithmetic Operators

+	addition
-	subtraction
*	multiplication
/	division
%	remainder
++var	preincrement
--var	predecrement
var++	postincrement
var--	postdecrement

Assignment Operators

=	assignment
+=	addition assignment
-=	subtraction assignment
*=	multiplication assignment
/=	division assignment
%=	remainder assignment

Relational Operators

<	less than
<=	less than or equal to
>	greater than
>=	greater than or equal to
==	equal to
!=	not equal

Logical Operators

&&	short circuit AND
||	short circuit OR
!	NOT
^	exclusive OR

if Statements

```
if (condition) {
  statements;
}

if (condition) {
  statements;
}
else {
  statements;
}

if (condition1) {
  statements;
}
else if (condition2) {
  statements;
}
else {
  statements;
}
```

switch Statements

```
switch (intExpression) {
  case value1:
    statements;
    break;
  ...
  case valuen:
    statements;
    break;
  default:
    statements;
}
```

loop Statements

```
while (condition) {
  statements;
}

do {
  statements;
} while (condition);

for (init; condition;
  adjustment) {
  statements;
}
```

Frequently Used Static Constants/Methods

```
Math.PI
Math.random()
Math.pow(a, b)
Math.abs(a)
Math.max(a, b)
Math.min(a, b)
Math.sqrt(a)
Math.sin(radians)
Math.asin(a)
Math.toRadians(degrees)
Math.toDegress(radians)
System.currentTimeMillis()
Integer.parseInt(string)
Integer.parseInt(string, radix)
Double.parseDouble(string)
Arrays.sort(type[] list)
Arrays.binarySearch(type[] list, type key)
```

Array/Length/Initializer

```
int[] list = new int[10];
list.length;
int[] list = {1, 2, 3, 4};
```

Multidimensional Array/Length/Initializer

```
int[][] list = new int[10][10];
list.length;
list[0].length;
int[][] list = {{1, 2}, {3, 4}};
```

Ragged Array

```
int[][] m = {{1, 2, 3, 4},
             {1, 2, 3},
             {1, 2},
             {1}};
```

Text File Output

```
PrintWriter output =
  new PrintWriter(filename);
output.print(...);
output.println(...);
output.printf(...);
```

Text File Input

```
Scanner input = new Scanner(
  new File(filename));
```

File Class

```
File file =
  new File(filename);
file.exists()
file.renameTo(File)
file.delete()
```

Object Class

```
Object o = new Object();
o.toString();
o.equals(o1);
```

Comparable Interface

```
c.compareTo(Comparable)
c is a Comparable object
```

String Class

```
String s = "Welcome";
String s = new String(char[]);
int length = s.length();
char ch = s.charAt(index);
int d = s.compareTo(s1);
boolean b = s.equals(s1);
boolean b = s.startsWith(s1);
boolean b = s.endsWith(s1);
boolean b = s.contains(s1);
String s1 = s.trim();
String s1 = s.toUpperCase();
String s1 = s.toLowerCase();
int index = s.indexOf(ch);
int index = s.lastIndexOf(ch);
String s1 = s.substring(ch);
String s1 = s.substring(i,j);
char[] chs = s.toCharArray();
boolean b = s.matches(regex);
String s1 = s.replaceAll(regex,repl);
String[] tokens = s.split(regex);
```

ArrayList Class

```
ArrayList<E> list = new ArrayList<>();
list.add(object);
list.add(index, object);
list.clear();
Object o = list.get(index);
boolean b = list.isEmpty();
boolean b = list.contains(object);
int i = list.size();
list.remove(index);
list.set(index, object);
int i = list.indexOf(object);
int i = list.lastIndexOf(object);
```

printf Method

```
System.out.printf("%b %c %d %f %e %s",
  true, 'A', 45, 45.5, 45.5, "Welcome");
System.out.printf("%-5d %10.2f %10.2e %8s",
  45, 45.5, 45.5, "Welcome");
```

APPENDIX F

JAVA MODIFIERS

Modifiers are used on classes and class members (constructors, methods, data, and class-level blocks), but the `final` modifier can also be used on local variables in a method. A modifier that can be applied to a class is called a *class modifier*. A modifier that can be applied to a method is called a *method modifier*. A modifier that can be applied to a data field is called a *data modifier*. A modifier that can be applied to a class-level block is called a *block modifier*. The following table gives a summary of the Java modifiers.

Modifier	*Class*	*Constructor*	*Method*	*Data*	*Block*	*Explanation*
`(default)`*	√	√	√	√	√	A class, constructor, method, or data field is visible in this package.
`public`	√	√	√	√		A class, constructor, method, or data field is visible to all the programs in any package.
`private`		√	√	√		A constructor, method, or data field is only visible in this class.
`protected`		√	√	√		A constructor, method, or data field is visible in this package and in subclasses of this class in any package.
`static`			√	√	√	Define a class method, a class data field, or a static initialization block.
`final`	√		√	√		A final class cannot be extended. A final method cannot be modified in a subclass. A final data field is a constant.
`abstract`	√		√			An abstract class must be extended. An abstract method must be implemented in a concrete subclass.
`native`			√			A native method indicates that the method is implemented using a language other than Java.

*Default access doesn't have a modifier associated with it. For example: `class Test {}`

Modifier	*Class*	*Constructor*	*Method*	*Data*	*Block*	*Explanation*
`synchronized`			√		√	Only one thread at a time can execute this method.
`strictfp`	√		√			Use strict floating-point calculations to guarantee that the evaluation result is the same on all JVMs.
`transient`				√		Mark a nonserializable instance data field.

The modifiers default (no modifier), `public`, `private`, and `protected` are known as *visibility* or *accessibility modifiers* because they specify how classes and class members are accessed.

The modifiers `public`, `private`, `protected`, `static`, `final`, and `abstract` can also be applied to inner classes.

APPENDIX G

SPECIAL FLOATING-POINT VALUES

Dividing an integer by zero is invalid and throws `ArithmeticException`, but dividing a floating-point value by zero does not cause an exception. Floating-point arithmetic can overflow to infinity if the result of the operation is too large for a `double` or a `float`, or underflow to zero if the result is too small for a `double` or a `float`. Java provides the special floating-point values `POSITIVE_INFINITY`, `NEGATIVE_INFINITY`, and `NaN` (Not a Number) to denote these results. These values are defined as special constants in the `Float` class and the `Double` class.

If a positive floating-point number is divided by zero, the result is `POSITIVE_INFINITY`. If a negative floating-point number is divided by zero, the result is `NEGATIVE_INFINITY`. If a floating-point zero is divided by zero, the result is `NaN`, which means that the result is undefined mathematically. The string representations of these three values are `Infinity`, `-Infinity`, and `NaN`. For example,

```
System.out.print(1.0 / 0); // Print Infinity
System.out.print(-1.0 / 0); // Print -Infinity
System.out.print(0.0 / 0); // Print NaN
```

These special values can also be used as operands in computations. For example, a number divided by `POSITIVE_INFINITY` yields a positive zero. Table G.1 summarizes various combinations of the /, *, %, +, and - operators.

TABLE G.1 Special Floating-Point Values

x	*y*	*x/y*	*x*y*	*x%y*	*x + y*	*x − y*
Finite	± 0.0	± infinity	± 0.0	NaN	Finite	Finite
Finite	± infinity	± 0.0	± 0.0	x	± infinity	infinity
± 0.0	± 0.0	NaN	± 0.0	NaN	± 0.0	± 0.0
± infinity	Finite	± infinity	± 0.0	NaN	± infinity	± infinity
± infinity	± infinity	NaN	± 0.0	NaN	± infinity	infinity
± 0.0	± infinity	± 0.0	NaN	± 0.0	± infinity	± 0.0
NaN	Any	NaN	NaN	NaN	NaN	NaN
Any	NaN	NaN	NaN	NaN	NaN	NaN

Note

If one of the operands is NaN, the result is NaN.

APPENDIX H

REGULAR EXPRESSIONS

Often you need to write the code to validate user input such as to check whether the input is a number, a string with all lowercase letters, or a social security number. How do you write this type of code? A simple and effective way to accomplish this task is to use the regular expression.

A *regular expression* (abbreviated *regex*) is a string that describes a pattern for matching a set of strings. Regular expression is a powerful tool for string manipulations. You can use regular expressions for matching, replacing, and splitting strings. regular expression

Matching Strings

Let us begin with the matches method in the String class. At first glance, the matches method is very similar to the equals method. For example, the following two statements both evaluate to true. matches

```
"Java".matches("Java");
"Java".equals("Java");
```

However, the matches method is more powerful. It can match not only a fixed string, but also a set of strings that follow a pattern. For example, the following statements all evaluate to true.

```
"Java is fun".matches("Java.*")
"Java is cool".matches("Java.*")
"Java is powerful".matches("Java.*")
```

"Java.*" in the preceding statements is a regular expression. It describes a string pattern that begins with Java followed by any zero or more characters. Here, the substring .* matches any zero or more characters.

Regular Expression Syntax

A regular expression consists of literal characters and special symbols. Table H.1 lists some frequently used syntax for regular expressions.

TABLE H.1 Frequently Used Regular Expressions

<table>
<tr><th>Regular Expression</th><th>Matches</th><th>Example</th></tr>
<tr><td>x</td><td>a specified character x</td><td>Java matches Java</td></tr>
<tr><td>.</td><td>any single character</td><td>Java matches J..a</td></tr>
<tr><td>(ab|cd)</td><td>ab or cd</td><td>ten matches t(en|im)</td></tr>
<tr><td>[abc]</td><td>a, b, or c</td><td>Java matches Ja[uvwx]a</td></tr>
<tr><td>[^abc]</td><td>any character except a, b, or c</td><td>Java matches Ja[^ars]a</td></tr>
<tr><td>[a-z]</td><td>a through z</td><td>Java matches [A-M]av[a-d]</td></tr>
<tr><td>[^a-z]</td><td>any character except a through z</td><td>Java matches Jav[^b-d]</td></tr>
<tr><td>[a-e[m-p]]</td><td>a through e or m through p</td><td>Java matches [A-G[I-M]]av[a-d]</td></tr>
<tr><td>[a-e&&[c-p]]</td><td>intersection of a-e with c-p</td><td>Java matches [A-P&&[I-M]]av[a-d]</td></tr>
<tr><td>\d</td><td>a digit, same as [0-9]</td><td>Java2 matches "Java[\\d]"</td></tr>
<tr><td>\D</td><td>a non-digit</td><td>$Java matches "[\\D][\\D]ava"</td></tr>
<tr><td>\w</td><td>a word character</td><td>Java1 matches "[\\w]ava[\\w]"</td></tr>
<tr><td>\W</td><td>a non-word character</td><td>$Java matches "[\\W][\\w]ava"</td></tr>
<tr><td>\s</td><td>a whitespace character</td><td>"Java 2" matches "Java\\s2"</td></tr>
<tr><td>\S</td><td>a non-whitespace char</td><td>Java matches "[\\S]ava"</td></tr>
<tr><td>p*</td><td>zero or more occurrences of pattern p</td><td>aaaabb matches "a*bb"
ababab matches "(ab)*"</td></tr>
<tr><td>p+</td><td>one or more occurrences of pattern p</td><td>a matches "a+b*"
able matches "(ab)+.*"</td></tr>
<tr><td>p?</td><td>zero or one occurrence of pattern p</td><td>Java matches "J?Java"
Java matches "J?ava"</td></tr>
<tr><td>p{n}</td><td>exactly n occurrences of pattern p</td><td>Java matches "Ja{1}.*"
Java does not match ".{2}"</td></tr>
<tr><td>p{n,}</td><td>at least n occurrences of pattern p</td><td>aaaa matches "a{1,}"
a does not match "a{2,}"</td></tr>
<tr><td>p{n,m}</td><td>between n and m occurrences (inclusive)</td><td>aaaa matches "a{1,9}"
abb does not match "a{2,9}bb"</td></tr>
</table>

Note

Backslash is a special character that starts an escape sequence in a string. So you need to use \\d in Java to represent \d.

Note

Recall that a *whitespace character* is ' ', '\t', '\n', '\r', or '\f'. So \s is the same as [\t\n\r\f], and \S is the same as [^ \t\n\r\f].

Note

A word character is any letter, digit, or the underscore character. So `\w` is the same as `[a-z[A-Z][0-9]_]` or simply `[a-zA-Z0-9_]`, and `\W` is the same as `[^a-zA-Z0-9_]`.

Note

quantifier

The last six entries `*`, `+`, `?`, `{n}`, `{n,}`, and `{n, m}` in Table H.1 are called *quantifiers* that specify how many times the pattern before a quantifier may repeat. For example, `A*` matches zero or more `A`'s, `A+` matches one or more `A`'s, `A?` matches zero or one `A`'s, `A{3}` matches exactly `AAA`, `A{3,}` matches at least three `A`'s, and `A{3,6}` matches between 3 and 6 `A`'s. `*` is the same as `{0,}`, `+` is the same as `{1,}`, and `?` is the same as `{0,1}`.

Caution

Do not use spaces in the repeat quantifiers. For example, `A{3,6}` cannot be written as `A{3, 6}` with a space after the comma.

Note

You may use parentheses to group patterns. For example, `(ab){3}` matches `ababab`, but `ab{3}` matches `abbb`.

Let us use several examples to demonstrate how to construct regular expressions.

Example 1

The pattern for social security numbers is `xxx-xx-xxxx`, where `x` is a digit. A regular expression for social security numbers can be described as

```
[\\d]{3}-[\\d]{2}-[\\d]{4}
```

For example,

```
"111-22-3333".matches("[\\d]{3}-[\\d]{2}-[\\d]{4}") returns true.
"11-22-3333".matches("[\\d]{3}-[\\d]{2}-[\\d]{4}") returns false.
```

Example 2

An even number ends with digits `0`, `2`, `4`, `6`, or `8`. The pattern for even numbers can be described as

```
[\\d]*[02468]
```

For example,

```
"123".matches("[\\d]*[02468]") returns false.
"122".matches("[\\d]*[02468]") returns true.
```

Example 3

The pattern for telephone numbers is (xxx) xxx-xxxx, where x is a digit and the first digit cannot be zero. A regular expression for telephone numbers can be described as

```
\\([1-9][\\d]{2}\\) [\\d]{3}-[\\d]{4}
```

Note that the parentheses symbols (and) are special characters in a regular expression for grouping patterns. To represent a literal (or) in a regular expression, you have to use \\(and \\).

For example,

```
"(912) 921-2728".matches("\\([1-9][\\d]{2}\\) [\\d]{3}-[\\d]
   {4}") returns true.

"921-2728".matches("\\([1-9][\\d]{2}\\) [\\d]{3}-[\\d]{4}")
   returns false.
```

Example 4

Suppose the last name consists of at most 25 letters and the first letter is in uppercase. The pattern for a last name can be described as

```
[A-Z][a-zA-Z]{1,24}
```

Note that you cannot have arbitrary whitespace in a regular expression. For example, [A-Z][a-zA-Z]{1, 24} would be wrong.

For example,

```
"Smith".matches("[A-Z][a-zA-Z]{1,24}") returns true.
"Jones123".matches("[A-Z][a-zA-Z]{1,24}") returns false.
```

Example 5

Java identifiers are the names that identify the elements such as classes, methods, and variables in a program.

- An identifier must start with a letter, an underscore (_), or a dollar sign ($). It cannot start with a digit.
- An identifier is a sequence of characters that consists of letters, digits, underscores (_), and dollar signs ($).

The pattern for identifiers can be described as

```
[a-zA-Z_$][\\w$]*
```

Example 6

What strings are matched by the regular expression "Welcome to (Java|HTML)"? The answer is Welcome to Java or Welcome to HTML.

Example 7

What strings are matched by the regular expression "A.*"? The answer is any string that starts with letter A.

Replacing and Splitting Strings

The `matches` method in the `String` class returns `true` if the string matches the regular expression. The `String` class also contains the `replaceAll`, `replaceFirst`, and `split` methods for replacing and splitting strings, as shown in Figure H.1.

java.lang.String	
+matches(regex: String): boolean	Returns true if this string matches the pattern.
+replaceAll(regex: String, replacement: String): String	Returns a new string that replaces all matching substrings with the replacement.
+replaceFirst(regex: String, replacement: String): String	Returns a new string that replaces the first matching substring with the replacement.
+split(regex: String): String[]	Returns an array of strings consisting of the substrings split by the matches.
+split(regex: String, limit: int): String[]	Same as the preceding split method except that the limit parameter controls the number of times the pattern is applied.

FIGURE H.1 The `String` class contains the methods for matching, replacing, and splitting strings using regular expressions.

The `replaceAll` method replaces all matching substring and the `replaceFirst` method replaces the first matching substring. For example, the following code

```
System.out.println("Java Java Java".replaceAll("v\\w", "wi"));
```

displays

```
Jawi Jawi Jawi
```

The following code

```
System.out.println("Java Java Java".replaceFirst("v\\w", "wi"));
```

displays

```
Jawi Java Java
```

There are two overloaded `split` methods. The `split(regex)` method splits a string into substrings delimited by the matches. For example, the following statement

```
String[] tokens = "Java1HTML2Perl".split("\\d");
```

splits string `"Java1HTML2Perl"` into `Java`, `HTML`, and `Perl` and saved in `tokens[0]`, `tokens[1]`, and `tokens[2]`.

In the `split(regex, limit)` method, the `limit` parameter determines how many times the pattern is matched. If `limit <= 0`, `split(regex, limit)` is same as `split(regex)`. If `limit > 0`, the pattern is matched at most `limit - 1` times. Here are some examples:

```
"Java1HTML2Perl".split("\\d", 0); splits into Java, HTML, Perl
"Java1HTML2Perl".split("\\d", 1); splits into Java1HTML2Perl
"Java1HTML2Perl".split("\\d", 2); splits into Java, HTML2Perl
"Java1HTML2Perl".split("\\d", 3); splits into Java, HTML, Perl
"Java1HTML2Perl".split("\\d", 4); splits into Java, HTML, Perl
"Java1HTML2Perl".split("\\d", 5); splits into Java, HTML, Perl
```

Note

By default, all the quantifiers are *greedy*. This means that they will match as many occurrences as possible. For example, the following statement displays `JRvaa`, since the first match is `aaa`.

```
System.out.println("Jaaavaa".replaceFirst("a+", "R"));
```

You can change a qualifier's default behavior by appending a question mark (`?`) after it. The quantifier becomes *reluctant*, which means that it will match as few occurrences as possible. For example, the following statement displays `JRaavaa`, since the first match is `a`.

```
System.out.println("Jaaavaa".replaceFirst("a+?", "R"));
```

APPENDIX I

ENUMERATED TYPES

Simple Enumerated Types

An enumerated type defines a list of enumerated values. Each value is an identifier. For example, the following statement declares a type, named `MyFavoriteColor`, with values `RED`, `BLUE`, `GREEN`, and `YELLOW` in this order.

```
enum MyFavoriteColor {RED, BLUE, GREEN, YELLOW};
```

A value of an enumerated type is like a constant and so, by convention, is spelled with all uppercase letters. So, the preceding declaration uses `RED`, not `red`. By convention, an enumerated type is named like a class with first letter of each word capitalized.

Once a type is defined, you can declare a variable of that type:

```
MyFavoriteColor color;
```

The variable `color` can hold one of the values defined in the enumerated type `MyFavoriteColor` or `null`, but nothing else. Java enumerated type is *type-safe*, meaning that an attempt to assign a value other than one of the enumerated values or `null` will result in a compile error.

The enumerated values can be accessed using the syntax

```
EnumeratedTypeName.valueName
```

For example, the following statement assigns enumerated value `BLUE` to variable `color`:

```
color = MyFavoriteColor.BLUE;
```

Note that you have to use the enumerated type name as a qualifier to reference a value such as `BLUE`.

As with any other type, you can declare and initialize a variable in one statement:

```
MyFavoriteColor color = MyFavoriteColor.BLUE;
```

An enumerated type is treated as a special class. An enumerated type variable is therefore a reference variable. An enumerated type is a subtype of the `Object` class and the `Comparable` interface. Therefore, an enumerated type inherits all the methods in the `Object` class and the `compraeTo` method in the `Comparable` interface.

Additionally, you can use the following methods on an enumerated object:

- `public String name();`
  Returns a name of the value for the object.
- `public int ordinal();`
  Returns the ordinal value associated with the enumerated value. The first value in an enumerated type has an ordinal value of 0, the second has an ordinal value of 1, the third one 3, and so on.

Listing I.1 gives a program that demonstrates the use of enumerated types.

LISTING I.1 EnumeratedTypeDemo.java

define an enum type

declare an enum variable

get enum name

get enum ordinal

compare enum values

```
1  public class EnumeratedTypeDemo {
2    static enum Day {SUNDAY, MONDAY, TUESDAY, WEDNESDAY, THURSDAY,
3      FRIDAY, SATURDAY};
4
5    public static void main(String[] args) {
6      Day day1 = Day.FRIDAY;
7      Day day2 = Day.THURSDAY;
8
9      System.out.println("day1's name is " + day1.name());
10     System.out.println("day2's name is " + day2.name());
11     System.out.println("day1's ordinal is " + day1.ordinal());
12     System.out.println("day2's ordinal is " + day2.ordinal());
13
14     System.out.println("day1.equals(day2) returns " +
15       day1.equals(day2));
16     System.out.println("day1.toString() returns " +
17       day1.toString());
18     System.out.println("day1.compareTo(day2) returns " +
19       day1.compareTo(day2));
20   }
21 }
```

```
day1's name is FRIDAY
day2's name is THURSDAY
day1's ordinal is 5
day2's ordinal is 4
day1.equals(day2) returns false
day1.toString() returns FRIDAY
day1.compareTo(day2) returns 1
```

An enumerated type `Day` is defined in lines 2–3. Variables `day1` and `day2` are declared as the `Day` type and assigned enumerated values in lines 6–7. Since `day1`'s value is `FRIDAY`, its ordinal value is 5 (line 11). Since `day2`'s value is `THURSDAY`, its ordinal value is 4 (line 12).

Since an enumerated type is a subclass of the `Object` class and the `Comparable` interface, you can invoke the methods `equals`, `toString`, and `comareTo` from an enumerated object reference variable (lines 14–19). `day1.equals(day2)` returns true if `day1` and `day2` have the same ordinal value. `day1.compareTo(day2)` returns the difference between `day1`'s ordinal value to `day2`'s.

Alternatively, you can rewrite the code in Listing I.1 into Listing I.2.

LISTING I.2 StandaloneEnumTypeDemo.java

```
1  public class StandaloneEnumTypeDemo {
2    public static void main(String[] args) {
3      Day day1 = Day.FRIDAY;
4      Day day2 = Day.THURSDAY;
5
6      System.out.println("day1's name is " + day1.name());
7      System.out.println("day2's name is " + day2.name());
8      System.out.println("day1's ordinal is " + day1.ordinal());
9      System.out.println("day2's ordinal is " + day2.ordinal());
10
11     System.out.println("day1.equals(day2) returns " +
12       day1.equals(day2));
13     System.out.println("day1.toString() returns " +
14       day1.toString());
15     System.out.println("day1.compareTo(day2) returns " +
16       day1.compareTo(day2));
17   }
18 }
19
20 enum Day {SUNDAY, MONDAY, TUESDAY, WEDNESDAY, THURSDAY,
21   FRIDAY, SATURDAY}
```

An enumerated type can be defined inside a class, as shown in lines 2–3 in Listing I.1, or standalone as shown in lines 20–21 in Listing I.2. In the former case, the type is treated as an inner class. After the program is compiled, a class named EnumeratedTypeDemo$Day.class is created. In the latter case, the type is treated as a standalone class. After the program is compiled, a class named Day.class is created.

Note

When an enumerated type is declared inside a class, the type must be declared as a member of the class and cannot be declared inside a method. Furthermore, the type is always `static`. For this reason, the `static` keyword in line 2 in Listing I.1 may be omitted. The visibility modifiers on inner class can also be applied to enumerated types defined inside a class.

Tip

Using enumerated values (e.g., `Day.MONDAY`, `Day.TUESDAY`, and so on) rather than literal integer values (e.g., 0, 1, and so on) can make a program easier to read and maintain.

Using `if` or `switch` Statements with an Enumerated Variable

An enumerated variable holds a value. Often your program needs to perform a specific action depending on the value. For example, if the value is `Day.MONDAY`, play soccer; if the value is `Day.TUESDAY`, take piano lesson, and so on. You can use an `if` statement or a `switch` statement to test the value in the variable, as shown in (a) and (b).

```
if (day.equals(Day.MONDAY)) {
  // process Monday
}
else if (day.equals(Day.TUESDAY)) {
  // process Tuesday
}
else
  ...
```

(a)

Equivalent

```
switch (day) {
  case MONDAY:
    // process
Monday
    break;
  case TUESDAY:
    // process
Tuesday
    break;
  ...
}
```

(b)

In the `switch` statement in (b), the case label is an unqualified enumerated value (e.g., `MONDAY`, but not `Day.MONDAY`).

Processing Enumerated Values Using a Foreach Loop

Each enumerated type has a static method `values()` that returns all enumerated values for the type in an array. For example,

```
Day[] days = Day.values();
```

You can use a regular for loop in (a) or a foreach loop in (b) to process all the values in the array.

```
for (int i = 0; i < days.length; i++)
  System.out.println(days[i]);
```

(a)

Equivalent

```
for (Day day: days)
  System.out.println(day);
```

(b)

Enumerated Types with Data Fields, Constructors, and Methods

The simple enumerated types introduced in the preceding section define a type with a list of enumerated values. You can also define an enumerated type with data fields, constructors, and methods, as shown in Listing I.3.

LISTING I.3 `TrafficLight.java`

```
public enum TrafficLight {
  RED ("Please stop"), GREEN ("Please go"),
  YELLOW ("Please caution");

  private String description;

  private TrafficLight(String description) {
    this.description = description;
  }

```

```
11     public String getDescription() {
12       return description;
13     }
14   }
```

The enumerated values are defined in lines 2–3. The value declaration must be the first statement in the type declaration. A data field named `description` is declared in line 5 to describe an enumerated value. The constructor `TrafficLight` is declared in lines 7–9. The constructor is invoked whenever an enumerated value is accessed. The enumerated value's argument is passed to the constructor, which is then assigned to `description`.

Listing I.4 gives a test program to use `TrafficLight`.

Listing I.4 TestTrafficLight.java

```
1  public class TestTrafficLight {
2    public static void main(String[] args) {
3      TrafficLight light = TrafficLight.RED;
4      System.out.println(light.getDescription());
5    }
6  }
```

An enumerated value `TrafficLight.red` is assigned to variable `light` (line 3). Accessing `TrafficLight.RED` causes the JVM to invoke the constructor with argument "please stop". The methods in enumerated type are invoked in the same way as the methods in a class. `light.getDescription()` returns the description for the enumerated value (line 4).

Note

The Java syntax requires that the constructor for enumerated types be private to prevent it from being invoked directly. The private modifier may be omitted. In this case, it is considered private by default.

Appendix J

Bitwise Operators

To write programs at the machine-level, often you need to deal with binary numbers directly and perform operations at the bit-level. Java provides the bitwise operators and shift operators defined in Table J.1.

Table J.1 Bitwise Operators

<table>
<tr><th>Operator</th><th>Name</th><th>Example (using bytes in the example)</th><th>Description</th></tr>
<tr><td>&</td><td>Bitwise AND</td><td>10101110 & 10010010 yields 10000010</td><td>The AND of two corresponding bits yields a 1 if both bits are 1.</td></tr>
<tr><td>|</td><td>Bitwise inclusive OR</td><td>10101110 | 10010010 yields 10111110</td><td>The OR of two corresponding bits yields a 1 if either bit is 1.</td></tr>
<tr><td>^</td><td>Bitwise exclusive OR</td><td>10101110 ^ 10010010 yields 00111100</td><td>The XOR of two corresponding bits yields a 1 only if two bits are different.</td></tr>
<tr><td>~</td><td>One's complement</td><td>~10101110 yields 01010001</td><td>The operator toggles each bit from 0 to 1 and from 1 to 0.</td></tr>
<tr><td><<</td><td>Left shift</td><td>10101110 << 2 yields 10111000</td><td>The operator shifts bits in the first operand left by the number of bits specified in the second operand, filling with 0s on the right.</td></tr>
<tr><td>>></td><td>Right shift with sign extension</td><td>10101110 >> 2 yields 11101011
00101110 >> 2 yields 00001011</td><td>The operator shifts bit in the first operand right by the number of bits specified in the second operand, filling with the highest (sign) bit on the left.</td></tr>
<tr><td>>>></td><td>Unsigned right shift with zero extension</td><td>10101110 >>> 2 yields 00101011
00101110 >>> 2 yields 00001011</td><td>The operator shifts bit in the first operand right by the number of bits specified in the second operand, filling with 0s on the left.</td></tr>
</table>

The bit operators apply only to integer types (`byte`, `short`, `int`, and `long`). A character involved in a bit operation is converted to an integer. All bitwise operators can form bitwise assignment operators, such as =, |=, <<=, >>=, and >>>=.

GLOSSARY

0 based A number in or index of objects where the first element starts at the index of 0.

algorithm Statements that describe how a problem is solved in terms of the actions to be executed, and specifies the order in which these actions should be executed. Algorithms can help the programmer plan a program before writing it in a programming language.

Application Program Interface (API) A set of classes and interfaces that can be used to develop Java programs.

argument A value that is passed to a method when the method is invoked.

assembler A program that translates assembly-language programs into machine code.

assembly language A low-level programming language in which a mnemonic is used to represent each of the machine language instructions.

assignment operator (=) Assigns a value to a variable.

assignment statement A simple statement that assigns a value to a variable using an assignment operator (=). When a value is assigned to a variable, it replaces the previous value of the variable, which is destroyed.

attribute A variable that stores a value for an object.

back-end application Part of a software design that handles the data and operations that communicate with the server.

biometrics The process of measuring a person's biological features for the purpose of identification. Examples are fingerprint scanners, retina scanners, voice recognition, or facial recognition.

bit A binary digit 0 and 1.

block A sequence of statements enclosed in braces ({}).

`boolean` data type A primitive data type for Boolean values (true or false).

Boolean expression An expression that evaluates to a true or false value.

Boolean value True or false.

`break` statement A program statement used to exit out of the current loop.

bugs Logic errors.

bus A system that connects all the components of the computers together.

business constraints Often involve project scheduling, budgeting, and security guidelines of a project.

business ethics Moral principles applied to business issues and actions.

byte A unit of storage. Each byte consists of 8 bits. The size of hard disk and memory is measured in bytes. A megabyte is roughly a million bytes.

`byte` type A primitive data type that represents an integer in a byte. The range of a byte value is from

-2^7 (-128) to 2^7-1 (127).

bytecode The result of compiling Java source code. Bytecode is machine-independent and can run on any machine that has a Java running environment.

bytecode verifier A program in the JVM that checks the validity of the bytecode and ensures that the bytecode does not violate Java's security restrictions.

career A chosen field of work in which you try to advance over time by gaining responsibility and earning more money.

case sensitive A characteristic of a programming language where uppercase and lowercase letters are read as different items.

casting The process of converting a primitive data type value into another primitive type.

CD-R A compact disc for read-only permanent storage; the user cannot modify its contents once they are recorded.

CD-RW A compact disc that can be used like a hard disk; that is, you can write data onto the disc, and then overwrite that data with new data.

central processing unit (CPU) A small silicon semiconductor chip with millions of transistors that executes instructions.

`char` type A primitive data type that represents a Unicode character.

CIA triad A principle used to define the three key components of computer security: Confidentiality, Integrity, and Availability,

class An encapsulated collection of data and methods that operate on data. A class may be instantiated to create an object that is an instance of the class.

class diagram A type of illustration used to describe the components of a class.

class loader A program used to load object classes into memory.

cloud storage A storage system in which data is stored across multiple servers and various locations, and is accessible from multiple devices.

cluster A group of similar items.

comment Comments document what a program is and how it is constructed. They are not programming statements and are ignored by the compiler. In Java, comments are preceded by two slashes (//) in a line or enclosed between /* and */ in multiple lines.

compiler A software program that translates source code (e.g., Java source code) into a machine language program.

computer crime Any act that either maliciously targets a computer system, or uses a computer to commit a crime.

computer abuse Bullying someone with the use of a computer.

computer fraud The act of using a computer to gain unlawful use of data or the computer system. Identity theft is an example of computer fraud.

Computer Fraud and Abuse Act (CFAA) A federal law that carries a penalty of up to $250,000 and 20 years in jail.

computer hacking The unauthorized entry into a computer system for malicious reasons.

concatenation The process of joining two or more strings together.

conditional operator Used in an expression that requires three operands and is represented by the symbol "?".

console Refers to the input and output device of a computer.

constant A variable declared final in Java. A local constant is a constant declared inside a method.

constraints Limitations on a project; typically falls into two categories of either a business constraint or a technical constraint.

constructor A special method for initializing objects when creating objects using the `new` operator. The constructor has exactly the same name as its defining class.

`continue` statement A program statement used to jump to the next iteration of a loop.

cookie Small text files that store sets of name-value pairs on the disk in the client's computer. Cookies can be used for session tracking.

core The part of the processor that performs the reading and executing of instructions.

cyber bullying The act of threatening, stalking, or harassing someone through social media or over the Internet.

dangling `else` ambiguity Describes a common mistake where an `else` clause is mismatched to an `if` clause.

data communication system The structure that communicates and transmits data back and forth from client to server.

data field A variable that stores a value for an object.

data structure A format for organizing and storing data. An array is an example of a data structure.

data theft The stealing or collection of personal data from someone without his or her consent.

data type Used to define variables to indicate what kind of value the variable can hold.

debugging To find errors in a program.

declare variable Defines a variable with a data type.

decrement operator (−−) Subtracts one from a numeric variable or a `char` variable.

default constructor If a class does not define any constructors explicitly, a `no-arg` constructor with empty body is assumed. This is called a default constructor.

divide and conquer Also known as stepwise refinement, used to decompose a large program into subproblems.

Unicode A code system for international characters managed by the Unicode Consortium. Java supports Unicode.

Unified Modeling Language (UML) A graphical notation for describing classes and their relationships.

unique address A specific location in memory that is used to locate and store data.

UNIX epoch January 1, 1970 Greenwich mean time (GMT) is known as the Unix epoch because 1970 was the year when the Unix operating system was formally introduced.

Unstructured Programming Style A type of programming style where code is written in sequentially ordered lines and includes GOTO statements.

USA Freedom Act A section of the Patriot Act that was changed stopping the NSA from collecting phone records from citizens not involved in a terrorist crime.

value type Stores a variable's values in physical memory.

value-returning method Terminology used when a method returns a value.

variable Variables are used to store data and computational results in the program.

`void` method A type of method where a value is not returned to the caller.

`while` loop A loop construct that begins with the keyword `while`.

Wi-Fi Protected Access (WPA) Formerly adopted by the industry as a standard in 2003; meant to improve the older WEP encryption policy.

Wi-Fi Protected Access II (WPA2) Was adopted as an industry standard in 2006, and provides a higher level of security than its WPA predecessor.

wildcard import Imports all the classes in a package and is denoted by an asterisk (*). As an example, `importjava.util.*` imports all classes from `package java.util`.

Wired Equivalent Privacy (WEP) The oldest of the three types of wireless encryption. Although it is widely used, it provides the least amount of protection.

work ethics Moral principles, or beliefs and behaviors about what is right and wrong in a work environment.

INDEX

C